Neil D. Isaacs

INNOCENCE & WONDER

Baseball through the Eyes of Batboys

MASTERS PRESS

A division of Howard W. Sams

Published by Masters Press
A division of Howard W. Sams & Co.
2647 Waterfront Pkwy. E. Drive, Suite 300
Indianapolis, IN 46214

Library of Congress Cataloging-in-Publication Data

Isaacs, Neil David, 1931–
        Innocence and wonder: baseball through the eyes of batboys / Neil D. Isaacs.
            p.   cm.
        ISBN 1-57028-000-2: $14.95
        1. Batboys -- United States -- Biography. 2. Baseball -- United States --History
        I. Title.
        GV865.A1I82   1994
        796.357'092'2--dc20   94-20268
        [B]   CIP

CREDITS

Cover photograph of Stan Strull, courtesy of Stan Strull.
Norman Rockwell's "The Dugout" printed by permission of The Norman Rockwell Family Trust, ©1948, The Norman Rockwell Family Trust.
Other photos courtesy of Tommie Ferguson; Hank Le Bost; Jim Ryan; Stan Strull; Tom MacDougal; Roy McKertcher (photo by Gene Tupper); Tony Atlas (photo by David J. Hopley); Jay Mazzone; Steve Winship; Wes Patterson; Kevin Cashen; George Catloth; Dennis Cashen (photo by Gene Boyars of the Baltimore News-American); Patrick Quinlan; Fred Weisman (photo by The Associated Press); Merritt Riley; Mike Macko; Tommie Ferguson (NBC photo by Paul W. Bailey); Chad Blossfield; Paul Greco.

Special thanks to: Christy Pierce (typography); Phil Velikan (cover design).

To David, Mickey, Anna, and Marjorie
—the sixth generation of Isaacs baseball fans—
from Grandpa with love

Boston Braves batboy Frank McNulty, now the President of Parade *magazine, posed for Norman Rockwell in a Cubs uniform in 1948 and became a central figure (he's the young boy in the foreground) in one of Rockwell's most famous paintings.*

PREFACE

It began like a scene from *The Graduate*, only instead of a pool party it was a Tuesday night poker game. My friend Burt Dietch, whom I've known since Mrs. McQueeney's fourth grade class at Roger Sherman School in New Haven, knowing that I was finishing up my book on Grace Paley and undecided about what the next project would be, said, "I have one word for you—*batboy*."

That word was father to much thought, grandfather to research, progenitor of the project. I discovered that no one had tapped the enormous resource of baseball lore and legend in the memory-banks of former batboys, that fears about the difficulty of accessing sources were groundless, and that the subculture of clubhouse and dugout has its own rites and myths and charm.

Everyone I talked to about it seemed to know someone who had been a batboy, and every one of them I tracked down knew three others. I did my usual backgrounding in the Library of Congress, wrote a hundred letters, made a thousand phone calls, prowled stadiums long hours before game time, drove a few tough interviews to Atlantic City after a Phillies game, and in Detroit against the advice of security people walked out Michigan Avenue to the corner of Wabash where someone thought Eddie Forester—who had batboyed for Ty Cobb—still lived.

Why hadn't anyone thought of it before, I was asked over and over again, and what can we do to help. With few exceptions, the former batboys of every era were receptive. Some chose to write me, some to tape-record their own reminiscences, some to be interviewed by phone, and some to welcome personal visits. Many followed up with additional installments. Of the exceptions, there were a couple of Californians who feared I would trash them by digging up scandalous material, a few bright younger ones who wanted to write their own books, a venerable historian whose failing health precluded interviews, and a Chicago television newsman who responds to neither phone nor fax.

Innocence and Wonder presents seventy-seven seasons' worth of batboys speaking in their own voices. It is primarily oral history, because most of the stories are taken from tapes and notes of interviews. Some are taken from written reports; a few are collations of oral and written material; and all have been edited to retain, I hope, the flavor of their sources' style. As the number of respondents approached 200, two general impressions became clear.

In nearly every case, the batboy has a unique story to tell, one that he has treasured throughout his life. And yet, from 1915 to 1991, there is a similarity in their stories that gives a sense of continuity and fellowship to the experience—and batboys value that just as highly. They were special. And they belong.

A follow-up book, *Batboys and the Subculture of Baseball*, scheduled for publication by the University Press of Mississippi in 1995, synthesizes and analyzes the material presented here (and more), from the perspective of a cultural historian with his own idiosyncratic biases and style. In that effort I have been blessed by the superb editing of Seetha A-Srinivasan and the generous guidance of Jerry Klinkowitz.

I have had a legion of helpers along the way, for which these expressions of thanks are but modest tokens. Burt Dietch not only whispered the original suggestion in my ear, but also wrote letters, made contacts, and conducted a couple of preliminary interviews, along with Phil and Marilyn Isaacs. Uncle Phil Taylor, the Orioles' Bob Brown, and Mel Proctor provided many good leads. Tom Dolan, Jim Walczy, and Clyde Taylor gave both pragmatic and psychological support. Phil and Marilyn Isaacs were active enthusiasts from the start, and without the help of my wife, Ellen Isaacs, who took me to a ballgame on our first date, nothing that matters ever gets done around here.

Once and (perhaps) future editors, whose encouragement kept me going—especially when expressed in the form of what my brother calls "rave rejections," include Eric Swenson, Ed Burlingame, Al Silverman, Ken Cherry, Mel Helitzer, Larry Malley, and Dick Wentworth. Some of the material was culled for an essay called "The Importance of Being Batboy," published by Peter Stine in the "Sports in America" issue of *Witness* (1992), which is now being reprinted by Wayne State University Press.

I doubt that I can remember everybody whose leads, advice, or remarks were valuable, but several come to mind: Harold Rosenthal, Bill Gildea, Jon Miller, Jack Buck, Stacy Berger, Dave Sislen, Seymour Steiglitz, Don Stevens, Bob and Mercy Coogan, Frank Mazzone, Tom Boswell, Ken Denlinger, Gerald Strine, Larry King, and Shirley Povich. A number of baseball front office or p.r. people gave more than routine attention: Jay Hinrichs, Bill Squires, Bill Beck, Barry Waters, Jim Ferguson, and Larry Shenk.

Equipment and clubhouse managers were the mainstream of support in identifying sources, lining up interviews, generously cooperating, and enthusiastically supporting the project. Special thanks, among them, to Butch Yatkeman, Frank Ciensczyk, Dennis Liborio, Frank Coppenbarger, Jim Ksicinski, Jim Schmakel, Jeff Ross, John Silverman, Joe Macko, Buddy Bates, Leonard Garcia, Mike Murphy, Brian Prilaman, Jim Wiesner, Cy Buynak, Willie Thompson, and last but not least, Yosh Kawano. A few primary sources extended themselves above and beyond their own interviews: Jim Ryan, Steve Winship, and Bob Recker.

Players, coaches, and other personnel at all levels of the game who were generous with their time and thought include Steve Garvey, Eddie Logan, Jimmy Reece, Ken Reitz, Pete Rose, Jr., Art (Caveman) Kusnyer, Ernie Tyler, Sr., Jim Tyler, Rob Ogle, Jim O'Neill, Bob Bauman, Bill Zeigler, George Brett, and Dan Schatzeder. Special appreciation and warmest regards for Brooks Robinson: I understand why they say that some players have candy bars or restaurants named for them, but Brooks Robinson has sons named after him.

The greatest debt is owed to the co-authors of this book, the men whose voices are heard in the following pages. Among the batboys whose very words are unheard this time around are John Baxter, Billy Coward, Ivan Crayton, Joe Dunn, John Dykowski, Jay Emiston, Ozzie Guillen, Jeff Hochberg, Chris Lehr, Chad Meyer, Jeff Risch, Gerald Rosen, Thomas (Snuffy) Ryza, Shannon Smith, Ray Tarin, Mark Thomson, Jimmy Tyler, Kurt Schlogo, Greg Grimes, Brad Grimes, Sid Holland and Barry Waters.

Finally, I am especially indebted to Tom Bast for his efforts in publishing this work, and to Mark Montieth, its editor, I am prepared to present a writer's MVP award.

Neil D. Isaacs
Colesville, MD
June 1994

CONTENTS

The Twenties and Before 1

The Thirties 13

The Forties 29

The Fifties 51

The Sixties 85

The Seventies 133

The Eighties and After 181

FOREWORD

Most fans believe that all the batboy does is handle the bats for the players, carry them to and from the plate and put them in the rack. But take a look at the on-deck circle next time you're at the ballpark. With the pine tar rag, the donut, the rosin bag, and the weighted bat—it's like an obstacle course, and the batboy is in charge.

It's really an exciting and a prestigious job for the kids, and they have to work very hard. They come early, and they leave late. They do a lot more in the clubhouse than you'll ever see them do on the field. I can remember a number of times when one of them would get involved in a play, trying to retrieve a bat when there was a play at the plate or picking up a passed ball when it was still in play. Usually you wouldn't notice them on the field but they were always there when you needed something to be done in the clubhouse.

I remember a lot of the kids we had working in the Orioles clubhouse, and all of them were real nice kids. There was Bill Little, who became a pilot for American Airlines—I still see him once in a while in California. There was Bobby Scherr, who became a lawyer. And there were all the Tyler brothers and the Cashen brothers.

Two who stick out in my mind are included in this book—Jay Mazzone and Roy Firestone. Jay amazed us all, with what he could do without his hands. When he got fitted with his hooks, he went through a six-week training course and complete it in half the time. But we treated him like anyone else in the clubhouse—got on him when he made an error, had him up before kangaroo court, and all that. He came to St. Louis as batboy for the 1966 All-Star Game, the hottest game I can remember playing. Jay lasted longer than most of the players—before he passed out.

As for Roy, he would entertain the whole team in Florida. We'd have an hour and a half ride to a game in West Palm Beach, and he'd come on the bus with the team and crack us all up all the way with his routines and imitations, including a great Earl Weaver. That story he tells here about our trainer Ralph Salvon is just right—I can just see Ralph, God rest his soul, getting in Roy's face and can hear his voice as he's putting him on.

You know, baseball players are pranksters, and they'd have to put every new kid through some kind of initiation, like sending them to find the key to the batter's box. But then the batboys would get to make one road trip, and players would take them to dinner and treat them like members of the club.

Of course there are some guys, when they get to the big leagues they want everything done for them. Curt Blefary was a good example on our club, and we'd always get on him for it. These are the guys who run the kids' butts off in the clubhouse. And as far as knowing what the players are really like, the batboys can give a better analysis than anyone else. They see them as they really are, day in and day out. That's why the stories Neil Isaacs has collected here should be a lot of fun for fans of all ages.

They're fun for me, because I actually got my start in baseball as a batboy. That's right. Long before I played for York or San Antonio, I would take care of the bats for the teams my daddy played on, when I was growing up in Little Rock. You won't find it on the back of any baseball card, but my first teams were the Fire Department and the Riverside Nursery teams. I was their batboy long before I was a player, and I loved being around the game then.

Brooks Robinson
Baltimore, MD
June 1994

Roster of Contributors

National League

Atlanta Braves
Payton Morris	1989-91

Boston Braves
Charlie (The Greek) Chronopoulos	1940-49
Tommie Ferguson	1946-52
Frank McNulty	1945-50

Brooklyn Dodgers
Hank Le Bost	1915-16
Stan Strull	1943-44, 1946-51

Chicago Cubs
Phil Cline	1965-66
Rich Eberle	1965-66
Bill Philips	1955-56

Cincinnati Reds
Rich Merschbach	1976-79
Mark Stowe	1975-76

Houston Astros
Carl Schneider	1989-91

Los Angeles Dodgers
Johnny Boggs	1977-78 and 1981
Rene Lachemann	1960-62
Gilly Lefebvre	1959-61
Jimmy Lefebvre	1961
Jim Merritt	1961

Milwaukee Braves
Chad Blossfield	1954-57
Mike Doyle	1963-65

Montreal Expos
Steve Friend	1986-88

New York Mets
Paul Greco	1984-87
Mike Rufino	1984-87

Philadelphia Phillies
Mark Andersen	1976-80
Kenny Bush	1949-66
Dan O'Rourke	1985-89
Tony Pastore	1987-90

Pittsburgh Pirates
Tracy (Red) Luppe	1985-90
Socko McCarey	1919-21
Art McKennan	1920-22
Bobby Recker	1959-62

St. Louis Cardinals
Buddy Bates	1969-71
Don Deason	1967-70
Jim Hackett	1944
Tim Murnin	1988-91
Jerry Risch	1966-69
Jerry Schroer	1955-58
Jim Schroer	1955-57
Tony (The Flea) Simokaitis	1985-90
Butch Yatkeman	1924-31

San Diego Padres
Bobby Alldis	1981-85
John Plein	1976-78
Brian Prilaman	1971-72

San Francisco Giants
Mario Alioto	1973-79
Fred Costello	1985
Bob French	1966-68
Roy (Red) McKertcher	1958-61
Mike Mullane	1983-86
Mike Murphy	1958-60
Patrick Quinlan	1976-79
Brad Tham	1965-72
Gus Tham	1963-67

American League

Baltimore Orioles

Dennis Cashen	1980-82
Kevin Cashen	1977-79
Michael Cashen	1972-76
Neil Cashen	1969-72
Roy Firestone	1971-72
Jay Mazzone	1966-73
Bob Scherr	1964-66
Jimmy Triantas	1984-88
Fred Tyler	1973-79

Boston Red Sox

John Donovan	1948-51
Tommie Ferguson	1945
Don FitzPatrick	1944-50
Dennis Liborio	1969-73

California Angels

Tony Atlas	1976-80
Bill Bush	1965-67
Tim Buzbee	1975-79
Bob Elder	1965-67
Leonard Garcia	1965-67
Roger Hailey	1965-69
Fred Mueller	1965-67

Chicago White Sox

Jim Sassetti	1984-88
Mark Sassetti	1985-88

Cleveland Indians

Jeff Sipos	1971-72
Bill Tofant	1929-31
Fred Weisman	1936

Detroit Tigers

Tony Antonio	1985-89
David Cowart	1980-84
Eddie Forester	1919-21
Bob Mical	1980-84
John Nelson	1979-82
William (Red) Willis	1947-51

Kansas City Royals

Wes Patterson	1984-91
Eric Winebrenner	1980-88
Steve (Stretch) Winship	1979-84

Milwaukee Brewers

Luke Fera	1987-89
Pat McBride	1970-74
Tony Migliaccio	1978-84
Ron Nedset	1983-85

Minnesota Twins

Steve Labatt	1982-86
Mark McKenzie	1968-70
Clayton Wilson	1987-90

New York Yankees

Paul Gonoud	1981-82
Mickey Morabito	1970-73
Thad Mumford	1968-69
Merritt Riley	1982-84
Mike Rufino	1982-83
Tom Villante	1943-45

Oakland A's

Rocky Maunakea	1969
Steve Maunakea	1977
Mike Pieraldi	1968-70
Ron Pieraldi	1970-73

St. Louis Browns

Billy Cahill	1937-39

Seattle Mariners

Craig Beatty	1988-1990

Texas Rangers

Ben Grieve	1989-91
Mike Macko	1983-87
Mike Wallace	1973
David Zeigler	1984-87
Kim Zeigler	1983-86
Ted Zeigler	1982-84

TORONTO BLUE JAYS

Mahendra Naik	1977-79

WASHINGTON SENATORS

Steve Altman	1951
Eddie Baxter	1967-71
Fred Baxter	1931-32
Johnny Boggs	1969
George Catloth	1932-38
David (Jigger) Cohen	1925
Ray Crump	1949-57
Bob Farmer	1957-58
Jack Hughes	1956
John Milne Kurtz	1957-58
Rick LaCivita	1970
Tom MacDougal	1957-58
Scotty MacDougal	1958-59
John Mitchell	1941-42
John Mitchell	1970-71
David Povich	1946-47
Maury Povich	1946-48
Jim Ryan	1956-58
Bill Turner	1956-59

MINOR LEAGUES

DECATUR COMMODORES

Frank Coppenbarger	1967-74

KANSAS CITY BLUES

Sid Bordman	1940-41

NORFOLK
(YANKEE TEAM IN CLASS B PIEDMONT LEAGUE)

Jim (Doc) Ewell	1934

PORTLAND BEAVERS

John Pesky	1932-37

ST. PAUL SAINTS

Jim Wiesner	1952-57

THE TWENTIES

THE TWENTIES AND BEFORE

Baseball fans take batboys for granted. But the position is of fairly recent vintage, a contemporary of the lively ball and the relief pitcher, though more venerable than such semi-fixtures as designated hitters and artificial turf. The batboy originates in the coming together of four separate elements or functions—the mascot, the support staff that accompanies commercialization of sports, the equipment that develops with professionalization, and the habit of boys to hang around ballparks and ballplayers.

At the turn of the century, these pieces might be found here and there (though players usually cared for their own stuff) but not in combination. John McGraw is said to have kept a humpback mascot with the Giants from 1903 on, and W. P. Kinsella presents a fantasy of 1908 baseball in which Frank Chance's Cubs have a "hunchbacked midget" who tends the bats while the Iowa Baseball Confederacy All-Stars adopt an "albino" youngster to do the same. But right up to World War I it was common practice for players, managers, and clubhouse men to choose boys on their way into the ballpark and give them free admission in return for running errands and helping out with equipment. But when clubhouse management stabilized, some boys became regulars who performed routinized tasks in the clubhouse and on the field. By the end of the 1920's they were uniformed, too, and though some were still called mascots they were mostly underpaid, under-age drudges who willingly served their heroes.

According to legend, Pete Sheehy began his nearly sixty years of service in the Yankee Stadium clubhouse one day during the 1927 season. Walking past the fence on his way toward the bleachers, an arm reached out through the fence (shades of *Field of Dreams*) to grab him, and a voice said, "Ya wanna be a batboy?" In some versions it is the arm and voice of Babe Ruth. It was actually clubhouse boss Fred Logan who saw Sheehy, asked if he would help out for the day, liked his effort, and asked him to keep coming back.

In *Baseball: The People's Game* historian Harold Seymour tells a similar story about the start of his three-year stint batboying for the Dodgers, 1924-26. In fact, Seymour's brief sketch—being hired, learning about baseball from the inside, and wising up fast among colorful men right where the action was—provides an early model of the standard batboy's story. The embarrassments, the superstitions, the surprising incidents, and the canny insights reverberate throughout the following pages down through the decades.

HANK LE BOST ....

I was born at the turn of the century, May 27th, 1902, and I remember watching the ballpark take shape at Ebbets Field. From my home on Schenectedy Avenue and Eastern Parkway I would walk cross-country, past squatters' huts, to Ebbets Field.

My father was a cigar-maker. Across the street was a market that made deliveries by donkey cart. I used to pet the donkeys and I was petting one in the street one day when my father called—when my father called, you came right away—and I was run over by a 1909 Ford. I walked away unscratched—I had flattened myself under the car and it passed inches over my head.

My parents were German immigrants, came over at 35 and 34 (they died at 95 and 77). I was a big strong kid. My first job was for a stationery company at $5 a week, which I brought home to my mother. She'd give me 25 cents spending money a day, 5 cents for subway and 5 cents for lunch. I also delivered newspapers, and I was a bouncer for the Dance Caprice in Brooklyn at 13, until I got my teeth knocked out by an angry customer who came back with friends after I escorted him out.

About this time, the kids used to wait at the entrance to the ballpark for players to take them in. I was 13 and was befriended by Casey Stengel, who was 25 or 26. He called me "carrot-top" and treated me as a good-luck charm, so I began to go regularly and run errands for him and others, for penny tips—beer and sandwiches mostly. You could go to the movies at that time two for a nickel, buy a knish at Nathan's for two cents.

I was very impressed with the players, but it was much different then. The manager had little to say about what they did, and many had beer bellies. Their only exercise was chasing flies in the outfield, and they'd often say, "Go get it, kid," if it wasn't hit right to them. There was little discipline in those days. The manager was Wilbert Robinson, himself quite rotund—he'd sometimes give me two cents.

My job was mostly retrieving bats, shagging flies, and getting hot dogs. You know, the players actually ate hot dogs during the game. I was playing ball myself at the time for the Brooklyn Union Gas team, and it was their uniform I wore to batboy. The Dodgers supplied nothing and didn't pay. My mother sewed long pockets inside my baseball uniform, so that I could take several used balls home without anyone knowing. I'd sell them, and that was my pay.

Stengel was a prankster even then—hotfoots, noisemakers on cushions. Jake Daubert I remember as a loveable person with a good personality. And Zack Wheat, good batsman and glove man, was liked by all the players. Of the visitors I got to know Pie Traynor pretty well. There were some players who shot their mouths off, but they played like a team—unlike today.

I batboyed for two seasons, 1915 and 1916, and the second year the Dodgers won the pennant. But the game of baseball didn't have as much meaning for the people in Brooklyn then, there were many immigrants. The World Series was no big deal, not like it is today, no big deal to the average baseball fan. I do remember Babe Ruth, though, as an outstanding pitcher.

There was a lot of betting, of course; gambling was rampant, cardplaying, even crooked gambling. So it didn't surprise me when I saw it going on at Grossinger's, where I got a job as a tennis pro, even though I didn't play very well. Part of the job was to dance at night with the homely girls. Jenny often caught me dancing with the prettiest girl and would tell me, "That's not what we're paying you for."

As far as baseball and being a batboy were concerned, I didn't pay it no heed. It just wasn't a big thing in my life. It's only in the last couple of years, when Marty Adler got hold of me for the Brooklyn Dodgers Hall of Fame and those articles were done about me as the oldest living batboy and that part of my life became known, that I became active in baseball again.

To tell you the truth, I'm disillusioned with the game now. It's strictly a money game, and that takes away from the old-time glamour when players played for the glory of winning. But I do have a business card that says I'm "New York's #1 Met Fan."

Hank Le Bost retired from a successful business career in 1962. Elected president of the Dorchester Senior Center in Brooklyn, he sang in the chorus, played championship bridge, and lectured on rejuvenation through nutrition. He died at 90.

Socko McCarey ....

I was born in Pittsburgh in October of 1902. I used to go to the ballpark every day I could as a boy, and I'd head right for the 25-cent bleachers. One day in 1919 the clubhouse man stopped me at the gate and asked if I wanted to be batboy.

Sure I did, and I worked as batboy until 1921, then began twenty years in the dressing room. As batboy I got paid $2 every two weeks plus 50 cents from the visiting side.

Well, let's see. I remember Pie Traynor, and I remember Paul Waner. The one I remember best is Jolly Cholly Grimm because he was the one that gave me the name Socko. They'd all fool around with me, see, slap me around. I'd slap 'em back, too. So Charlie Grimm called me Socko.

Socko McCarey still lives in Pittsburgh, but in 1942 he left the Pirates and began scouting for the Boston Red Sox. In the high schools, American Legion teams, and sandlot games in the area, he scouted such future big-leaguers as Glenn Beckert, Eddie Sadowski, and Russ Kemmerer.

Eddie Forester ....

I was hired in 1919 by Mr. Frank Navin. I'd be there every morning, he'd say, "Ain't you got no school?" and I said, "No, I ain't goin' to school—my teacher's sick." He said, "You better come up with a new story, that one's old." Every time the team was home I'd go to school—there was 88 kids—they'd check me in and I'd go out the back door. Was born in May 1909. Lived on Wabash Avenue all my life, near the corner of Michigan Avenue, just a short walk to the ballpark. Three or four years I batboyed, then went to the ground crew till '73. Fifty-three and a half years I worked at the ballpark.

I thought I was gonna be a ballplayer. I'd go out and practice with 'em and everything and they'd say, "What are you doin'?" I'd say, "I'm gonna be a ballplayer, I'm gonna play for the Detroit Tigers." They said, "You think you are." That's when I was twelve years old.

Batboys had no uniforms. Then a kid got killed in Chicago, was playing on the field, got hit in the head with the ball. His family sued and won. After that they said everybody on the field had to be in uniform. Got $15 a week plus two balls a day. Third year got $35. That was Mr. Navin. He said, "Eddie, how much are we paying you?" "Fifteen dollars." "That's not enough, we gotta raise that." He was the best man that there ever was. He was a good guy. When he died my heart went out for the man. Always good. He'd say, "What do you think of this player, what do you think of that player?" "They're all good," I'd say. He'd say, "That's what I want to hear. You treat 'em right, now." "I always do," I'd say. Mr. and Mrs. Feltzer were good people too.

I got kids for the visiting team, but sometimes had to do both. There were washing machines in the clubhouse. I'd shine shoes every day. Cobb was a fussy guy. "Look at that insole, you didn't get in there." I'd say, "It's all wore out, won't hold the polish." I took care of the umpires every day, too. Four dozen balls, with that mud. Cobb got hold of a couple dozen once and froze them, pulled a trick on the umpires. They were like hitting big balloons. When they found out, the umpires were mad as hell, but what could they do?

Ty Cobb, he was the worst damn manager there was in baseball. Swear at the players, fight with 'em, and everything. He fired me twice. I said, "You can't, I have the clubhouse." "Well, you ain't gonna be batboy today." I'd say OK and I took care of the clubhouse. Twice he did that to me. He sent me for orange juice—I was the only one could get it because the man at the store gave me a special brand. "I want that good orange juice. I don't want the kind the other kids get for me—you get it." So I got him a gallon. Special brand, you know. And it was better, too. He said, "I like that. That's good."

Oh but he was terrible, swear at the players, call them all kinds of names. Wasn't for Gerry Walker he'd a got knocked cold. Charlie Gehringer grabbed him—Cobb called him a sonofabitch—"Mr. Cobb, don't ever call me that name—I have a mother." And I was right there alongside of him. He said, "Don't ever call me that" and he shook the hell out of him. Gerry Walker, he said, "Come on, come on." That was the first time Gehringer ever did or said anything. He was the quietest guy on the club, real quiet man, always talked to everybody, signed autographs and everything. But Cobb was a son of a gun. I said I don't want any part of him. After he called Gehringer that I never did like him. Swear at ballplayers— "sonofabitch," "bastard"—I didn't like that. He wasn't treating those guys right.

I used to play ball with Hank Greenberg all the time. He was the best damn ballplayer, I'll tell ya. Played catch every day with him. Greenberg—you couldn't do a favor for him without getting paid. Go get a sandwich, he'd give you a buck. Sandwich cost 75 or 80 cents then. I'd go to Robison's across the street—got the bar now on Trumbull next to the cab company. Ham and egg sandwich—and he was Jewish, wasn't supposed to eat ham, ya know. He'd say, "Get me a special sandwich," I'd say OK, and he'd always tip me a dollar. Course he made a lot of money, hundred thousand dollars. But he was the best guy there ever was. You couldn't do anything for him without getting paid.

Two or three players would drink, mostly beer. Howard Ehmke was drunk every goddam day, had a bottle of whiskey all the time in his locker—only one I ever seen in all my years. He'd go in the locker between innings. They had to wait for him sometimes, he made believe he had to go to the toilet or something, and he'd take a big swig out of the bottle—a quart or a fifth. Helluva pitcher, though.

Women? They were waiting for 'em to come in, over here at Michigan Central Depot. They never had to worry about women. Women were always there looking for a ballplayer, they wanted to marry a ballplayer. I used to take money to the bookie, Joe something—I never learned the last name—at 8th and Broadway at the bar. He'd give me a receipt. Horses, ten, fifteen, twenty dollars. Lots of times they won, too—big! He'd say, if you hit, you meet me here in the morning. Greenberg, Walker were bettors. Eldon Auker bet heavy, fifty dollars all the time, every time. He won lots, too. He got tips or something from somebody.

They called me "The Kid" and "Tigers' Kid." There's been so much change. The games take so much longer. I like it better now. Used to be, two hours and you were on your way. When I retired I got a pass for any American League park. They give me that and I said, "I'll use it, don't worry." I love baseball, can't get it out of my blood.

Eddie Forester still lives on Wabash Avenue,
and when the Tigers are playing at home he
walks down Michigan to the Stadium every
other day or so.

ART McKENNAN ....

My dad was a doctor who worked for Jones & Loughlin for thirty years. He was a great baseball fan, and he'd schedule his appointments in time to get to the ball games. He took great offense at those he called "knockers" who would badmouth the hometown players.

The games started at 3:30 and I'd come after school, whether my dad took me or not. You had to get an adult to take you into the ballpark, and I was about eleven when Billy Southworth, who was the Pirates right fielder then, was the first one to take me into the field. In 1919 I started to run errands in the clubhouse.

Then in 1920 I was in the right place at the right time. A batboy didn't come back and I was hired. From 1920 to 1922, while I went to Schenly High School, I was the Pittsburgh batboy. The pay was a ball or two a game—at the end of one season I had eighty balls in a trunk. In the middle of the '22 season I had a chance to move to the scoreboard at a dollar a game, so of course I took it.

There was no Sunday ball in Pittsburgh, but the Pirates got all holidays on their schedule. They would play a morning game at 10:45, clear the stands, and play the afternoon game at 3. It was heaven on earth for me to eat a meal between games with the players.

It was a good ballclub but too frivolous. There was horseshoe pitching, craps games, and hitting golf balls in the outfield in the morning. I remember Max Carey, Carson Bigbee, and Racehorse Dave Robertson. Rabbit Maranville and others seemed never to go to bed. They knew all the "holes" where they could get drinks during Prohibition. Charlie Grimm was the comedian. He kept everyone laughing. He claimed to be the only lefthanded banjo player. But he was the greatest fielding first baseman I ever saw.

When Grimm came back with the Cubs he always walked a wide circle around me. I don't know why—maybe he was afraid of his earlier reputation. One year he wanted more money from the Pirates and went to see Barney Dreyfuss, the little man behind the big desk. When he came back we asked him, "How'd you make out?" "Well," he said, "I told him I wanted more money, and he said, 'I want more base hits.'"

Dreyfuss never talked to an agent in his life. As an owner he personally scouted the minors, and he signed both Waners himself. Not so many of the fellows were married back then, and Branch Rickey would try to guide them into marriage, to make them more stable.

It was Judge Landis who broke up Rickey's farm system. Baseball was more fun before it got commercialized. Three things were the major changes—artificial turf, TV, and free agency.

Back in 1920, Babe Ruth and the Yankees came into Forbes Field for an exhibition game late in the summer. It was so crowded people were standing in the outfield. In three times up Ruth did nothing. The fourth time he hit a foul pop, and Possum Whitted, playing third, responded to the yelling of the crowd and deliberately dropped it. Jimmy Zinn was pitching—I remember him well, because he looked like Jack Dempsey and I used to break in his shoes and gloves for him. Well, he grooved the next pitch and Babe hit it over the right field wall.

After the game I was allowed into the visiting locker room to get Ruth to sign a ball. There he was, stark naked and a little grumpy, but he signed it. Would you believe I later used that ball to play with?

As a batboy you got to play some in the field, but no one ever gave you a time at bat during batting practice. I got to shag flies, sometimes even take infield, and I'd get a big hand from fans when I made a play. I also got to sit on the bench and work the scoreboard for the Homestead Greys, with Josh Gibson and Abe Kennedy, against such teams as the Baltimore Elite Giants and the Kansas City Monarchs. I remember Goose Tatum's clown team, too, and their off-color routines.

I was stricken with polio in 1930, at 23, but recovered enough to run the electric scoreboard in '42. Then in '48, I started doing the public address. Ray Scott really helped me with announcing. One of my most treasured mementos is an inscription from the day Forbes closed: "Thanks for all the beautiful years we spent together at Forbes Field. Love, Roberto Clemente."

Art KcKennan worked both scoreboard and p.a. through the '86 season, but broke his wrist and missed some games in '87, was replaced, and retired.

DAVID (JIGGER) COHEN . . . .

I was thirteen years old when Frank Baxter hired me. That was 1925, when the Senators won the pennant and lost the Series in seven games to Pittsburgh. I remember Sam Rice, Joe Judge, and Walter Johnson. He was a great pitcher, all right, but he was a champion cardplayer, especially cassino. The players I liked best were Buddy Lewis and Cecil Travis, but they came along ten years later, when I was already in dental school.

Buddy Myer came up as a rookie that year, and I kind of liked him. I felt bad when they traded him a couple of years later. I heard that he had a fistfight with Bucky Harris and that's why they traded him. But he became a better second baseman than his old playing manager.

I did a lot of things. I shined shoes and retrieved foul balls, climbing up a ladder into the grandstand and over into the lumber yard behind the stands. They didn't pay anything, either. I got tips and I'd steal balls, which I'd sell along with old gloves they gave me.

I really didn't care for the job very much. They were always yelling at me. I guess I didn't understand their superstitions. One time I happened to cross some bats when I laid them out for the game, and I got yelled at. Another time I was in the visiting dugout when the Yankees were in town, and I noticed that Joe Dugan always walked all the way down to the end of the dugout for the rosin bag before going out to the on-deck circle. So the next time he was due up I hustled down to get it for him and brought it to him. I thought I was just saving him some steps, but I got yelled at again.

When Mr. Baxter asked me if I wanted to come back and work the next year, I said, "No, I don't want to get yelled at any more."

Dr. David Cohen practiced dentistry in the District of Columbia from 1937 to 1977. Nowadays you might catch him on his weekly junkets to Atlantic City, and if the subject of baseball comes up near him on the bus he may tell about his year as Senators batboy.

Butch Yatkeman ....

Boys travel in twos, you know. One batboy brings in another. That's how I got started and that's how I hired a lot of my kids.

It was 1924, I was not quite sixteen, and Sam Lott, my neighborhood friend from across the street, brought me in. I'd go out to the ballpark in my street clothes and help out on the visiting side. Then, when Sam had to work in his father's furniture store, I went over to the Cardinals side in mid-season. Altogether I was a batboy for eight years.

My father was an American Jew of Russian descent who was brought over to this country as a child and settled in St. Louis. I'm the youngest of five children, and I was named Morris. My father wanted me to be a lawyer, but after two years of pre-law at St. Louis University and one semester of law school, I knew he was just wasting his money. The family was disappointed at first in my choice of a career in a baseball clubhouse, but they grew to be proud of me.

I remember the 1926 team very well, with Jim Bottomley, Rogers Hornsby, Bob O'Farrell, Billy Southworth, and young Bill Hallahan. The fourth game of the World Series that year I'll never forget, when Babe Ruth hit three home runs. But we won in seven games—the Cardinals beat the Yankees in three of five World Series, and won nine of the thirteen we've been in.

As a youngster I had a habit of whistling all the time I was in the dugout, things like "Ain't Gonna Rain No More No More" over and over again. One day a player yelled from the other end of the bench, "Hey, kid, stop that whistling." But the player sitting next to me said, "Don't worry about it, he's probably got a headache from the night before." Who were they? Oh, you know better than to ask me to name a player when I can't say something good about him.

During the off-season in 1932 I got to go barnstorming. With Paul Derringer's team in the Thirties there was catcher Jimmy Wilson, the two Deans, and Pepper Martin. We'd sit around after the games, count the take, and divvy up the money. Pepper took me on lots of fishing and hunting trips, but I never shot a gun.

Frisch as a manager? Well, I worked for eighteen managers over the years, and they were all great. Red Schoendienst and Ken Boyer were great friends. Whitey [Herzog] was the best man I ever worked for, he looked out for *everyone*—players, clubbies, clerical staff.

In '81 I was ready to retire, give up the traveling, after fifty years with the club, and Whitey asked me to stay one more year. "Maybe we'll win you a pennant," he said, and they won the World Series. The '82 World Series ring is the one I'm wearing, but I have the '42 ring handy—over here next to this ball from the '31 Series signed by Herbert Hoover.

You know, you hear a lot about drugs and drinking, but most kids are good kids, and I can prove it. I am proud of every one of my batboys. They have all turned out to be fine gentlemen and good citizens in the community.

September 12, 1982 was Butch Yatkeman Day at Busch Stadium, the only former batboy and equipment manager so honored. The Cardinals have named their home-team facilities the Butch Yatkeman Clubhouse.

THE THIRTIES

The Thirties

As the pre-game drills of the players became more firmly fixed as ritualized routines, so did the participation of batboys. It became common to see them shagging fly balls during batting practice, as well as gathering and carrying the buckets of balls and the bags of bats. On occasion, you would see them taking some infield practice after the starters finished their drills, and a few might even get to pitch some batting practice—especially to pitchers.

Batboys were likely to be wannabes, and these opportunities to perform, however marginally, on a professional field made the long hours and menial chores worthwhile. Some, like Johnny Pesky, grew into Major League uniforms. Others, like Bill Tofant, found that the economics of the game and the time would not allow them to be players.

Unsurprisingly, the reminiscences of batboys of this period—the era of the Great Depression—tend to focus on money. The scrambling for tips, the standard pay of two used balls per game that could be sold for change, and the idolizing of those players who were free spenders all become staple elements of the batboy's story.

BILL TOFANT ....

Bill Lobe and I both served as batboys for the visiting teams at old League Park, the original home of the Cleveland Indians. This was in 1929, 1930, and 1931. At the time I was working nights at a bakery and Lobe was a truckdriver.

We would report to League Park at 11:00 a.m. for the home games. I would pitch batting practice and Lobe would catch. Some of the Indians players would come out early for batting practice. We had a couple of neighborhood lads shag flies in the outfield. One was a Jimmy Wasdell, who worked his way up to the big leagues playing with Washington, Brooklyn, Pittsburgh, Philadelphia and with the Indians, a total of eleven years in the big leagues.

Lobe and I were scouted by the White Sox, who wanted us to go to one of their farms for sixty dollars a month. I refused, as I was making 72 dollars a month in the bakery. Lobe also refused. Lou Fonseca was the White Sox manager at the time. I was an infielder, but Eddie Rommel, a pitcher for Philadelphia, showed me how to throw a knuckleball and I perfected this pitch throwing batting practice.

Also at the time I was writing a sports column for an ethnic newspaper. One day, while the Yankees were in town, I approached Babe Ruth about giving me an interview for the paper. He said, "OK, Kid." He called everyone "Kid." We sat in a corner of the dugout and I asked him to give some batting tips to the kids in the area. For 15 minutes he answered my queries. I thanked him, and he said, "Hey, Kid, save me some copies of that paper." The next time the Yankees came to town I had six copies for him. When he entered the clubhouse in his camel's hair coat and cap, he stuffed the papers in his pocket and took them back to the Big Apple. One of my duties when the Yanks came to town was to go to a drugstore right across from the ball park and buy a bottle of "Eye Lo," which Babe used to wash out his eyes prior to a game.

I also recall that I had to have two copies of the score cards ready for Connie Mack. The Indians printed their own cards in their own print shop. He used the cards to position his outfielders. Mack was the manager for the Philadelphia team.

Another recollection involved the Yankee first baseman, Lou Gehrig. Prior to the game the Yanks warmed up right next to their dugout. A man came down to the gate with a youngster holding a ball. He asked me to have Lou sign the ball. I told him the players did not want to be disturbed so he and the lad went back to their seats, not far from the playing field. Lou quit warming up and wanted to know what the pair wanted. He could see he was the object of their attention. He said to me, "You little so and so, go up there and get the ball." I did and he signed it and I returned it to the man. He then handed me a dollar bill. I returned to the dugout and asked Lou if he wanted to split the dollar. He told me to be nice to people and that I would be rewarded not monetarily but in self-satisfaction. I never forgot this advice and it served me well in my career.

When the visiting teams would conclude a series and were going out of the clubhouse, they would tip the clubhouse man. Lobe and I usually got a dollar apiece. Ruth gave us two dollars and Fred Firpo Marberry of the Washington Senators was good for a deuce. We also got two baseballs each for tending the bats, etcetera. You can imagine that Lobe and I were the envy of all the neighborhood kids for the three years we were at League Park, and when we played sandlot ball on Sundays it was easy to find friends to fill in for us. We reached 21 years of age toward the end of our tenure, and it was time to go out into the world and make a living. Lobe stayed with the Indians and spent many years as bullpen catcher, getting a Major League pension when Bob Feller went to bat for him.

We lived close by to League Park and my mother was a baseball fan and a good cook. I remember inviting some of the St. Louis Browns players to our house for her soup, sausage and other ethnic foods. Jack Burns, Larry Bettencourt, Oscar Melillo, George Blaeholder were frequent visitors and enjoyed the repast. Joe Vosmik of the Indians also came. He was Ma's favorite, being a local lad.

Being a batboy and so close to the inside of the game and dealing with many of the top players at the time, served me well in my thirty-five-year career in the police department.

William J. Tofant is a retired Cleveland Police Lieutenant. He was a lieutenant in a 101st Airborne Division intelligence unit and treasures two rolls of 16mm film liberated from Hermann Goering in 1945.

Jim (Doc) Ewell ....

It all started when I went to see a parade. The Ringling Brothers Barnum and Bailey Circus came to Norfolk, and when I heard the calliope I started to follow it. It was 1932. I was nine years old.

When we got near the circus grounds I heard a roar. I'd never been to a ballgame, but I followed the roar of the crowd to the ballpark. It was the Norfolk team in the Piedmont League. A guy asked me, "Hey, kid, you wanna see the ballgame?" I said yes and he said, "You're gonna have to pick up the cushions after the game." So I did and he paid me a dime. Of course I came the next day and the next day.

The next year, I was ten, and I got the job of picking up the bottles—for a quarter. I got a big raise. But one day when I was under the stands a bottle hit me on the head. Next day I took my quarters and went down to the Army-Navy store and bought a World War I helmet, so that the bottles would just bounce off. I believe I'm the first guy ever to wear a hard hat in the ballpark.

When I was eleven, my third year at the ballpark, 1934, they needed a batboy. I applied to the manager, Barnacle Bill Skiff, and got the job. It was a Class B team in the Yankee organization, and that spring the Yankees stopped on their way north for an exhibition game.

I was ready, as usual, with water on the bench, looking after the bats, and running errands. I was wearing a pin-stripe uniform, passed down from Frank Crosetti, and a pair of old spike shoes two sizes too large and stuffed with paper. But I really didn't know what any of the Yankees looked like.

Around the second inning I look out and see a guy hit in the head by Ray White. So I go out there with a bucket of cold water with Coca-Cola written on the side. The trainer was back in the clubhouse. A gruff voice said to me, "Put a cold towel on his head, kid." The next day in the paper there was a picture of me putting a cold towel on Lou Gehrig's head with Babe Ruth leaning over watching.

There was talk that it was deliberate because White had gone to Columbia, like Gehrig, and there was some hard feeling. But I don't believe he'd ever do that. Anyway, that was the moment that started me toward a career as a trainer. Babe Ruth was my first instructor, though I studied for many years, not only in clubhouses but at colleges and medical schools as well.

I've come a long way in this game, from the bottom to the top. I've trained four All-Star teams, been to the World Series, and was the first guy Charlie Finley ever fired.

Doc Ewell was senior trainer for the Houston Astros until his death in 1993. In his career he had trained the Yankees, the Athletics, two presidents, and champions in half a dozen pro sports, and had been a popular raconteur with several appearances on "The Tonight Show with Johnny Carson."

Johnny Pesky....................................

I grew up in Portland, Oregon, and I was one of about a dozen kids who would hang around the Portland Beavers. The groundskeeper, Rocky Benevento, would let us help out by keeping the bullpen and coaching boxes in order. It was just a way of getting into the ballpark. We had a team of our own, called the Baby Beavers, and they let us use the facilities when they were on the road.

Eventually I got to help out in the clubhouse, I guess that would be around 1931 or 1932—I was twelve or thirteen, and then be a batboy. I especially remember Bill Posedel, our third baseman Fred Bedore, and the manager Bill Sweeney—nice, nice men.

Two of our outfielders were Berger and Bongy, but another was a big mean guy who was hitting about .120 and taking it out on everyone, including us. The other batboy and I sawed off a broom handle and put it in his locker with a note that said, "Maybe you can hit with this."

Later on I got to play against some players whose bats I'd carried in Portland, but no one ever teased me about that. One time in Philadelphia, though, Bob Johnson, who had been in Portland, was with the A's during my rookie season in the league. I hit a triple and he was laughing, looking down at me, and said, "You looked like you thought someone was chasing you."

I never forgot that my first job in baseball was as batboy and shining players' shoes. In Boston, in 1941, as a young-looking rookie, I'd get to the ballpark early, and Johnny Orlando, the clubhouse guy, would say, "Grab a brush." And I did.

John Pesky played ten years in the American League, mostly in Boston, and has remained active in the Red Sox organization, including stints as manager throughout the system.

FRED WEISMAN ....

My dad was Max David Weisman, better known as Lefty, who was the trainer for the Cleveland Indians from 1921 to 1949. He had grown up in Chelsea, Massachusetts, and learned as a boy selling newspapers that he had to fight his way to the choice locations to peddle his papers. Well, he had fought his way up to the prime corner of Boylston Street and Mass. Avenue, not far from Fenway Park, where he was befriended by Tris Speaker of the Red Sox. Speaker promised him that if he ever got to be a manager, he would make Lefty his trainer. And so he did.

My dad took that job seriously, though he knew very little about it when he started. He went to school nights to study training techniques. And I believe he became an excellent trainer. I was born in Cleveland in 1926. Six years later my brother Jed was named for Joe Vosmik, Earl Averill, and Dick Porter.

My batboy experience was limited to a single road trip in 1936—Washington, Philadelphia, New York, and Boston. I got to wear a uniform with Hal Trosky's number 7 on it. In Philadelphia, my dad took me to a Chinese restaurant. I'll never forget, because he told the waiter, "This kid is the team owner, and I'm his guardian." To prove it, he left tickets for the waiter and his girlfriend at the ballpark.

That's where Bob Feller joined the team. He was sixteen, and I guess we were about equals intellectually, so we got to be friends. When Feller got his uniform he complained to Lefty, "My hat's too large." My father answered, "Make sure it stays that way." And Feller did, working hard, quietly learning his trade, getting to the park around 9:30 instead of eleven o'clock.

It was a great trip for the Indians, and I was called a good luck charm. The highlights were in Boston. I got to run out to the outfield with Earl Averill while the infield was being dragged, and I caught a fly from Lloyd Brown's fungo. Averill told me to doff my cap at the crowd, and I did—to great applause. I was actually written up in the Boston *Globe*, with three pictures, including one with Trosky, one with my dad, and one kneeling with a bat in "classic batboy form."

Those are some of my treasured memories. Baseball provided some wonderful acquaintances, like our good neighbor Steve O'Neill and a classy gentleman named Jim Hegan, but my glimpses of life in the clubhouse were limited. Lefty, for example, was known far and wide as a handicapper, but I never saw any gambling, or drinking for that matter, among the players. Now my mother was a very tolerant woman, but she wouldn't let Babe Ruth in our house, called him "vulgar, rotten, and degenerate." But many baseball people would come, and after Mom's chicken soup and Dad's twisting of their backs they would always leave feeling much better.

Fred Weisman heads a firm of eleven trial lawyers in Cleveland where he's been a litigator for more than forty years.

FRED BAXTER ....

I was a Washington Senators batboy in 1931 and 1932, under Walter Johnson. My brother Frank was much older, and he'd first batboyed in 1912. He was hired by Mr. Griffith. He had a bad hip, from falling off an ice truck as a kid, and he stayed on with the club, running the home clubhouse until he died in '49. He was much loved by all, from the time he started as mascot.

The home batboy was called mascot, and I continued that when I moved over from the visiting clubhouse in '49. Two kids were needed on the visiting side to lug bats, then one in the dugout and one down the line as ballboy. There'd always be lots of applicants, and I'd work them all during the spring, then pick the ones with the best work habits and attitude. My two sons and their friends always had the inside track.

The first job was to clean shoes, then do the towels and other laundry. Only nine players had extra uniforms, you know, not the other scrubini whose uniforms were usually hung up unwashed. Not much cleanliness, but it's different now on account of stupid television. You can always tell the difference between bush-leaguers and major-leaguers. Bushers threw uniforms on the floor, major-leaguers hung 'em neatly. I don't much care for today's players—it's all speed now, not all-around ability. Too many shoemakers.

Clark Griffith was a great humanitarian. He let every man do his job without interference. Bob Short was the opposite. He meddled, had favorites, one little bobo or another.

Tips were small change when I was batboy. I remember that Ted Lyons of the White Sox always tipped a deuce and tipped everyone, but mostly I made money by selling used balls; we called them "old rockets."

One batboy I had was a cocky kid named Pat. I called him an angle-shooter. He'd take orders from the players for lunch and come back from Friedman's drugstore with an extra milkshake no one ordered. Someone would finally take it, but the gimmick was that there was always half a shake left over that wouldn't fit in the cup, so Pat would have it before coming back. I never stopped it—more power to him. But he did get his comeuppance. I sent him to Baltimore to get the bat-stretcher. Tommy Thomas, with the Baltimore club, then in the minors, had been briefed, and he told Pat he'd come a day too late, that he'd just sent the bat-stretcher up to the Yankees. He put Pat on the train to New York, but at Yankee Stadium they turned him away, thought he was nuts. He came hangdog back to D.C., apologizing for his failure. He was not so cocky after that.

There was no serious gambling, and never on baseball. Oh, the kid who followed me, mascot in '33 under Cronin, later became a bookie. They played hearts and pinochle in the clubhouse, a little poker once in a while, nickel-dime. Mr. Griffith had a pinochle tournament in the office on New Year's. Rogers Hornsby and Al Simmons loved to bet the horses. Piersall loved to play gin rummy. There was a bookie named Joe who hung out at Bass's in Mt. Ranier, place run by three brothers, Jack, Benny, and Sol Bass, where a lot of us went. One night coach Ellis Clarey comes in for a beer, dressed in coat, tie, and hat. Joe doesn't recognize him, thinks he must be a cop, flushes all his numbers slips down the toilet. Pete Rose? I think it's a crime to crucify the man.

Booze and women ruined more good ballplayers, but I never saw much drinking in the clubhouse, just some beer, but I never saw anyone drunk. Paul Casanova smoked some marijuana on occasion, but he's the only one. Charlie Dressen liked his Early Times, kept a bottle in his office, said he needed to have a drink to give the newspaperman or he'd never come to see him. Joe McCarthy liked his Black and White. Art Fletcher did the X and O managing for the Yankees. The great managers were Bucky Harris, who could make something out of nothing, and Jimmy Dykes, who would accurately predict the standings in the spring.

Oh, there were great guys. Cecil Travis, who got frostbit in the Battle of the Bulge, a great player who never regained his form after the war. Bobo Newsom with his superstitions, his glove always opened toward the dugout. He never smoked the first or last cigarette in a pack and always threw matchsticks behind him. George Case with his rabbit's foot. Alvin Crowder kept black widows in a jar in his locker, stuffed with grass—he caught flies for them. Frank Howard with his size 54 shirt and 36 pants. DiMag—the greatest player and a perfect gentleman. He'd never argue or badmouth anyone. And Eddie Yost, another gentleman, a great salad-eater. He's the godfather of my sons, John and Eddie, who were both batboys.

Now Goose Goslin was a player who drank a little bit but always gave a hundred percent on the field. He smoked a lot between innings, would stuff the unfinished butt in his back pocket and burn holes in his uniforms. Gave me problems that way. He'd always take a Dr. Pepper from the same corner of the case before a game, then in the second or third inning would take a pee in the urinal down the tunnel behind the dugout. One day I doctored his Dr. Pepper with a pyridium pill, you know, a kidney flusher. And when Goose goes down in the third inning he starts to piss bright red. He runs up into the dugout holding his pecker and yelling to trainer Mike Martin, "Please help me, I think I'm bleeding to death."

Buddy Myer, our second baseman, used Fitch hair tonic, but too many others borrowed it. So when there was an inch left in the jar, he pisses into it and leaves it out. Sure enough, it got used anyway, so he stands up in the clubhouse and announces to the team, "This much was Fitch, the rest my piss, and I hope you enjoyed it."

That wasn't the worst. Gerald Walker our left fielder used to be buddies in Detroit with Slick Coffman the relief pitcher. The first time the Tigers came in after Gee was traded to us, Coffman filled his glove with dirt for a joke. Walker got even the next day. He comes in early and takes a healthy one and then, with a sharp stick, fills Coffman's glove with it. You should have heard Slick roar when he stuck his hand in it.

Yeah, they were all great in those days. There's only one player I'd ever badmouth, that no-good bum Denny McLain, another one of Mr. Short's little bobos. I'll tell you the kind of guy he was. One day he was denied entry to the team parking lot—he'd given his ticket to some bimbo—and he lied to Short about it and had the parking attendant fired. When he was traded he left town owing me $67, and he never paid. I got even, though. I kept his golf clubs, gave them to my son.

Fred Baxter retired to his Bethesda, Maryland home with his wife Doris after one season in Texas with Short's Rangers. His batboy sons are both mailmen.

George Catloth ....

I lived just a block from Griffith Stadium and I used to make some money during ball-games by asking people, "Watch your car?" when they parked. Then I sold papers, first outside, then inside the ballpark, got to know everybody, until Frank Baxter hired me as visiting batboy in '32. From '34-'38 I was the mascot—the home-team batboy of the Washington Senators.

I think I was responsible for the first organized strike in baseball history. The Browns had come to town, with Rogers Hornsby as manager, and we had unloaded their hundred and two bats and been paid two dirty old balls. So the two of us refused to work the next day—and enjoyed it when Monte Weaver shut them out with only two hits from all those bats.

Not everyone was so cheap. Al Simmons was a good, generous guy. Babe Ruth was crazy. He'd throw cherry bombs in the shower room, knocked me on my ass once, but tipped five bucks when leaving town. When teams left, we'd have to go to Union Station with them to help load the equipment on the train. One time, Lefty Gomez gave me a buck to buy a three-cent stamp for an envelope. The stamp machine was about ten yards away, but he told me to keep the change.

Then there was Dutch Leonard who was always bitching and complaining about the price of things. He didn't like it that he'd be charged 25 cents on the tab for ice cream, so he'd send kids to Koss Drug Store at 7th and Florida instead. We fixed him when we brought him one little scoop in a big dixie cup and told him that was 40 cents' worth.

I used to earn Cokes for pitching batting practice to the yannigans, you know, the re-serve players. And then there was the time I got my World Series cut, batboying for the Giants in '33. See this C-shaped scar on my right index finger? I was piling warm Coke bottles in the ice box before the game, and when one of them exploded I got my World Series "cut." By the way, that was the only game the Senators won in the Series, Earl Whitehill shutting out the Giants. Monte Weaver was almost as good the next day, but lost it in the eleventh inning, to Carl Hubbell, who pitched two complete games for wins. They were real gentlemen, those Giants, Hubbell and Mel Ott and Bill Terry.

Walter Stewart, called him Lefty, who pitched for the Senators that year, was a hunt-ing man from Sparta, Tennessee. On closing day in '32 he had brought his bluetick hounds into the clubhouse, in their cage, so he could take off for home right after the game. Well, Alvin Crowder, called him General, was quite a dandy in those days, and he let it be known that he resented the dogs' presence in his dressing room. You should have heard him bitch and moan after the game when he found the clay dog turds in front of his locker that we had put down during the game.

They did some crazy things back then. Oscar Melillo, the Red Sox coach, was scared of insects, so they were always putting worms in his shoes. One day they sent me down to Garrison's Novelty Store for a fake snake, put it in the coaching box and then made it move with a thread running from the dugout. And I'll never forget the day they had me put a pyridium pill in Goose Goslin's Dr. Pepper after I'd pitched batting practice. It was against Detroit, and in the third inning, two things happened almost at once. Goslin was pissing in the corridor behind the dugout and the crowd was roaring because Hank Greenberg just hit the shit out of one, and then Goslin comes running into the dugout calling to trainer Mike Martin that he was bleeding to death.

Of the visiting teams, of course, the Yankees stand out most clearly in my mind. Besides the Babe, I remember Ben Chapman—a fancy dan who always knew his own average but not where the team stood; Lou Gehrig—a sedate, pompous man; Pat Malone—a crazy pitcher who once pissed in the fire in the pot-bellied stove that stood in the center of the visiting clubhouse; Myril Hoag—an outfielder with small feet, who'd have me break in a new pair of size 6 1/2 or 7 spikes until he came back to town; and Joe DiMaggio—the gentleman's gentleman, who came to a Redskins game with Edward Bennett Williams a few years ago and said he remembered me.

The Yankees always gave their rookies a hard time. When the old clock was removed from the right field wall in Griffith Stadium, they'd sit on the bench talking about the clock running slow or fast, teasing the rookies who'd be trying to find a clock among the welter of billboard ads. One of their favorite tricks was to hire a little black boy for a buck to stand at the clubhouse entrance and holler, "Daddy, Daddy," at a rookie.

Joe Cronin was really good with kids, even after he became president of the American League. One day he called a Red Sox team meeting and told me to keep everybody out. I ended up barring Tom Yawkey from the clubhouse—I didn't know he was the owner. And then Ted Williams. What a rebel! He was refused meals in the Shoreham when he'd go in there wearing a T-shirt.

Charlie Gehringer was the player I loved most. When he dropped a pop fly in the '37 All-Star Game I almost cried.

Bucky Harris was another manager who was great for the clubhouse kids. After a loss he'd have us call his wife, Liz, and say he'd be late, then give us a couple of bucks each to sit around and play hearts with him.

The best athlete on those Senators teams was Wes Ferrell. He could do anything—horseshoes, golf—but he was also very hot-tempered. One day in Orlando he threw his clubs and bag in a lake and then warned his caddy, "If you go down there for them, I'll throw you in the lake." He and his brother, Rick, got into an argument in the clubhouse after a tough loss one day, and when Wes took his watch out of the money box and found it had stopped, he threw it on the floor and stomped on it.

Zeke Bonura was good to kids, too. On off-days he'd take us fishing down at Solomons Island. But he took a fancy to Thelma, Mr. Griffith's adopted daughter, and we thought that was why he was traded.

I remember a couple of left-handed pitchers, Joe Krakauskas and Ken Chase. They were so wild you had to wear shin guards and a mask just to warm them up. It was funny to see them pitching batting practice to each other, getting a taste of their own medicine.

Remember speedy George Case? When he was training for a match race with Jesse Owens, he'd get me to run with him. I was pretty fast, but he'd give me a ten-yard start and catch me within fifty yards.

In '39 I got my chance. Clark Griffith sent me to Ashland, Kentucky, to play in the Mountain State League, as a shortstop and then second baseman for $75 a month. I could run and field but I couldn't hit. I got to play third base during batting practice against Greenberg and Jimmy Foxx, and have the broken fingers to prove it. Buddy Lewis, a lifetime .300 hitter, gave me two of his bats, but that didn't help. At least, later, I could blame him for my inability to hit.

Working in Griffith Stadium, I got to see Joe Louis and Max Baer, FDR and John Nance Garner, who was at the ballpark almost every day after 3. What else is a vice-president supposed to do? I also got to keep the scoreboard for the Homestead Greys and see Josh Gibson, one of the greatest ever and as good a player as I've ever seen. One day in Griffith he hit five home runs in a doubleheader—three in the left field stands, one over the right field fence, and one over the fence in dead center. One spring, when the Senators came to Tinker Field in Florida to watch him, Gibson threw a runner out at second from the crouch and they all said, "OK, we believe."

I'll be honest with you. The game of baseball is so slow now, I only go to a couple of Orioles games a year.

Long since retired, George Catloth retains a
professional connection with the ballpark.
Joined, in turn, by his son and his grandson,
he has run the scoreboard for the Washington
Redskins' home games since 1937.

BILLY CAHILL ....

I was St. Louis Browns batboy from 1937 to 1939. I went into the service in 1941, but as soon as I got out I went back with the team and caught batting practice until '49. I loved baseball and I still do.

My best memories are my first game and a two-week road trip I went on when I was 15. We hit all seven cities. I roomed with Bob Bauman, who for sixteen years was the Browns trainer.

The pay was two balls a game, used, that I sold for fifty cents each. Tips, too. Red Kress, Don Heffner, and Harlond Clift were the big tippers I remember.

One day I was in the on-deck circle rooting for the Browns batters, and Cal Hubbard was the umpire. He yelled at me, "You will stay back by the dugout and you will quit yer hollerin'." So I did, but I had a longer run to retrieve the foul balls coming off the screen. Then Bauman said to me, "Why don't you just shortleg a couple of balls?" So I did, twice, and the balls rolled back toward the plate and onto the field. Then Hubbard turned around and said, "You win, you can go back to the circle, but you will keep yer mouth shut!"

I'm a retired man now, but I still have my uniform—not the service one, the baseball one.

Billy Cahill still lives in St. Louis. He's a
Cardinals fan.

THE FORTIES

THE FORTIES

World War II thinned the ranks of Major League players in their prime, at the same time extending the careers of older and marginal players. Batboys, too, experienced both extremes.

Some, like Dan Scanlon of St. Louis, enlisted in the Navy before the '42 season and served several years in the Pacific, or, like Art Peters, waited until after the Cardinals won the '42 World Series and then served in the Army in Europe. But for those who were ineligible for service, the job could extend through additional seasons as baseball struggled to maintain whatever stability it could. At war's end, clubs welcomed back former batboys, finding or making jobs for them in patriotic gratitude.

In the post-war period, as baseball coverage expanded in the media, batboys were regularly pictured greeting home run hitters as they crossed the plate. Two in particular achieved a more substantial modicum of fame—Charlie Di Giovanna of the Dodgers and Garth Garreau of the Giants.

Charlie, better known as "The Brow," spent fifteen seasons in Dodgers clubhouses in Brooklyn and Los Angeles, on the road and on tour in Japan, all but the last few as batboy. When he died in 1958, at 28 (rheumatic fever had damaged his heart as a child), he was eulogized in *Coronet* magazine by Dick Young, who focused on the warm laughter that surrounded his presence in the clubhouse.

As the practice of getting signatures on balls became a regular part of the batboy's duties, it was The Brow who perfected the benign forgeries that spared the players and inspired generations of clubhouse hands. It all began because his manager, Burt Shotton, had a tremor in his writing hand and told his eager batboy to sign for him. Batboys have been easing the chore of collecting signatures by their handy efforts ever since.

Garth Garreau's writing hand was taking notes all through the 1946 and 1947 seasons, and the result was a book called *Bat Boy of the Giants*, in which he told his story (with assistance from sportswriter Joe King) from first interview to fond farewell. Written for a juvenile audience, it established the model for several subsequent books, with its depiction of heroic players, amusing incidents, and young emotions. Garreau, following graduation from Michigan State, was killed flying a training mission during the Korean War.

SID BORDMAN ....

Except for a few years in Minnesota, virtually all my school life and adult life was lived in Kansas City. I was hooked on baseball. Even in grade school when I had themes to write I wrote them on baseball. The ballpark was at 22nd and Brooklyn, and we lived around 28th or 29th and two or three blocks east. It was a safe neighborhood, and we'd walk over and find a way to get in, usually climbing a concrete fence. There was a guard we called "Tarzan" with a bullwhip, and I'll never forget the day he almost got me, that whip so close I could feel it going past. I got a job selling newspapers and *The Sporting News*, and that sort of led to the batboy job because I got to know the clubhouse guy. I was fourteen during the 1940 season, and he asked me to fill in for the Kansas City Blues when the regular kid was out for a few days. They won all three games, so when the regular came back he was sent to the visiting side and I stayed on.

The manager was Billy Meyer and we had an American Association infield that could have been in the majors—Billy Hitchcock, Phil Rizzuto, Gerry Priddy, and Johnny Sturm. Hitchcock and his wife used to pick me up in his brand new '41 Plymouth to drive me to the ballpark. That was really something. Rizzuto took a liking to me, treated me like a younger brother, took me out for haircuts and dinner. When he moved up to the Yankees we corresponded, and the next season I visited New York and stayed with him for two weeks.

Sometimes I'd get to throw batting practice to the pitchers. One day an outfielder, Arthur (Bud) Metheny, asked me if I wanted to be a player. I said yes, so he said, "You gotta learn to chew tobacco." He gave me a plug of Beechnut, and I ended up passed out on the trainer's table. I never saw the game that day. That was my only initiation trick, I guess.

Johnny Lindell was the only player who ever irritated me. He'd come up—6'4" and 220 pounds—and cork you in the arm or mash you in the back and laugh about it. If you said, "What did you do that for?" he'd say, "I want you to be tough."

Part of my duties as batboy would be to run up to get new balls from the general manager's office during late innings when the original eighteen were running out. I'd go up to Roy Hamey's office and say, "We need some more balls, Mr. Hamey," and he'd say the same thing every time: "Those damn umpires!" Now the balls are a dime a dozen, even if they cost a lot more.

I got paid 50 cents a game, plus a cut from the sales of soda pop, tobacco, and candy that we'd buy from the concession stands and sell in the clubhouse, with the players marking down what they took on a cardboard list in the training room and settling up before leaving on road trips. There were tips too, the best tippers being the players who had been in the big leagues and knew what it was all about. Buster Mills, who'd played for five Major League clubs, was the best tipper we ever had. But there were fringe benefits. I'd get up close for home plate action and get my picture in the papers. And there was a Mr. Wilson, a district manager for Standard Oil whose box was right behind me, who'd feed me hot dogs and peanuts every game—the fans were real nice. The ballplayers chipped in eighty or eighty-five dollars for each batboy the years they won the pennant, which was very decent for that time. They still gave a case of Wheaties for home runs, but the players couldn't be bothered, so my neighborhood had all the Wheaties it could eat.

And equipment. My local team, the Spring Valley Cardinals, was the best-outfitted team in town, with balls and gloves. A lot of us still had cracked bats from the '38 season, when Joe (Muscles) Gallagher, who led the American Association in cracked bats, was going with a girl in our neighborhood. We'd be hitting ourselves in the belly trying to swing those heavy bats in the playground. And there was a coach with the Minnesota Millers who wore size five shoes and kept me supplied with his extras.

For the '42 season I moved up to clubhouse boy and got a 100 percent raise to a dollar a game. I shined twenty-five pairs of shoes a day, with very little help from the batboy. And I had a new duty. One of our starting pitchers, Rinaldo (Rugger) Ardizoia, had me run up to the stands and give his wife a kiss before every game he started. And she was a beauty, too!

I made one road trip that season, to Milwaukee, where we won the pennant by sweeping a doubleheader the final day. We stopped in Chicago on the way home for a party at the Blackhawk. It was one of the first times in my life I wore a tie.

In '43 I got to go to spring training for the first time, but it was just in Excelsior Springs, Missouri because of wartime travel restrictions. My roommate was Yogi Berra, a rookie who was assigned to Norfolk that year. Ironically, the year before my American Legion team had played in the finals against his and got beat 11-8. Yogi drove in the eleven runs. But he never acknowledged me. He was always sort of spacy. Year after year he'd see me in clubhouses and in Florida, even last year, and he'd only say one thing—"You still working?" As soon as I turned seventeen that season I went into the service. Once a month throughout the war, even in the South Pacific, I'd get a box from the Blues with food and cigarettes, which I sold or traded. And as soon as I got back in February of '46, Frank Lane, who was then general manager, hired me to go to spring training at $25 a week, on condition that I live in the clubhouse, not the hotel. Actually, my accommodations were better than the players'.

Then I entered Rockhurst College, but I was also managing and playing for a semipro team. We'd manage to get a couple of paragraphs in the paper, and then I got to report on my college's teams. As a senior I told my editor, who'd covered the Blues when I was in the clubhouse, "I'm gonna try to get a coaching job." "No," he said, "you're coming to work for us. And not right away, but eventually, you'll be covering baseball." From '55 on I was at the ballpark, from '64-'67 I was the Kansas City *Star* beat reporter for the A's, and then the Royals until '80, also serving as official scorer most of that time.

I might be the only writer who started as a batboy, and it certainly helped. Players I had batboyed for, like Eddie Bockman and Lloyd Christopher, turned up later as scouts on the West Coast. And when I was in Cincinnati covering a World Series, Buzz Boyle—the coach who gave Rizzuto the name Scooter—took me over to see Tommy Reis, whom I'd known as a pitcher and who was an employee relations guy in a department store. Mostly I had learned what players and managers think—it was never a mystery in the clubhouse. I learned how players talk, when they meant what they were saying and when they were pulling somebody's leg.

More than anything else, what I gained from my time in the clubhouse was insight, insight about people, about players, about baseball.

Sid Bordman, retired from sportswriting, runs the Royals press box during spring training at Baseball City Stadium in Haines City, Florida, and returns to Royals Stadium in Kansas City as official scorer.

John Mitchell ....

I lived on 13th Street in Washington, a block north of Central High. Early in the summer of '41 I started cleaning shoes and running errands for Fred Baxter in the clubhouse at Griffith Stadium. After I while I took over as visiting-team batboy, and I stayed on through the '42 season. I got paid fifty cents a game plus tips. Joe Cronin was good for ten cents a game. I remember Ted Williams and Joe DiMaggio as tippers, but the tip I remember best was from Bob Harris, a right-handed pitcher for the St. Louis Browns. He gave me twenty-five cents for getting him a quart of High's ice cream, which he ate between games of a double-header—and then went out and pitched six innings of relief.

In those days, we used electric heaters in the locker room to dry out uniforms between games on humid summer days in Washington. Williams used to put two bats in with the clothes— thought the ball went off dry bats harder. I'll never forget the day Doc Cramer robbed him of home runs twice at the fence, in left center and right center. Williams said in the clubhouse they were "the two best catches I've ever seen."

I remember Rudy York sitting there in his two-piece blue underwear. He was part Indian and regarded himself as a great strongman. Barney McCosky—remember him, with that Charlie Gehringer look-alike batting stroke?—bet York he couldn't stand on a bat and lift himself up. He tried to do it for fifteen minutes before he figured out it couldn't be done.

The Red Sox had a pitcher named Broadway Charlie Wagner. He had grown up poor in Reading, Pennsylvania, but he had a new suit for every day of the week when he played baseball. Connie Mack, of course, always wore a suit and a hat, in the clubhouse and in the dugout. Then there was Jimmy Foxx, who'd sit in the clubhouse playing gin rummy, wearing just jock, socks, and shoes.

I remember stoic Lefty Grove, sitting in the lobby of the old Shoreham Hotel, smoking a foot-long cigar. George Case, Red Ruffing, and Lou Gehrig also stand out in my mind. And Bobo Newsom, with his superb sense of humor. Jeff Heath, too, who took great pride in his muscular build and did resemble a small Arnold Schwarzenegger. I can still picture the clubhouse scene with Doc Cramer sitting on the toilet and guys throwing burning rolls of paper over into the stall.

Two things I remember from the field: One was realizing for the first time the speed of a fast ball, when from up close I saw Virgil Trucks throwing—it was absolutely frightening. The other was a play I saw the Yankees make and have never seen since. It was Joe Gordon racing out into short center to field a Texas-leaguer, flipping the ball to DiMaggio, who then threw the runner out at the plate with Bill Dickey making the tag.

I learned to appreciate the players more from being around them. The game has changed. I think the train rides were good for baseball. But I love the d.h. rule—Williams could have played another ten years. You know, during the war, when I was with the Third Fleet in the Pacific theater, I used to love getting the long letters my father regularly wrote, and they were mostly about baseball.

John Mitchell recently retired as Chief Administrative Judge of the Circuit Court for Montgomery County, Maryland.

TOM VILLANTE ....

At Stuyvesant High School in Manhattan I became friendly with Chester Palmieri, who was a ballboy for the Yankees in the summer of '43. I'd help out occasionally in the clubhouse, but the day of the first game of the World Series, I saw Chet at school and asked him why he was there. "I can't work today," he said, "because I'm taking the Regents Exams." "Can I take your place?" "Sure." I got to the Stadium at 10 a.m. and saw Pop Logan, who with his son Eddie ran the clubhouse, and he said to suit up in a Cardinals uniform. I thought it was a mistake, a Yankee ballboy in a Cards uniform, so when I dressed I hid in the bathroom. But then I actually got to work the game. Later I asked Logan for a job as batboy, and Joe McCarthy heard and asked if I'd like to be the home batboy and told me to write him a letter at the Senator Hotel in Atlantic City. On March 17, 1944 I received a letter telling me to report to the Polo Grounds for the Red Cross game versus the Giants, but not to say anything because there would be a press release. I showed up, carrying my own spikes and some yellow socks. Frank Crosetti told me they were "bush" and had me change into black socks.

At Yankee Stadium I found my name on the locker next to Crosetti. He asked me then if I played ball, and I said I was a shortstop. I took some ground balls with him, and the throw was really too long for me, so I moved to second base. Cro taught me switch-hitting. George Stirnweiss taught me to pivot. And pretty soon I was taking second infield.

I was shocked, stunned by the clubhouse language, but the players were regular, terrific guys—Johnny Lindell, Red Rolfe, Red Ruffing, Stirnweiss, Crosetti. Phil Rizzuto was always the butt of jokes—they liked to scare him with insects in his shoes.

Joe DiMaggio always had a bobo, a buffer for the outside world. First it was Lefty Gomez, then Joe Page, and finally Billy Martin. "He tips more than I make," Billy would say. After a game, DiMag would walk into the clubhouse, hold out his hand, and Pete Sheehy would have a cup of coffee in it just like that.

Tommy Henrich used to practice his jumping and balancing act at the right field fence every day. When I asked him why, he said, "One day I know I'll make this play and it will save a run, a game, or maybe a pennant." No wonder they always won.

On the road I usually roomed with the trainer. One warning I got was about Washington, that they would try to keep the visitors' bat bag in the shower. On one trip to Chicago

I had a room to myself, except that I woke up in the morning to see a large, hairy-chested man shaving at my sink. It was Charlie Keller, just out of the Merchant Marines.

Joe McCarthy was always "Mr. McCarthy." The clubhouse was his domain. When Ed Barrow wanted to confer with him, it would be at the Harry M. Stevens office in the Stadium, not the manager's clubhouse office. If he suspected a player of fooling around, he'd go up to him with a cigar in his mouth and ask for a light—the matchbook would clue him in, as well as a shaky hand.

If he were worried about a player, he'd use psychology, tell Gehrig to help Rolfe out with throws by being especially careful, tell Rolfe to get throws up to help out the troubled Gehrig. If he wanted to see the catcher, he wouldn't say "Get Mike," he'd say to me, "Tell Mr. Garbark I'd like to see him," and Mike would go into his office and close the door.

We had a hard-throwing, wild right-hander named Bill Zuber. On one of his rare good starts, McCarthy was briefing him every half inning to keep him focused on what to throw to whom. In the sixth inning, Zuber forgets his glove when he goes to the mound. So he bends over and deliberately breaks his shoelace for an excuse to walk back to the dugout for his mitt. McCarthy just nodded at him, as if to say, "Sure you're in control." When McCarthy left New York for Boston, he acquired Zuber, because he was afraid he'd learn control and come back to beat him.

In the summer of '45 Lou Boudreau asked me if I was ready for college and offered to get me a scholarship at the University of Illinois. But Joe McCarthy said, "Pick your school, we'll send you. I ended up at Lafayette, on a William P. Coughlin Scholarship, played basketball two years, baseball four, and worked summers with the Yankees. Finally I made it to Yankees spring training in 1950. First day on the field, this fresh kid told me, "Move over to short—I'm the second baseman. Later I heard the same voice in Miami Stadium yelling at Jackie Robinson, "You old pigeon-toed bum." It was Billy Martin.

That summer my decision was easy. Rather than spend years in the minors trying to make the bigs as a marginal infielder, I'd grab the media moment with my idea for a United Features column, "My Day in Baseball" with Joe DiMaggio. By fall I was also ghosting a World Series column for Rizzuto for I.N.S. and then accepted a position with B.B.D.O., where my sports marketing career began.

Carmelo Villante was nicknamed Commie, which he changed to Tommie in 1950, for obvious public relations reasons. His résumé includes the jobs of Executive Director, Major League Promotions, and producer of "Lasorda at Large" and "Yogi at the Movies."

JIM HACKETT . . . .

I was born and raised within three blocks of Sportsman's Park. The Cardinals organization developed the nucleus for a staff from among the boys in the neighborhood, and it was a good education in life. At thirteen or fourteen you could be sitting with Sam Braden, the president of the club, in his office or in his box. In '44, I was hired by Butch Yatkeman to work in the clubhouse, but before I ever got a chance to suit up as batboy on the field I was moved up to the front office in '45 as a messenger boy.

In those days, the traveling secretary and the visiting team's traveling secretary would go around to all the stiles and tally the total attendance for the game. It would be written on two slips, and I'd run the first one to Mr. Braden's box. Harry Caray would be on the air and say, "I see Jimmy down in the president's box—he'll be up here in a minute with the attendance." And I'd deliver the second slip to the press box.

After we won the pennant in '46, I was sitting with Bill Walsingham, Leo Ward, Sam Braden, and Mr. Goldschmidt, the ticket man, as they were deciding when to put the World Series tickets on sale. There's a pounding on the glass door on Dodier Street. Mr. Braden said, "You better go down there, Jimmy, before whoever it is breaks the glass." I went and there was a man, his big car parked outside, who said, "Is Sam here?" I nodded yes and he said, "Tell him Machinegun Kelly is here from Chicago and wants a set of tickets." I didn't know who Machinegun Kelly was, but I brought the message upstairs. They all jumped up and went over to the window. "Let's give him a set of tickets," someone said. They were $18.75 a set. I ran down with a set, he gave me a twenty, and that was that.

You ask why so many batboys become policemen. Well, there are a lot of police around a ballpark, they make contact with personnel, and a relationship develops. It's the same type of job anyway, dealing with people. Certainly it was a great experience for me, dealing with people around the ballpark. The park gave tremendous background in trying to evaluate people of every class. It taught me the ability to spot a phony.

James J. Hackett rose through the ranks to be Chief of Detectives of the St. Louis Police with the rank of Lt. Colonel.

CHARLIE (THE GREEK) CHRONOPOULOS ....

Ten years I hung around the ballpark, Braves Field, from 1940 till 1949 when I graduated high school. I tried playing professional ball, got as high as Class B, Evansville in the 3-I League, where Wes Covington, Hank Aaron, and Eddie Mathews started. My greatest claim to fame, though, is that I played with Bob Uecker.

Stengel was the Braves manager when I started. Of course the high point was being the batboy when we won the pennant in '48. I still wear my ring. Bob Elliott was there, and Jeff Heath, Tommy Holmes, Sibby Sisti, Johnny Sain, Phil Masi. The worst thing that happened was the day that season when Heath broke his ankle sliding home against Brooklyn. I was right there, heard the snap, and saw the bone protrude. He missed the Series, might have made the difference. It was funny to get to play with guys whose shoes you'd shined. In a spring training game once, I got to pinch run for Earl Torgeson. Bucky Walters was coaching at first base, and he says, "Two away, you gotta go." Willard Marshall was up, and he lined the ball to the outfield. I was digging hard and following the signals all the way, and I remember Johnny Cooney especially laughing as I rounded third and slid home—long after Del Ennis had caught the ball and doubled me up at first for the third out.

The one time I remember they got me when I was a batboy was during a rain delay when someone said, "Greek, run out to the bullpen and get the rubber for the pitcher's mound," and I did. What seems really funny to me now is that in all those years in the clubhouse I never thought of doing police work.

Charlie Chronopoulos has been a police officer for more than thirty years, and for more than a decade he has been the Chief of Police of Tyngsborough, Massachusetts.

Tommie Ferguson ....

I worked in the Red Sox clubhouse when I was 15, in '45, but Braves Field was to be the first ballpark in Boston to get lights, so I moved over the Braves as a ballboy in '46. On the first day I showed up at the ballpark at six a.m. and reported to George Doc Young, the equipment manager. Sailor Bill Posedel took me under his wing, but there was a grand bunch of guys there. Tommy Holmes, Sibby Sisti, and Jeff Heath were all super. Eddie Stanky was wonderful to me. And Bob Elliott, "Mr. Team"—when I was in the service in Korea he used to send me The Sporting News and peanut brittle. Now, by the way, I've had a chance to scout Elliott's grandson. Sisti was the clubby's hero because he always tipped everyone. Bill Rigney, too—in '47 I remember he would tip everyone fifty cents every time.

That first year I got to travel to Philadelphia and New York, but from '47 on I took a western trip, riding the trains to St. Louis and Chicago, etcetera. I was given meal money on the road but I never was allowed to pick up a check. Lunch, breakfast, anything—someone on the team always took care of me.

Warren Spahn was always spitting tobacco juice on people's shoes, and I wanted to learn to do that. The first day I tried chewing tobacco I was the ballboy at the plate, and one of my duties was fielding the foul balls off the screen. Well, there was a ball coming down off the screen and there I was with a mouth full of chew. I looked up and swallowed some, and I promptly went down into the tunnel and threw my guts up.

Nineteen Forty-eight was a perfect year. I graduated Brookline High School, lettered in hockey and baseball, went on a western trip with the Braves, got to the World Series and got a ring and a big enough share to buy a car for my parents, and I had my first butterfly girl—you know, just to look at her gave you butterflies. But I think that was also the year pitcher Red Barrett set up all three of us kids with some Baseball Annie named Pearl in Cincinnati. The whole team knew about it. Jeff Heath was banging on our door claiming to be the hotel cop, and on the train back home Bill Voiselle kept walking by and saying, "Yep, ol' Pearl's got the clap again." Voiselle was a character. Whenever anyone got a box of Wheaties for hitting a home run, Voiselle would take it and save it. Then at the end of the season he'd load them into his truck and drive home to 96, South Carolina. One winter a writer for *Collier's* magazine went down there for a story and told how Voiselle would feed those Wheaties to his dogs. When the Chairman of the Board of General Foods read that story, it was the end of the "box of Wheaties" promotion.

In '52, the station wagon was all loaded with equipment and I was ready to drive as usual to Bradenton for spring training when I received a letter from Harry Truman that said, "Greetings." I played a little service ball, was a football trainer, and played baseball at Fort Myers—Johnny Antonelli was there. When I got out in February of '54 I went right back to the visiting clubhouse, though the Braves had moved to Milwaukee. I had thought about becoming a newspaperman then, and I was accepted in college at Xavier, but Hy Hurwitz wrote a story about me in the *Globe* and also called John Quinn in New York. That's why I was offered the chance to stay in baseball instead of going to college.

The best advice came from Eddie Stanky. He told me never to go to the minors. Even if you have to be an usher at the ballpark, he said, at least you'd be there if there was another opening. I moved up to equipment manager for the Braves, and in '58 I married Lois Petey Collins, the only Irish girl I could find in Milwaukee. But I still lived in Boston and sold ties in a Boylston Street haberdashery.

In '61, Gene Autry, Bill Rigney, and Fred Haney walked into the store and offered me the job of traveling secretary for the California Angels. Haney was a marvelous human being, who always made the little people feel important, and he gave me the biggest break of my life. From there I went to the Seattle Pilots in '69 and the Milwaukee Brewers in '70 as traveling secretary and vice-president for administration. I guess it helped that in my Milwaukee Braves days I used to get Bud Selig into Green Bay games when he was an undergraduate at the University of Wisconsin.

Hank Aaron came to the Braves in Milwaukee when I did. Did you know I was the one who gave him No. 44? He wanted to change numbers and that happened to be available, just a random thing. And then I was back in Milwaukee, in the other league, when Robin Yount arrived—there's no more professional person in the game. Some of the umpires stand out, too, like George Majerkerth, Lou Jorda who never cut his fingernails, Jocko Conlan who wore little polka dot bow ties a' la Bill Klem, Artie Gore—a nervous guy but a wonderful man, and especially Beans Reardon—a super guy who always gave an extra ball to the batboys after games.

Being a batboy is a wonderful job for a kid. It's a great teacher of human nature to be in the clubhouse.

Fergie retired from the Brewers to Santa Ana in 1983, but has continued in baseball as a Phillies scout.

DONALD JAMES FITZPATRICK ....

I was born in Brookline and went to Brookline High. Frankie Kelly, my friend and classmate, became a batboy our freshman year and he brought me in in our sophomore year, '44. I was visiting batboy till '50, was in the service '51-'54, came back as Red Sox batboy a couple of years and then became assistant equipment manager to John Orlando. He'd always say, "Give me the dead-end kid, that's what I like" for batboys. When I took over, I hired blacks, had as many as four at one time, and Mr. Yawkey liked that.

The umps were generally good fellows in my day, and that's changed. Bigger changes are expansion, which diluted the product, and the escalating money, which reduced incentive. But the biggest change of all is the black athlete, which added more to the game than anything else, with their talent, their intelligence, and their attitude, for example, men like Tommy Harper, Don Baylor, Willie Randolph, Jim Rice, and Frank Robinson.

I had always been a fan. I can remember how I struggled in the bleachers for Lefty Grove's three-hundredth win, and I grew up hearing "and a case of Wheaties for Jimmy Foxx." So '49 was a heartbreak on the bench. I cried. But history is written by victors. We lost. Go ask the Yankees about that season. Pete Sheehy was the best clubhouse man ever. He treated all others well, no matter how many times the Yankee won.

Dave Ferris was one player who took an interest in Kelly and me. I'll never forget that he bought shirts for us both for our high school graduation. Hank Greenberg was a wonderful man, the gentleman of all time. I batboyed for Pete Gray. He was not too happy a person, to be kind about it.

People talk about the difference between the real person and the media image of the person, as in the case of Ted Williams. But that can be carried out of context. Baseball is a difficult job because every day has tremendous peaks and valleys, your emotions go up and down, there are failures and successes daily. Of course Ted Williams was different when he was among his friends. But I was there at the moments of his life when he really betrayed his true self.

Among the managers, I thought that Steve O'Neill was wonderful, a fine man. But Joe McCarthy was a giant, a ballplayer's manager. When you win is when you look at mistakes, not when you lose—that's one thing I learned from him. When he took over the Red Sox, he kept saying to Bobby Doerr, "Make the double play, turn it, come on, Bobby, turn it," because Bobby always wanted to make sure of one. It was on a road trip in '49, staying at the Chase Hotel in St. Louis, that I learned how knowledgeable McCarthy was about the theater.

One day in Anaheim I saw Bill Rigney throw his hat to the ground and get chased by Ed Hurley. Later the batboy goes out to the plate and throws *his* hat, and Hurley chases him. Well, the next day, the kid was working as ballboy down the foul line, but he starts blasting his radio down there and gets chased again.

I used to run around a lot, on the road, with Yaz and Reggie Smith. One day, when we were in Oakland, '67 or '68, we drove over to Berkeley, along with Joe Foy. Well, we walk through Sather Gate and around the campus, and we sit on the wall there. I'm talking animatedly about something or other and I get up, and I'm demonstrating Williams' batting stroke, and a crowd starts to gather. It was amazing—anyone who got up to speak there at that time drew a crowd. We couldn't stop laughing about it, but we ran into traffic driving back and were almost late to the ballpark for the game, and Dick Williams was furious. That's a good idea for a book you have there, because baseball is so much a part of America, and batboys are so much a part of the game.

*Fitzie retired as Boston Red Sox equipment
manager in 1991.*

JOHN DONOVAN ....

My basketball coach in Chelsea recommended me to John Orlando, who ran the Red Sox clubhouse, and I started working there in 1946. In '48 I was visiting batboy, and the next three seasons was a ballboy. From '52 through '57 I worked summers for Dick O'Connell in the ticket department and as a night watchman winters. That saw me through Holy Cross (class of '54) and Boston College Law School.

When I started in the clubhouse I was elated and awestruck, being around Johnny Pesky, Bobby Doerr, Dom DiMaggio, Birdie Tebbetts, and Ted Williams. I was too overwhelmed to let anything shock me. When the Red Sox won the pennant in '46, Filene's was giving camel's-hair coats to the team. The tailors came to the clubhouse to measure them, and Williams wanted the kids taken care of. They're not on the list, the tailors said (one of them was the father of rookie Eddie Pellagrini, by the way). Williams said, "Take care of the kids, and then you can measure me." You know, I still have that coat.

Pesky was particularly good to batboys. Doerr was always a gentleman, and so was Dom DiMaggio. But the daily intensity of Ted Williams was electrifying. Joe DiMaggio was a quiet man; in '47, after I packed his trunk on getaway day, he called me over, saying just "Donny," and tossed me his cap as a souvenir. He had a special shoe to protect his bone spur that was designed by a Mr. Kaufman of Quincy. Now his son Ron is a White House aide. Mr. Yawkey always called me Donny, but as long as she lived Mrs. Yawkey called me Donnybrook.

One game I'll never forget was against the Browns when I was working down the right field line. Williams hit a liner that I gloved on one hop and threw to Dick Kokos at second base. It was a fair ball. Umpire Cal Hubbard called me out from a corner of the dugout to tell me to pay attention, but Manager Joe McCarthy just said, "Don't let it bother you." A telegram from Will Harridge, the American League President, said "talk to the kid."

Baseball is much more complex now. But the law business, like baseball, is based on preparation.

John Donovan, until shortly before his death
in 1993, was Executive Vice-President and
Counsel for the Boston Red Sox.

Stan Strull ....

I started working in Ebbets Field as a turnstile boy, at 50 cents a game plus free admission, at age thirteen. I had to get working papers to do it. I became a batboy when Harry Rudolph broke his ankle, and I was replaced by Charlie (The Brow) Di Giovanna. I joined the Navy in '44, and when I got out in July of '46 I went right to the visiting clubhouse.

I worked "off the books" because as a vet I was a member of the "52-20 Club," but from '47-'51 I made three dollars a game plus five from the clubhouse man. Later I did stats for NBC when the Game of the Week was in New York. But eventually I took the civil service exams and qualified for the police. I was always very low-key, as opposed to The Brow who was a colorful guy. Throughout my career I was always known as "so-and-so's partner."

High points on the field were seeing Lavagetto break up Bevens' no-hitter in the '47 Series and batboying for Rex Barney's no-hitter against the Giants in the rain in '48. Rex had eaten a hot dog, thinking there would be a rain-out, and it kept repeating on him during the game. In '49 I got a one-quarter World Series share, and I bought my first car with it. My first road trip was in '47, and I roomed with that great pitching prospect Elmer Sexauer. His career was all of two-thirds of an inning in '48—two walks and two outs. On later trips I roomed with either The Brow or our boss, Johnny Griffin. He was known as "the Senator" and was the kind of miserable guy you had to check every little thing with, like "So-and-so wants a Coke, OK?" I also got to go to spring training from '49-'51.

I met a lot of outstanding people, like Pee Wee Reese. Roy Campanella was A-1. Jackie Robinson was a great competitor—no one else could have stood up to such abuse. Clyde Sukeforth is still a friend, and Sam Narron, who was blinded in one eye by a firecracker thrown by a fan. I still exchange Christmas cards with George Shuba. There were a couple of players who were worshipped by people who were pains in the ass in the clubhouse. And there were some that people didn't like but I never had a problem with, like Eddie Miksis and Dick Williams. Leo Durocher? He was aces in the clubhouse and always a big tipper.

Stan Strull, nine years a cop and twenty-four
a detective, mostly in Bedford-Stuyvesant, is
now a private investigator.

DAVID POVICH.....................................

As a batboy during spring training for the Washington Senators in 1946 and 1947, my clearest memory is of being introduced to Dr. Pepper in the clubhouse. I remember that clubhouse in Orlando and the Angebilt Hotel and Berger's Tavern, where my dad hung out with Arch McDonald and other writers, and the endless hearts games they'd play.

I remember learning the art of dressing properly in a baseball uniform, so that both pairs of socks and the pants fit right. Among the players, I remember Early Wynn, how tough he was and all business, with the philosophy that the batter was a guy trying to take money out of his pocket.

Most of all I remember Eddie Yost as a rookie. He was clearly my biggest influence. I used to stay with him, doing everything he did, spending hours learning how to slide. We'd slide till the skin came off our ass. I'd stand next to him when he was getting coached, be next to the cage when he was getting batting instruction, and run the bases with him learning to round them the right way. Watching Yost start from nothing, with *some* talent of course, and make himself into a star was a great lesson for me. He was a model of hard work and he taught me never to flinch from obstacles or challenges.

After four years as varsity third baseman at the Landon School, David Povich went to Yale and Columbia Law School, has practiced as a litigator in the Washington firm of Williams & Connolly since 1962.

MAURY POVICH..

With the Washington Senators, in the late Forties, during spring training at Tinker Field in Orlando, I was clubhouse boy, ballboy, and batboy. My father, Shirley Povich, covered the team for the Washington *Post*, so every February we moved to Florida. My brother David and I were taken out of school and put in school in Florida, which was so bad that they let us out at noon. So it was arranged with Clark Griffith that we could work for the team.

I was nine years old and I learned how to swear and smoke—Lucky Strikes.

I was in awe of the managers—Ossie Bluege, then Joe Kuhel, were both scary to us kids—and some of the players. Gil Coan was the fastest man in the league then, and I remember him laboriously wrapping his ankles, tender from eczema, every day. And the old catcher Jake Early—I thought he was the strongest man alive because he could throw one Povich kid over one shoulder, the other over the other shoulder, and then pick up a third kid between his legs.

In '48, his last winter, Babe Ruth came to the ballpark in a camel's hair coat from shoulders to shins and a camel's hair cap. I knew he must have been very sick to be so covered up in the March heat of Florida.

I lived out the classic batboy's nightmare one day. There was a play at the plate, and everything seemed to arrive at the same time—the runner, the throw, the catcher, the umpire, and the batboy. I was so mesmerized by the play that I forgot to clear the bat out of the way, I was just standing there, and the runner slid right through me to the plate. Clark Griffith, sitting in the stands with my mother, turned to her and said, "Ethel, this boy of yours is gonna get hurt if he doesn't pay more attention to what he's supposed to do."

Baseball was good for me. When I was sixteen I became a gofer for Bob Wolf, who was the Senators broadcaster, and from him I first learned the importance of accuracy in broadcasting. As assistant director and stats man, I had to keep him up to the minute on factual matters, who was warming up, etcetera. But now free agency and long-term contracts have changed the game. In the baseball I remember, nobody ever *didn't* put out all the time.

Maury Povich hosts a daily television talk show on NBC.

William (Red) Willis...........................

In 1947 I was a visiting clubby with Detroit, but even before that I had been a batboy on the sandlots with Federation teams. From '48-'51 I was the Tigers batboy. The next couple of years I spent in service, with the Army, mostly in Alaska, and when I got out I went right back to the ballpark. I ran errands, read stiles, and by the late '60s was selling tickets. It got in my blood.

The players were great. They nailed my spikes to the floor, threw me in the whirlpool, uniform and all—it was always fun when they were winning. Vic Wertz was a wonderful person, Virgil Trucks too—I barnstormed with him and Gene Bearden after the '51 season. Fred Hutchinson and Diz Trout were swell, and Hoot Evers a favorite of mine. Gehringer was a great, great man. Red Rolfe was quiet but a tough customer and a good manager. Among the umpires, Bill Summers was a standout—he always let you know. The biggest change from then to now is the d.h. Otherwise it's still baseball and still the Tigers. No, I wouldn't change it, but I wouldn't want a son to do what I did—it's not good for two people in the same family to work in the same outfit.

William Willis worked his way up to Director of Ticket Sales at Tiger Stadium, retiring on disability after his stroke in late 1990, marking 43 years with the Tigers.

FRANK MCNULTY ....

My start was serendipitous. When I was fourteen, Lou Scalponetti, a friend of the family who worked for the IRS but had connections in baseball with the Boston Braves, had promised to get me a job working concessions at the ballpark. He was driving me out to Braves Field but stopped on the way to pick up two players—I forget who—at Copley Square. And they took me in to meet Shorty Young in the clubhouse, suggesting that I could work there, which I did, as clubhouse boy, in 1945.

The four years after that, while I went through Boston College High School, I mostly batboyed on the visiting side, and then in '50, after my freshman year at BC, I replaced Charlie (The Greek) Chronopoulos as the regular Braves batboy. I graduated in '53—batboying had paid for my college education.

It was during the '48 season that I became, according to Billy Sullivan who did p.r. for the Braves then, "the most publicized batboy of the time." Norman Rockwell came down from the University of New Hampshire to Braves Field on a Sunday. They dressed me in a Cubs uniform and he gave me a single instruction—"look sad"—and took about twenty-five individual shots. I got five dollars for it and, later, a signed copy. In September, there I was on the cover of the *Saturday Evening Post*, standing in front of the dugout with Charley Grimm and others sitting behind me. A couple of years later, I was also featured in a *Sport* magazine story called, "Everybody Envies the Batboy."

At first I was just so in awe of the whole experience. Those were the Braves of Southworth, Spahn, Sain, and Bob Elliott. I also remember Chuck Workman, Whitey Wietelmann, Butch Nieman, and Connie Ryan. Southworth arranged for me to go on my first road trip, the last western swing in '46. After two years in the Marine Corps, although my college degree was in marketing, I started a career in business. Before coming to New York with McCall Publishing, I worked for General Motors, and I got my first job there—in part—because of my experience in baseball. I answered an ad for a job in their comptroller's office in Framingham, and the comptroller turned out to be a sports nut. I think the key to the interview that opened the door for me was the fact that I was wearing my 1948 World Series ring.

To sit through a pennant-winning season is an experience like no other. It feels like destiny has taken over, that everything is pre-ordained to work out right. Amazing things would happen for the Braves in '48. In Chicago, for example, when our lead over St. Louis had shrunk to a game or two, we lost the first game of a doubleheader. And we were losing the second when Jeff Heath hit a drive over Hal Jeffcoat's head. Jeffcoat, a rookie playing center field at Wrigley, ran back and hit his head on the ivied wall. And Heath, who'd normally take two and a half days to run around the bases, had an inside-the-park home run.

Frank McNulty is the president of Parade *magazine.*

THE FIFTIES 50

THE FIFTIES

If ever baseball could be said to reflect the culture at large it was during the Eisenhower Era. Looking forward to great changes to come and initiating some of the processes that would lead to those changes, it essentially held to its comfortable traditions. The Yankees and the Dodgers dominated the decade, though the Brooklyns became the Los Angelenos. Blacks and Hispanics came to the Majors as players in increasing numbers, but clubhouses, like management, remained majority bailiwicks.

Batboys were paid by the game, the long hours made tolerable by their associations with the game and their heroes. Among their perks, it became common to be taken on one road trip during the season. This, in turn, contributed to the establishment of closer relationships with some players. In part, this may also account for the notion of batboy as an entry-level job for a baseball, usually clubhouse, career track. At the same time a pattern emerges in which batboys often go on to pursue careers in law enforcement.

The movement of franchises opened up many new doors for batboys in the new cities, but the kids who had worked for the minor league clubs in those cities had the inside track. And among the treasured souvenirs of batboys of the era are a ceremonial first ball signed by President Eisenhower, a ball stained by shoe polish that changed the course of a World Series, and a life-long friendship with Willie Mays.

CHARLES (CHAD) BLOSSFIELD . . . .

From the first, I lived a baseball life. My father was general manager of the Hartford Chiefs from 1938 to 1952, and when the club folded the Braves organization brought him to Milwaukee as assistant ticket director. When I was fourteen, I interviewed for a clubhouse job with Joe Taylor and got to be visiting batboy.

My first game, which I worked in my street clothes, was an exhibition with the Red Sox—Ted Williams, Dick Gernert, Parnell, Pesky, Doerr, Dom DiMaggio, Sammy White. Then on Opening Day I was in uniform for the Cards under Stanky, with Jerry Staley, Raschi, Musial, Schoendienst, Garagiola. Fergie [Tommie Ferguson] was back from the 45th Infantry Division and running that clubhouse like a good sergeant. The Braves won the game on a Bruton home run, and Stanky threw Fergie's radio right across the room.

I was on the field June 12, 1954, when Jim Wilson no-hit the Phillies. The Braves won 2-0 on homers by Smalley and Aaron. I remember that the attendance was 28,215, and I remember the Phillies locker room afterwards. The Whiz Kids were terribly depressed (many beers' worth, as I recall) for not getting any runs for their great pitcher, Robin Roberts, who threw a two-hitter back at Wilson.

That was Henry's rookie year—he was still wearing No. 5—and when the Dodgers came in they hadn't seen him before. He went four-for-four against Don Newcombe. He was a kind of mouthy guy and when Hank got his fourth hit, a double, Newk threw his glove down and walked out to second base. We didn't know what was going on as we watched him stand nose-to-nose with Aaron. Later we heard that what he said was, "You sonofabitch, what did your wife feed you for dinner? I can't get you out."

Somebody lodged a complaint with the Wisconsin Industrial Commission about my working under age, and I was taken off the field that June. But I stayed on in the clubhouse the rest of '54 and '55 until I turned sixteen in '56 and could suit up again. Then I ballboyed through '57 till I finished high school. The pay was $2.50 a game, and there was also a $500 World Series share. At the end, each player gave me five bucks for a going-away-to-college gift. Eddie Mathews gave me twenty extra and said, "Have a good time with the girls in college."

We got to take the last road trip of the year with the team, and they gave us $12 a day meal money. In 1956 in Cincinnati, there were four of us kids stuffing ourselves in a fine restaurant, when Frank Torre saw us. He was dining with this gorgeous blond named Sally, and of course he picked up our check. He didn't know that we'd each ordered two steak dinners plus strawberry shortcake. Back home in Milwaukee, Torre stands up in the club-house and announces, "Don't ever pick up the check for these guys."

The players were a bunch of unique, intense, mostly high school educated guys, but very few of them were mean or nasty. There were people like Musial, Hodges, Snider, and Campy, who were not only big tippers but genuinely acknowledged that you existed. And there was a Danny O'Connell, who was a kind of counselor for all the batboys and told us funny stories. There was the Kingfish, Wes Covington, who said of Tom Wilson of the Los Angeles Rams, "He couldn't make our high school team." And there was "Pruschka," quiet, work-manlike Andy Pafko, who was just not one of the boys. But guys like Torre, Mathews, Bob Trowbridge, and Red Murff (later the Mets scout who signed Nolan Ryan in 1964) would play basketball against us clubbies in a game we arranged at the Elks Club.

Some things happen in the clubhouse you never hear about. There was the time Lou Chapman of the Milwaukee *Sentinel*—they called him Gumshoe—wrote a story that em-barrassed the players. The next time he came back there, Spahn and Burdette picked him up, carried him into Doc's [training] room, and threw him head first, suit and all, into the whirlpool. "Write what you want," they said, "But you're soaking wet." He showed up later in the press box wearing a short-sleeve trainer's outfit.

And interesting things seemed to happen with visiting teams. Like the time when I was carrying a stack of equipment so high I couldn't see, and Big John the doorman was steer-ing me into the Giants' locker room. I stumbled, nearly fell, and sat down in the lap of a woman sitting on a folding chair in the corridor. It was Laraine Day, Durocher's wife,   who just laughed like a lady and helped me up.

I guess some of the wild stories you hear are true. Joe Adcock took me fishing with him one day, and I asked him if he had gotten a good night's sleep the time he hit four home runs in a game. "Broomsage," he said—that was the best he could do with my name, "I was up till five the night before, had one hour's sleep." But I think most are exaggerated. What I remember most vividly was being in a hotel room next to Mathews' one night, with walls thin enough for me to hear him come in at night, call his wife back home, and tell her he loved her. No doubt he was my biggest hero, and I was there at the All-Star Game in Mil-waukee in '77 when, at 47, he hit one off the wall in the old-timers game.

The best memory, of course, is October 6, 1957, the fourth game of the World Series, when I played my most important part. I had shined maybe 12,000 pairs of shoes from those cookie-tin sized containers of polish in my four years, without thinking much about it, un-til that day, the last time I would ever shine the shoes, when the Yankees were about to put the Series out of reach. Leading two games to one, they had tied this one up with three in the ninth and gone ahead in the tenth. Then Nippy Jones was sent up to hit for the Braves, with instructions to just get on.

Tommy Byrne's pitch hit him on the foot, but Augie Donatelli said no, just a wild pitch for a ball. I retrieved the ball at the backstop, and Jones said, "Gimme that ball, Bloss." I did, and he showed the ump the shoe polish on the ball. He changed his mind and awarded him first base. Then Logan's double tied it, and Mathews' homer won it and turned the Series around.

It was decisive, like the third day at Gettysburg. The picture of Nippy, Yogi, Augie, and me, standing at the plate studying the ball with the shoe polish I'd put on, was in all the papers next day. I still have that ball. You know, I once caught one of the ten most wanted fugitives, but the biggest thrill of my life was that home run by Mathews.

*Charlie Blossfield retired from the FBI in
1993, and is now Manager, Special Investiga-
tions Unit, Kemper National Insurance Co.*

RAY CRUMP ....

In 1949, as a ten-year-old, I was hired as visiting clubhouse boy. I got 50 cents a day, and it cost 34 cents carfare to get there and home. It was like going to a boys' club for me. The next season I was the youngest batboy at the time. I wore number 97. Bucky Harris gave it to me. Calvin Griffith was my only boss, and he retired my number 97—that was the guy who didn't even want to retire Killebrew's number.

My biggest thrill as a batboy was always making road trips. My first was at 12, to Boston, New York, and Philadelphia. After Jackie Jensen was traded to Boston in '54, he always entertained me when I came with the club. I'll never forget the time when I was 16 and was kneeling in the on-deck circle with Jensen. A big blonde with a beautiful body walks into the stands, and I says to him, "Jackie, how'd you like to go to bed with that?" "I go to bed with that every night," he says, "that's my wife."

In 1961, I wanted to stay in Washington with the new franchise, but when I was told I couldn't have the clubhouse job I went to Minnesota. The club ran a contest, with *Look* magazine, for twins to be the first Twins batboys. They promised all contestants personal interviews, so I had to fly up from spring training to interview 326 sets of twins. I eliminated them on several criteria—lived too far away, too young, too old, and too much baseball experience. I didn't want kids who wanted to play or watch baseball. I hired Peter and Richard King, who lived on a farm, did chores from five to nine in the morning, had never been to a ballgame, and wanted the job because if they won they wouldn't have to do their farm chores. They did well, worked four years, but there were no more contests.

I have lots of stories to tell, and many pictures to go with them, but I can't share them with you because I'm writing my own book.

Ray Crump has a store and baseball museum
across the street from the Metrodome.

STEVE ALTMAN . . . .

A friend of mine was a Senators batboy and got me a job as ballboy for the '51 season. Bucky Harris was the manager, and I wore Willie Miranda's old uniforms.

TV was a novelty then, and the players sat around watching TV before games. Communication was difficult on that team. There was a language barrier in the clubhouse, with half a dozen Cubans on the club.

I found that the superstars were aloof. I had more to do with the mediocre players, who seemed to be more kid-oriented, Connie Marrero, for example, or Mickey Grasso, a nice guy and big tipper.

It was Mantle's rookie season, and I found him easy to tease—handing him the bat and then pulling it back. The Mick was not amused. I remember a pre-season exhibition game with the Dodgers, when I was sitting on a chair behind the plate, tending the screen for foul balls, when Roy Campanella caught a foul ball off the screen, but the umpire called the batter out.

My whole life revolved around the job that year, and I missed it the next year when I moved from Southeast (Sousa Jr. High) to Northwest (Coolidge High). My mother was not pleased about the job in the first place. But I won't have to tell my grandchildren what it was like, because Mom and Dad brought a movie camera to a game and filmed me in action as a batboy.

Steve Altman is Senior Vice-President for
Commercial Leasing of the Charles E. Smith
Co.

KENNY BUSH....................................

I sold newspapers around the ballpark, Connie Mack Stadium, and got to know everybody in the Phillies organization. At 12 or 13 I got a chance to be batboy, and I been there ever since. I started in '49 and I was Phillies batboy for eighteen years.

I wanted to be a player. I took infield all the time. But I never could hit. It's a different game now. The money makes the difference.

Used to be, there'd be a super guy like Robin Roberts, a gentleman like Richie Ashburn. Now, you gotta cater to 'em. You gotta babysit millionaires.

My most vivid memory is '64, a bad year, the collapse in September. The manager, Gene Mauch, comes into the clubhouse after a loss in Houston, the post-game spread is all laid out, and he overturns the whole table.

Kenny Bush was visiting clubhouse manager
at the Vet in Philadelphia until 1991.

JIM WIESNER ·······································

I was the batboy for the St. Paul Saints, the Dodgers' AAA club, from 1952-57, and then the next three seasons ran the clubhouse. Because Mr. Griffith was moving the Senators franchise to Minnesota, the Dodgers were planning to move the Saints to Omaha. I was negotiating to move with them, but then I heard that Fred Baxter was not coming, that Ray Crump would move from the visiting to the home clubhouse, and so there might be an opening with the major league team. So I applied.

Now, in those nine years, I had always hoped to get to Florida for spring training, but it never happened. That winter, the Golden Gophers were in the Rose Bowl, and I was out there, staying with Norm Larker, who'd just hit over .300 as the Dodgers first baseman. I'd left word at home for all calls to be relayed to me. And it was while I was there that the offer came from Washington. It had one provision—that I'd have to go to Florida for spring training. I've been every year since, 24 as visiting clubhouse manager until Crump retired, and equipment manager since then.

That first year in Minnesota, the Twins ran a contest for twin boys to be batboys. The winners were the King boys, OK kids, but I'm glad I didn't have to do that again. I like to interview and then hire, the main requirement being honesty. They tend to stay several years, into their twenties. I haven't had many legacies, but now there's Mr. Kelly's son, Tom, Jr., and even at eleven he's very knowledgeable about his duties.

*Jim Wiesner is equipment manager for the
Minnesota Twins.*

JACK HUGHES.....................................

I was hospitalized as a boy for a long period of time with a brain tumor. My dad was a newspaperman and he kept me diverted by having famous people write me, send autographed pictures, etcetera. That began a lifelong habit of collecting celebrity autographs, memorabilia, etcetera, but I soon focused on baseball.

I worked around Griffith Stadium for about sixteen years, mostly in concessions, but for one year, 1956, I worked for the Senators as the batboy for the visiting club. And that included the National League for the All-Star Game. Ah, the pleasures and wonders of being on the field. I was allowed to shag flies during batting practice, and the first time I was amazed at how the balls carried. I would break in toward the plate and the ball would carry far over my head. The ball was yours if you could get it past the coach in charge—I developed a technique for doing that.

Wayne Belardi, an infielder for the Tigers, had designs on being a pitcher. He had me catch for him and scared the living daylights out of me with the speed of his fastball and the break of his curve. I even got a chance to hit off Iron Mike, the pitching machine, from around second base, and hit one over the right field fence. George Susce, Sr., was a coach for the Kansas City A's, and he said, "When you finish school, let me know and I'll arrange a tryout—you've got potential." He endeared himself to me forever. Another kid broke the pitching machine by seeing how far it could throw him.

I was an avid Yankees fan. They were the only team regularly to bring a uniform for the batboy. I can still hear some of the weird voices, especially the ridiculously high-pitched sound of Frank Crosetti. I swore that when Mickey Mantle and Whitey Ford were inducted into the Hall of Fame I'd be there, and I was, with signed pictures of us together to prove it. I went to great lengths to get that life-size cutout of Gil McDougald from a shoe store. I loved seeing Mantle and Billy Martin in the clubhouse, wearing cowboy hats and staging mock quick-draw gunfights. I also remember Mantle tediously, painfully, wrapping his legs. And I remember the day Martin was ranting and railing and cursing out Casey Stengel, marching up and down in front of the manager's office, with the rest of the club cowering in front of their lockers. Later we discovered that Stengel wasn't in the office.

I was impressed with the young, cordial Cleveland team, especially Rocky Colavito. Friendly and instructive, he would sit next to me on the bench and educate me about the fine points of play, why throws from the outfield went where they did, etcetera. On getaway day, he took that long walk *back* into the clubhouse from the Griffith Stadium parking lot through the tunnel, because he had forgotten to leave me a tip. Four bucks and all the change in his pocket.

They were the nicest team, overall. Manager Al Lopez treated everyone as people. He autographed a ball for me and said, "If we win the pennant, you're going to the World Series as our batboy." My allegiance immediately changed over from the Yankees, but the Indians fell short in the stretch. It was a great team, though, with Bob Feller, Al Rosen, Bobby Avila. I used to sit on Feller's ankles while he did sit-ups. One day I accidentally broke his wrist-exerciser in the locker room, but neither he nor anyone else said a word about it.

The player who made the most profound impression on me was Jimmy Piersall. He came into the clubhouse early one day and found me, twelve years old, reading a girlie magazine I had found in one of the Red Sox lockers. He grabbed the magazine out of my hands, threw it against one wall and me against another, and said, "I don't want to see you with this kind of stuff anywhere, anytime." Later, during the same series, kneeling in the on-deck circle, he told me he was gonna hit a home run—and he did.

I made $2.50 a day, plus tips. Players would leave a buck or two on getaway day. All-Star tips were more bountiful. Ted Kluszewski and Stan Musial each tossed twenty into the hat. A few years later, after the club moved to Minnesota, I visited the Twins clubhouse. What a stark comparison. It was night and day. There was a quality food spread in the Twins home clubhouse, and I could remember taking visiting players' orders for lunch between games of a doubleheader, running to the greasy spoon. You were lucky to have the bag intact when you got back, there was so much grease on the burgers.

As a collector I saw different sides to people. Ty Cobb, for instance. I had heard many bad stories about him, but I didn't really know what he looked like. I hung around outside the Touchdown Club when he was a guest honoree, and I kept asking men as they were leaving if they were Ty Cobb. Finally, someone took me inside to meet the great man, who sat me down and told me stories, affably demolishing the negative image and signing a picture and a ball for me.

Baseball has been central to my life. I regret not following up on two opportunities, first, going to Minnesota with the club when offered a job, despite the lack of specifics, and second, not going to graduate school in sports management at Ohio University when I graduated Mount St. Mary's.

Jack Hughes has made a successful career in public relations and is a volunteer "Designated Hitter" for the Baltimore Orioles. The basement of his Columbia, Maryland, home is a veritable museum of baseball memorabilia.

JERRY SCHROER ....

From 1955 to 1958 I worked for the Cardinals at Sportsman's Park in St. Louis. Before that, at twelve or thirteen, I used to hustle soda pop at the ballpark, for Cards and Browns games. The streetcar was a nickel if you could pass for under twelve, and then at the park I had to pass for sixteen. I moved up to peanuts, which was a better seller, and then in '54 got the chance to be a batboy.

I was fifteen years old when the man who ran the visiting clubhouse couldn't continue, and I was asked to take over. The next season, because Butch Yatkeman asked me to be the Cardinals batboy, I got my father to take over the visiting clubhouse job. He was a machinist by trade, but he did it until his death in 1974. And I kept batboying until Butch said I was too big for the job—I was already bigger than Solly Hemus when I started.

Mr. Busch had bought the club and in '54, for $300,000, he bought three players who were supposed to turn things around—Alex Grammas, who became a journeyman infielder, Tom Alston, a big black first baseman who was rarely used, and Memo Luna, a Mexican lefthander who pitched only one game in the majors. Still, they became contenders after Fred Hutchinson became manager in '55.

I had seen Bobo Holloman pitch a no-hitter for the Browns, I was hustling pop the day Bill Veeck brought in the midget, Eddie Gaedel, and I remember Satchel Paige's La-Z-Boy chair in the bullpen. I remember Ned Garver, Marty Marion as manager, and Clint Courtney, who was kind of aloof in those days. But the only reason I was upset when the Browns left was because it meant a loss of income for me.

There were tight quarters in that visiting clubhouse. The black players were crowded into corner lockers called "Shithouse Row." I remember blacks being only in the upper right field stands and how I rooted for the Dodgers and Jackie Robinson. He got a death threat in St. Louis and left town early, and two weeks later he *mailed* tips for the clubhouse kids.

Stan Musial was a big tipper, twenty bucks every time. I loved seeing him hit five home runs in a doubleheader, but the hardest ball he hit that day was caught. Leo Durocher was a good tipper, too—he seemed a cold man but he always looked out for the little guys.

And then there were the cheap guys. Willie Puddin' Head Jones was a blowhard, who'd always say, "I'm a little short of cash but I'll catch you next time, and I'll get you a sport coat wholesale"—but he never did either. Enos Slaughter—I was the one who was sent to tell him, during the second game of the "City Series" prior to the '54 season, to see the G.M. That was when he heard about the trade to the Yankees. "I'll catch you next time, Jerry," he said, but there was no next time and I had learned not to expect anything from him. Red Schoendienst was another one. Even though he came from Germantown, Illinois, where my dad had a farm, he was cheap with me. I was surprised at how ungenerous many of them were, but the awe I had for them never left.

I remember Floyd Wooldridge, who started eight games for the Cards in '55, his one big-league season. He injured his shin and the other players laughed at him, called him "The Goat." He'd put the rosin bag at the extreme edge of the mound area, and when asked why, he said, "I want it there so I can have time to think." And they'd say, "With what?"

I liked Bill Virdon, Ken Boyer, and Joe Torre. And Joe Frazier, who tried to teach me to throw a curve. And Wally Moon, whose hand I got to shake when he hit a home run in his first at-bat. I was friendly with Luis Arroyo, who lived in a hotel the whole '54 season while his family stayed home in Puerto Rico. And I was friendly with the "Polish Pride"—Rip Ripulski, Steve Bilko, and Ray Jablonski, who fixed me up on a date with his babysitter.

Among the umpires I remember Jocko Conlan, who'd grab your hand when you delivered balls and then not let go, and Al Barlick, who I thought was too bossy. I remember Charlie Jones, the p.a. announcer who kept the ballbag at the screen, who pulled me away from a brawl between the Cards and the Giants. I remember Earl Weaver, Sr., whose cleaning business handled the uniforms for the team—Earl, Jr.'s first contact with baseball. And I remember the St. Louis trainer, Bob Bauman, the best person I met in baseball.

My best memory is how much fun it was. When I was on the field I always thought everyone was watching me, and I always got a lump in my throat when running out to catch foul balls off the screen. There were three main lessons. First, that hard work pays off. Second, that I want to share my success with people who help, and so I'm a generous tipper. And third, I have been extremely sensitive to bigotry ever since.

Jerry Schroer's career with Allied Chemical took him to Charlotte, Chicago, and Cleveland as regional sales manager. He now owns and operates a nursing home company with some 1,600 beds.

JIM SCHROER ....

My dad managed the visiting clubhouse in St. Louis, did it until his death in '74. I worked for him in '55 and '56, was visiting team batboy in '57. The Browns were already gone when I started, but I didn't care—I was a Cardinals fan.

The two biggest tips I got were from Giants. When Orlando Cepeda was a rookie he dropped an envelope in the clubhouse on getaway day full of 50s and 100s. My dad and I told Butch Yatkeman and drove to the airport to try to catch him. Cepeda, meanwhile, comes back in a cab. We didn't see him till their next trip in, and he gave me fifty bucks.

The other was Dusty Rhodes, who had just come up to play for Leo Durocher. He gave me fifty on getaway day. What I remember best about Leo was him giving Willie Mays a lesson in gin rummy during a long rain delay. Danny Murtaugh's Pirates, though, were the Hearts kings of the National League. The manager, the coaches, and the bullpen catcher would play for hours.

There were lots of memorable guys. Julian Javier—I pitched batting practice to him and he couldn't hit my curve ball. Joe Garagiola—the only guy who could always get a smile out of Yosh Kawano. Jocko Conlan—who'd always grab my hand when I delivered balls to him at the plate. Fred Hutchinson—when he was the Cardinals manager, whenever I came over to the home dugout he'd harass me about stealing their signs.

A few incidents stand out, two of them involving Sandy Koufax. He and Roger Craig came up late in the '55 season, and I saw Koufax pitching batting practice to Carl Furillo. He keeps whiffing him, and Furillo says, "You dumb sonofabitch, this is supposed to be batting practice." Later, hotshot young Koufax is pitching against the Cards and gets two strikes on curves to Musial. I was sitting next to the trainer in the dugout, and he says to me, "Now he'll throw a fastball thinking he can get it past the old man and he'll hit it out." He does—grand slam. "What did he expect?" the trainer says, "he's only been doing it for eighteen years."

The best one was the end of the '56 season. Milwaukee comes in with the pennant on the line. Friday night, Warren Spahn loses 2-1 on a Joe Adcok error. Saturday afternoon they lose again. Sunday the Dodgers win the pennant. After the Saturday game a clique of five stayed around in the clubhouse drinking beer and some of the champagne—Spahn, Lew

Burdette, Eddie Mathews, Toby Atwell, and Bob Buhl. They were playing "clubhouse ball" with Spahn pitching beercans to Mathews catching, and I remember Burdette hit one off Buhl's head. Well, before they finally left they splintered all of Adcock's bats and nailed his spikes to the floor.

In '57 I got to batboy for the American League All-Stars, with Yogi Berra and Mickey Mantle. A thrill? No. That game was more of a pain in the ass than anything else. It was extra work, with dozens more balls to get signed.

*Jim Schroer served as an officer in Vietnam
and had a career as a metallurgical engineer
before joining his brother in the nursing home
business in Cleveland in '86.*

BILL PHILIPS.....................................

At first I tried to get a job as batboy through connections.

My father knew golfer Chick Evans, who knew the Cubs business manager. But he said no, lots of friends have sons and we can't take care of them all. At twelve, I was very small and my application was rejected. The next year, '55, when I was hired, the decision was based on nothing apparent. So I worked for Yosh Kawano that season, subbed when needed—about twenty games—in '56, and that was all.

At first in the clubhouse I was amazed that the players' physiques were not that athletic. Most of them smoked, and many looked like they had been drinking the night before. The only thing that distinguished them was amazing hand-eye coordination.

'Fifty-five was the first superstar year for Ernie Banks, who hit five grand slam home runs but was still a shy guy then. On May 12th, I was the Cubs batboy when Sad Sam Jones pitched his no-hitter against the Pirates. In the ninth inning he walks the first three men, and Stan Hack—the manager who was a wonderful man—says in the dugout, "One more and I'm taking him out." Sam proceeds to strike out Dick Groat, Roberto Clemente, and Frank Thomas. I was the first to the mound to congratulate him.

I had different kinds of embarrassments. One day I kept missing balls coming off the screen and the ump got on me, saying, "Are you trying to be on television?" Another time I was shagging flies during batting practice when a ball went through my glove and hit me in the eye. The fans are real close to the field in Wrigley and they all got on me. I had to be assisted to the clubhouse, got iced down, and ended up with a big black eye. Hank Sauer said, "All these players we got on the d.l., now even the fucking batboy is on the d.l." Ironically, they used my picture in a Wilson glove ad in *Sport* magazine. Two pages away in the same issue, advertising Rawlings gloves, was Stan Musial.

Bill Philips trades commodities on the Chi-
cago Board Options Exchange, not far from
Glenn Beckert, former Cubs second baseman,
who trades in the wheat pit.

MIKE MURPHY ....

I used to love baseball as a kid. I'd sneak into Seals Stadium and steal the balls off the field, and one day the trainer, Doc Hughes, said, "Look, rather than you steal balls from me, I'm gonna put you on as a batboy starting tomorrow." So that's how I got my first job, in 1952. I worked all through junior high and high school. All the kids were envious of me.

When the Giants came out in '58 I started working on the visiting side as batboy, through 1960, when I took over the visiting clubhouse. I was just out of high school but Eddie Logan gave me the chance. I was so green, so scared about how to handle it, but Mr. Logan kept saying, "You'll do it, kid, don't worry, you'll do it."

On the visitor's side I got to meet such great stars as Stan Musial and Bill Mazeroski, all the old guys. Everybody kind of liked me. They called me "Bobskin" or "Junior" because I looked like Bob Skinner, very thin, skinny, whittley like Bob, and I couldn't catch a ball out there either. To this day every time I see Stan Musial he calls me "Skins" or "Skinner." He used to play catch with me and give me thirty bucks for doing it.

When I was a batboy in the old Coast League I used to stay late to help the clubhouse man who worked another job at the railroad. He'd hand me the keys and say, "Murph, finish up," and I'd be cleaning the shoes, washing all the stuff, and hanging it all up. At that time we were run by the Boston Red Sox. Late one night I was leaving the ballpark, just a kid, twelve or thirteen years old, and I see Johnny Murphy and Joe Cronin arguing. Next thing you know Cronin takes off his jacket and takes a swing at Mr. Murphy, and I'm trying to break up a fight in the lobby.

They'd been at the press room all night drinking and I think it was about a ballplayer. But I guess there was a feud between them because they all wanted to be Mr. Yawkey's favorite, so they could run everything. I finally broke it up, and Cronin says, "Who are you?" and I says, "I'm Mike Murphy, sir." He says, "So you're a relation to this guy." And I said, "No, no, I just don't want you two gentlemen to get hurt." Then Jerry Donovan, the president of the ball club, came down and got the guys straightened out.

Mr. Logan took good care of us, treated everybody nice. He'd get the cigars out of Harvey Kuenn's office, and we'd play cards all night with Herman Franks. He'd let us stay over in the clubhouse on Friday nights. So whoever lost the card game, we'd throw them out the door in Candlestick with no clothes on.

Players used to sit around the clubhouse after games telling stories. You don't see that no more. Ballplayers now, they all rush out. Before, they used to sit around, drink a case of beer between all of them, and sometimes I'd have to drop everything to run and get them another case. I'd have to say Steve Bilko was the best storyteller. My job was to take care of Steve, make sure there was a case of beer in his locker after the ball game.

And then there were the red-asses. I dreaded to see Gene Mauch come to town. I'd put the bats up and he'd strike out and knock them all down. I'd put them back up, he'd knock 'em all down, and so who got a job managing the Phillies but Gene Mauch. He knocked over a few of my spreads, so I got mad at him. We didn't talk for years. Recently I saw him, and I said, "Gene, how are you?" "Oh," he says, "you're finally talking to me, huh?"

His was the worst temper I ever saw, but a couple of others came close, like Joe Nuxhall. After a tough loss, when Tom Haller hit a home run in the twelfth off Joe to beat Cincinnati, he was walking down the ramp, knocking things down. At that time there were rugs all the way around the clubhouse, and underneath it was concrete. Nuxhall meant to kick a stool, but the rug slipped and he went up in the air and fell right down on his ass. Everyone laughed. He says to me, "You son of a bitch, you put that carpet there, didn't you?"

Ballplayers of yesteryear were great. I used to go out with Harvey Kuenn. And after a day game with the Dodgers, Don Drysdale and Bob Miller wouldn't leave with the team. "I'm not rushing," Drysdale used to say, and I'd say, "No, I'll take you guys back into town." After I'd get through all the stuff, they used to say, "Murph, sit down and have a beer with us." Next thing you know we'd climb in the car, they'd say, "Let's go over to the Iron Gate and have a few beers." I'd say, "Yeah, I'll go with you." Next thing you know they started drinking the hard stuff. I look at my watch, it's almost two in the morning, and I'm still drinking with these guys. I'd stay with Drysdale, sleep on the floor in his room.

In 1962 we had our first World Series in Candlestick, and that was the greatest experience for me. I had the New York Yankees there—I had Yogi Berra, Whitey Ford, Mickey Mantle all on my side. It was just something to have the Yankees. I idolized these guys when I was a kid, and now I got to see them really up close. They gave me half a share, about $1,500. At that time ballplayers came out to play—they didn't make the millions that they do now. When I started with the Seals I was paid two bucks a game. When the Giants came out, it was seven bucks. Now batboys get fifty bucks a day, for about ten hours' work.

My first time to spring training was 1961, in Arizona. I used to beat Logan to the ballpark every morning, six a.m., and I'd have the coffee ready. Mr. Stoneham, the club owner, came up to me and said, "I'm building a minor league complex in Casa Grande. I want you to go down there and help Mattie Schwab the groundskeeper build fields out there." I thought, How are they gonna build fields in the middle of a desert? Nothing out there but sand. After the baseball season I spent the winter there, building grass, and Mattie showed me how to make a ball field. I'd never worked with the ground crew, and it was very good seeing grass grow out of nothing. "Field of Dreams" was just like Mattie Schwab.

I made one good road trip as a batboy. Mike McCormick and Ray Sadecki took care of me. Willie McCovey still comes to see me occasionally, still the same old Stretch, still moody as hell. I learned to stay away from him when he's moody, and he seemed to like you more the more you stayed away. I learned to know his moods, to stay away and let him make the first move.

Willie Mays is the best, the best ballplayer I've ever seen in my life. And I love the man. Even now when he comes with us in spring training he gives me a hundred dollars. I tell him, "I don't want to take nothing from you, because you've been great to me all my life," which he has, and he just says, "Here." You know, after Mr. Logan had his heart attack in '72, he says, "I'll see you and Doc Hughes in New York." We didn't know what he meant, but when we go to New York he sends over $300 for me and $300 for Doc.

We went out that night and blew all the money. Bought dinner for Joey Amalfitano, Johnny McNamara, a couple of sportswriters, and were drinkin' till four in the morning. We went to the 21, we started early, it was an off day the next day, and things ain't too cheap in New York. Anyway, we get back to the Hotel Commodore, and all we have left are these two big long five-dollar cigars. I says, "I'm broke, maybe Mays'll lend us some money." So we go up there and knock on his door, he comes out in these silk pajamas, and I says, "Hey, Will, you got a coupla more hundred dollar bills you could let me borrow?" And he did give us some money. That was Willie Mays.

We'd have a lot of stars come and see us. Bobby Darin used to be a favorite of the Giants. We got to meet him, and his son liked Willie Mays. After Bobby died, Sandra Dee used to bring little Bobby around. Before that, I remember Jeff Chandler, who loved the Giants. He used to give me a buck to go get him a hot dog. A hot dog cost 25 cents but he told me to keep the change. I always looked for him, and I'd say, "Mr. Chandler, want a hot dog?" He'd say, "Yes, and call me Jeff, son." You meet mighty interesting people around baseball. Even Hollywood people, big wheels, politicians, they love the game.

I got good experience working, hanging around baseball. But it's just seasonal work for most people. Off season I still do some police work, helping to keep kids off the street. And I always try to put my kids, my batboys and clubbies, in law enforcement. It's a good choice. It's year-round, never have to worry about it, civil service, just keeps you going.

I've always tried to help bring them up as good citizens. I've had a couple of rough kids like Brad Tham and his brother Gus, and Bob Fenech. We were all wild, tried to drink with ballplayers, and I could empathize. I did all that. But I'd indicate that you've got to go on with a better life or get an education. Like Mario Alioto, who worked as a batboy for many years and wanted to hang around the ballpark, but he got a chance to go to St. Mary's and now he's got a college degree and he does a good job in the front office.

I've worked all my life around baseball and I love it. It's the best education you can give a kid, working with a ball club. I wish there were a million clubs, to give a million kids the chance to be a batboy, to let them see what it's like working with ballplayers.

Murph is equipment manager of the San
Francisco Giants.

Roy McKertcher ....

I was the first batboy for the San Francisco Giants, from 1958-1961. I was fifteen when I started, going to Lowell High School, and I had already been visiting batboy for the Seals in the PCL. I talked with Jerry Donovan about the job, and on the day that spring training broke I was waiting at the clubhouse at 5 a.m. Murph [Mike Murphy] came along later. When Eddie Logan and George Natriano showed up they hired us right away and then tossed a coin to see who got first batboy pick. Logan won and took "the redheaded guy," me, and Natriano took Murph for the visiting side.

We got five dollars a day, seven for night games, eight for a doubleheader. You know, there are many people valuable to a club, the backbone of the organization, who don't get the credit they deserve. But we were made to feel we were important, part of the organization. That was the most impressive part—the attitude, professionalism, and temperament.

Everybody called me "Red"—Mays, Lockman, Daryl Spencer, Antonelli—and they were all good to me. Bill Rigney was the classiest guy in the world. In the showers he'd always ask my opinions about things, and I'd always agree with him. One day, he says, "What should I do with McCovey and Cepeda?" I said, "I don't know." He says, "I think I'm gonna put McCovey at first, he's a natural first baseman, and play Cepeda in the outfield. Now I want to know what you think and I don't want any bullshit answer this time." So I say, "That would be the greatest move in the world." The next day after he makes that move, Rig is fired, and on his way out of the clubhouse he stops to say to me, "It's not your fault."

Rigney got me in trouble with an umpire once. Chris Pelakoudas was just up from the PCL, where I knew him, and I told Rig his first name. So he's yelling out of the dugout at him—by name—and the next time I was close to the plate the ump says to me, "How does he know my first name?" "I don't know." "Well, don't ever tell anyone my first name again."

I got along well with most umpires, though, and I liked them. That may have helped influence me to start refereeing basketball a few years later. Lou Summers often commented on the way I ran quick and hard to do my job. I knew Emmett Ashford from the PCL, and I got along with Shag Crawford, Ed Vargo, and Al Barlick. One day there was a bench-clearing brawl against the Cubs. They had their batboy, Frankie, on that road trip, and he and I squared off on the field. Barlick says to me, "You hit him, you're gone."

Sometimes I ran too hard. On one road trip, in Cincinnati, I slipped on Crosley Field and slid into the dugout, bat in hand, and got a standing O from the players. Another time, at the Coliseum, a player changed sunglasses, and I was running off the field with his otherglasses in my back pocket, when I slipped on a step and sat down on them, crushing them. "That's the most expensive fall you made all year," is the message I got.

I remember the feeling of sitting in the visiting clubhouse, playing cards, and wearing your favorite player's jersey—Drysdale or Koufax. And I remember the day Willie McCovey arrived. I went over to introduce myself to him as he was sitting in front of his new locker, and he looked at me deadpan and said in his slow Alabama way, "Aren't you the one they call Red because the hair on your head is as red as a dick on a dog?"

It was during July of that first year when the Giants were playing at Seals Stadium that I was flown to New York to be on "What's My Line?" There I was, with John Daly, Bennett Cerf, Robert Q. Lewis, and Dorothy Kilgallen. But it was Arlene Francis who guessed me, easily. When I got back and the team got back from their road trip, Mays saw that I had a stack of mail. He said, "Why did you put my mail in your locker?" And when I told him what it was, he said, "One television show and you get more mail than I do."

Horace Stoneham had seen the show and liked the idea of promoting the Giants with a batboy, so they took me along on a trip to Portland for an exhibition game—I roomed with Andre Rodgers—and then on a 22-day road trip. (It included a long losing streak, so it was never repeated.) I always sat with Mays on the plane, and he always tapped my ankle with his bat for luck before he went to the plate. In '61, he promised me a new suit if he hit 40 home runs, and when he did, barely, right at the end of the season, he insisted on buying the best available for me. But they were all generous—on one trip, the players chipped in more than a hundred dollars for spending money for me in Chicago.

I guess Charlie (The Brow) Di Giovanna of the Dodgers was the best loved of the batboys. When he died, *Coronet* magazine started giving a batboy-of-the-year award in his name. I won it in 1959, not for anything on the field, but because I had been beaten up resisting a holdup in a hamburger joint. It was a hard way to be a hero, but what I remember was the basket of fruit that the club sent to the hospital for me. There was an apple missing and a note in the basket said, "IOU one apple, Johnny Antonelli."

I don't go to games now. I was spoiled by being on the field, and I don't like fighting the crowds and the weather anyway. They once offered me a front office job as statistician, but it didn't pay well and I got married at 20 and couldn't afford to take it. I understand what people go through when they have to quit playing. I was devastated when I left. A big part of me was left behind. As a batboy I was taught how to handle people, how to say hello, how to take kidding. And any success I've had since I attribute to the Giants organization.

Since 1969 Roy McKertcher has been a
Deputy Sheriff in San Mateo. He was also a
Pac-10 basketball referee for 14 seasons.

BILLY TURNER ....

I worked four years, 1956-59, on the home side for the Washington Senators, a year and a half as ballboy, two and a half as batboy. It was a fantasy job, a dream come true. I could have pinched myself.

I went to Blair High School, but I knew Moss Collins, the football coach at Carroll, who directed summer school playground activities and worked concessions at Griffith Stadium. When a ballboy left, Coach Collins introduced me to equipment manager Fred Baxter, who hired me. It was hard juggling that job and playing ball at Blair. One day I decided to skip practice to work a game, telling my coach I was sick. Next day the coach handed me the paper with my picture in it, in uniform and congratulating Roy Sievers on a home run. That same scene, me shaking Sievers' hand, is in the movie *Damn Yankees*, shot in Griffith Stadium, with Sievers as Joe Hardy and me as batboy.

My last two years I pitched batting practice for the pitchers and took infield with the utility players three or four nights a week. The players taught me fundamentals. Winning or losing didn't matter—it was just being there that was important. At the University of Maryland I played all four years, an infielder as a freshman, a relief pitcher as a sophomore, and starting center fielder as junior and senior. I was invited to a Pirates tryout camp, but my career as a paid player lasted just two years in the semi-pro Shenandoah Valley League. Law school became a higher priority.

The best times as batboy were listening to stories late into the night, usually told by Rocky Bridges. Sievers was a friend to me, tossing me his keys to drive his car. When he asked me to get Yogi Berra to autograph a ball for his son, Yogi had a one-word response to me: "Why?" Russ Kemmerer was another friend; he gave me a hand-painted ball as a farewell present.

There weren't many readers on that club, except maybe Lou Berberet and Faye Throneberry, but there was a lot of card-playing in the clubhouse, mostly pitch and cassino. And it was a lively bunch, sending me with notes to girls in the stands. Pete Ramos used to to do cup-checks, bouncing a ball off his teammates' uniforms. I'll never forget the time he caught Camilo Pascual not wearing his. But the most obstreperous guy was Clint Courtney. He owned a horse farm in Louisiana, and one day in the on-deck circle he said to me, "See that kid in the stands? He looks like he'd be a good jockey—get him after the game." I did, and after the season that kid went to Louisiana with Courtney. Once Cookie Lavagetto sent me to find Courtney and after a search I found him huddled in a storm drain behind the tarp. "What're you doing," I asked. "Just hiding from the manager," he said.

Among the umpires I remember Bill Summers as being gruff and Ed Runge being very nice. Nestor Chylak would go out of his way to be nice, to call you by name.

Two other high points, with political associations: catching an Opening Day ball thrown by President Eisenhower, and being there when the Nixon family visited the clubhouse and hearing Tricia say in an interview, "I don't like the game but the batboy is cute."

I have no regrets about my career as an attorney, though I never got to be an FBI agent as I had once hoped. I go to maybe three or four Orioles games a year. But if today I was offered the job of batboying for a month I'd take it in a minute.

Bill Turner is a Judge in the Circuit Court of Montgomery County (Maryland).

John Milne Kurtz ....

I was Washington Senators batboy from late in the '57 season through the '58 season. I went to Blair High School, was a friend of Jay Ryan, played some sandlot ball with him, and he had been working in the clubhouse, got me in when there was an opening.

I collected baseball cards, but I was shocked by the environment, the difficulty of the life, and the anxiety of the young players. The profanity was shocking to me. It was new to a sheltered suburban kid, the off-color humor, the amount of drinking and smoking. I got paid $2.50 a game. There were some tips, but not much. But I got to go to the All-Star Game in Baltimore, visit the National League clubhouse, and meet Stan Musial. Now that was a big deal. And later in the summer, vacationing in Wisconsin, my family's original home, I got to visit in the Milwaukee Braves clubhouse and meet Warren Spahn.

I admired Mickey Vernon and Roy Sievers, Ted Williams and Al Kaline. Clint Courtney was a scrappy, fun guy, who liked the batboys. Harmon Killebrew I fondly remember as a bonus baby, a scared young kid from Idaho who talked with me in left field during batting practice. I liked Whitey Herzog, who was young, energetic, enthusiastic. When he was traded to Kansas City he greeted the news as a big break for him.

I had some perception of racial, or perhaps more accurately, cultural bias, since there were Cubans but no blacks on the team. Pete Ramos was actually one of the players I was closest to, Ramos not being fully included in the team-as-society.

I learned that you have to look below the glitz. From the inside it's not as glamorous. The life of a ballplayer is *not* romantic. Certainly it was not a life for me. I had little interest afterwards. Eighty-two games is a long season. It got routine, tedious. The aesthetics of it was appealing—clear, moonlit summer evenings, the green field, the white of the uniforms. In retrospect there's a nostalgic appeal, a *Field of Dreams* quality. But it's probably a nostalgia for a golden age that never was.

John Milne Kurtz has dual Masters degrees in Architecture and Business Administration from Carnegie-Mellon and is Senior Vice-President for Marketing of the Charles E. Smith Co.

Bob Farmer ....

While I was at Blair High School and playing varsity ball there, I spent two seasons working for the Senators, '57 on the visiting side, '58 as home team batboy. I made $2.50 a game, and the first tip I got was a quarter from Whitey Herzog for getting him a sandwich from the Plymouth Restaurant.

The first time I was in the field for batting practice, I learned the difference between baseball at their level and mine. There came a drive off Minnie Minoso's bat and I charged in for it—it carried so far over my head it hit the wall. Later a Jim Lemon line drive went past my ear so fast my life flashed past too. I guess my worst embarrassment, though, was the time I ran out to meet the relief pitcher to take his warm-up jacket, and he wasn't wearing one.

The Yankees were my favorites. It was fun having Sal Maglie tossing pebbles at me in the dugout, and it was a sad day for me when they traded Billy Martin. Casey Stengel chewed me out once in the dugout, I forget why, but Enos Slaughter consoled me. That didn't stop me from naming my miniature schnauzer "Casey," and the one I have now is "Mickey" for Mantle. Sometimes the players would have us break in new gloves for them—they'd never use a new one in a game. I remember that Mantle's glove had a hole in the pocket the size of a fifty-cent piece. The other memorable Yankee was Yogi Berra. He would sign only his name on balls, and if you said, "Please sign it to...," he'd say, "Why?"

On the Senators side, Ted Williams wouldn't sign them at all. One lesson I learned was to treat everyone with respect, the opposite of the way Williams acted. I don't want to make people feel the way he made others feel. As a training officer for police officers my lesson is to treat people like you want to be treated.

I was interviewed once in the Washington *Star* and I made the mistake of saying, "Some of them don't look like ballplayers." I was really thinking about an old pitcher, Harry Byrd, but Jim Lemon thought I meant him and he got mad at me. At least I didn't tell how Pedro Ramos carried a gun. And I didn't tell how Clint Courtney and Rocky Bridges made our nights so long in the clubhouse, because at 2 a.m. they'd still be drinking beer and telling stories and betting they could knock a beer can off the trash can with another beer can.

The only time I ever had a brush with the law was with another batboy, a kid with a screw loose who had quit while I was still working. I was in town, all dressed up for my high school graduation picture, when he jumped me and started a fight. I was the one who got arrested. Years later, when I was at my final interview for a police job, talking about batboying put me at ease and helped get the job.

It was the greatest job I ever had. I learned dedication, teamwork, and to give a dollar and a quarter of effort if someone's paying a dollar. Baseball seems different now, too much like a business, the goal is money, not winning. In my time they played for the love of the game, enjoyed themselves more than they seem to now. As a ballplayer you knew you were lucky enough to be a kid all your life.

Bob Farmer played some ball at Montgomery College and the University of Maryland and for Buffalo Sand & Gravel in the Southern Maryland League before starting in law enforcement in 1971. He is a Montgomery County Police Officer.

JIM RYAN ....

I ate and slept baseball even before I became a batboy, played every day after school till dark, all day summers and weekends. Bob Farmer, Tom MacDougal, and I played baseball every free moment at Pinecrest Field. In '56 I went to work at Griffith Stadium, as an errand boy without pay, just to be around the game, and I got to fill in as batboy when needed. Then I was a regular in '57 and '58.

I got the job through my father, who knew equipment manager Fred Baxter as a boy. In fact, he had been a Senators batboy in 1924-25 under Frank Baxter, Fred's brother. When my son batboyed for the Phoenix Firebirds in the summer of '89 that made three generations of Ryan batboys. By the way, he made $12 a game instead of the $2.50 I got.

My first game was an exhibition game, the Senators against the Dodgers, in the spring of '56. The clubhouses were crowded with 40-man rosters, but I remember Eddie Yost telling a funny dirty joke and Roy Campanella with a cigar in his mouth on the field before the game. And I remember Jerry Snyder playing shortstop and getting kicked out of the game— he was complaining in the clubhouse that he only said "piss."

I found out that players are like you and me, just have a different kind of life. I also found out that working at the ballpark was not a help to me as a ballplayer. I got to take throws at first one day for Vic Power. And one of the young Red Sox taught me technique for fielding ground balls—though to this day I'm not sure if it was Ted Lepcio, Billy Klaus, Billy Consolo, or Marty Keough. But it got in the way of playing, and some of us batboys were good. Billy Turner was a great infielder. Bob Farmer homered for Blair High School one season to beat Northwood and then transferred to play at Northwood. Tom MacDougal played at Arizona State, was put under contract by Kansas City.

As for me, when I was a senior at Blair, the coach put us under curfew so I couldn't batboy, but I won the outstanding senior trophy. At Montgomery Junior College I was the leading hitter, and later at Maryland I hit .375 one season to earn my scholarship for Jack Jackson. But I didn't pursue it, followed my father's footsteps into the FBI as special agent. I have an idea of why so many batboys end up in law enforcement. People in law enforcement, if they're fans, can get out to the ballpark often, meet people connected with the game, and get their sons jobs as batboys. The kids then follow in their dads' footsteps into law enforcement.

According to Dad, Babe Ruth was the best ever. He saw him hit one over the old oak tree out of Griffith Stadium. But Stan Musial was a favorite of us both. And we were there to see him hit a home run and make a diving catch in the '56 All-Star Game in Washington. Willie Mays homered in that one too and also lined a shot off the third base bag. Mays and I talk every spring in Phoenix. You know he has a big knot on his index finger from signing autographs? It was Ken Boyer's fielding that really won that game, but it was Ted Kluszewski's arms that I was most in awe of.

Mickey McDermott had bought a house around the corner from Bob Farmer, and in '56 when he was traded to the Yankees, a young pitcher named Connie Grob lived there. I'll never forget the day he drove Rocky Colavito home for dinner, and I rode in the back seat.

On Opening Day in '58, President Eisenhower was on hand to throw out the ceremonial first balls. He threw the first one to Whitey Herzog. On the second, Frank Sullivan, a 6'7" Red Sox pitcher, reached out for it and deflected it right into my hands. I followed Whitey to the presidential box, but Piersall intercepted me and gave me another ball to get signed. Ike said, "You're the first batboy I have ever met," and the picture of him signing my ball was in papers all over the country the next day.

There were several memorable Senators from those years. Albie Pearson, who came up in '58, at 5'5" and 140 pounds, a real gentleman, who always said "Yes, sir" and "No, sir" but was never really accepted by the players. Ken Aspromonte, who'd complain about a speck of dirt left on his spikes. Clint Courtney and Rocky Bridges, who used to bet on their skills at spitting tobacco juice, both for accuracy and for distance. Joe Black, who saw me swinging a bat and said, "You look just like Ted Williams." Tex Clevenger, who had to be carried from the field after getting hit in the head with a shot off Billy Cox's bat. Pete ᵀ innells, who got so frustrated one day in '57 he took a bucket of ice with ammonia and dumped it over his head. The next season, with Boston, he and Ted Williams were in Washington tied for the batting title on the last day. I remember Williams sitting in the clubhouse reading a newspaper before the game, then going two-for-four while Pete went hitless.

Most of all I remember Pete Ramos, who called me "Feo." I remember him challenging Mantle to a 100-yard dash, and I remember his great rivalry with Camilo Pascual, who had the greatest curve I ever saw. Ramos loved to hit and would get me to pitch batting practice just for him. One day he threw some gum down my back and then felt so bad about it that he bought me a new shirt. I loved it when I'd get a postcard from him, in Spanish.

Among the visitors, I particularly remember Mudcat Grant, because there was one fan who always yelled "Sowbelly" at him. I can remember Early Wynn showing up in no condition to play, drinking many cups of coffee, and then pitching a great inning. And I remember Jimmy Piersall, kneeling in the on-deck circle with me but talking to a woman in the stands about sewing buttons on his shirt, and later making the greatest catch I ever saw off Roy Sievers on a ball that was over the fence in left center field—he led the league anyway with 42 in '57, but it should have been 43.

Of course there was a different atmosphere in the ballpark when the Yankees came to town, with Mickey Mantle, Yogi Berra, Moose Skowron, Whitey Ford, Gil McDougald, and

Billy Martin. I got a silver dollar from a fan for Yogi's autograph on a program in '58, and another for Mantle's on a cup-holder. My most vivid images of Mantle are of him being in such a hurry to end a game on getaway day that he batted righthanded against a righthanded pitcher and of him screaming "I ain't signing no more balls" in the clubhouse.

I formed some of my most lasting friendships as a batboy, including one I struck up by mail with Mike Murphy who was then a San Francisco Giants batboy. Now I see him every spring because he's their equipment manager. In '91 Murph and I went over to the Scottsdale Fashion Square Mall where several former Yankees were signing autographs— Ryne Duren, Don Larsen, Mickey Mantle, Whitey Ford, Bill Skowron, Hank Bauer, and Bobby Richardson. I took three photographs with me, one of Mantle and myself, one of Skowron and myself, and one that I had taken in '58 of Ford posing with a bat in his hand.

We saw Harmon Killebrew there, and I stuck out my hand and reintroduced myself to him. He was very friendly. The line around Mantle was so long we couldn't get close to him, so Murph and I went on to talk with Don Larsen, who's a very good friend of his. Then I found Skowron and placed the photograph on the table. He shook hands with me, asked me how I'd been and if I'd like him to sign the photograph. He signed it, "To Jim, best wishes, Bill Skowron," and we continued to talk. He was always very friendly to the batboys, and he treated me as if we were old friends meeting again.

Then I went back to find Murph, and he and I went back to attempt to have Mantle sign my photograph. The line was so long I couldn't get close to him. I held up the picture of him and me in the air and called out, "Hey, Mick, hey, Mick." There was a woman sitting next to him with a counter, clicking it off every time he signed his autograph. He looked up at the photograph and said, "Who's that, Nellie Fox?" I said, "No, Mick, that's you and me." The woman came and got the picture, took it back to Mickey, he looked at it, looked up at me, and said, "Oh, you were the batboy." To Murph and me it sounded like, "You were only the batboy," and the photograph was handed back to me unsigned. I suppose he would have signed that picture if I had stayed in line and paid him the ten dollars.

We found Ryne Duren and talked, and he promised to give my regards to Roy Sievers, who he said never forgets anyone. Then I found Whitey Ford and showed him the photographs. Duren had said to ask him if he remembered Jim Lemon, because Lemon, on September 1, 1956, had hit three home runs off Ford, with President Eisenhower at the game. I asked him, and Whitey said, "Yeah, he hit three home runs off me, but those were the only runs they got and we won the game." I talked to him for a few minutes, but he never volunteered to sign the picture. He was getting five dollars per signature that day.

That day in Scottsdale, Larsen got Mantle, Duren, Ford, and others to sign a ball for Murph, but even for him they wouldn't sign any pictures. Not much changes in baseball. The batboy experience changed my attitudes about baseball not at all. I still love the game. It was the best job ever.

James J. Ryan, Jr., is with the FBI in Phoenix.

Tom MacDougal ....

I was the Washington Senators visiting batboy in '57 and '58, when I was fourteen and fifteen in the ninth and tenth grades, then ballboy on the home side in '59. I got the job through batboy Jay Ryan—we'd been friends since seventh grade. Ray Crump was the one who hired me. On the eve of Opening Day I couldn't sleep, I was so excited. My dad, who was a cousin of Cincinnati Reds pitcher Ken Raffensberger, came up and talked me to sleep. It was a tender moment.

I loved it. Every day was like a first trip to Disneyland. I had started playing ball at five or six. Major League baseball had always been a dream for me, but batboying taught me the reality, with all the frustrations.

The Indians were my favorites. Minnie Minoso would take my brother Scotty and me out to a Mexican restaurant, treated us like gold. Rocky Colavito always cared about us. One day, when the trainer sent me to get something off a shelf, a whole set of lockers came falling down, pinning me. It was Rocky who lifted them off and carried me into the training room and laid me on the table. Herb Score was also very good, real people. And Vic Powers, who came to our house and visited with our parents. Shagging flies in batting practice was always great fun, but especially with the Indians when Bobby Avila would bet me nickels on who who could come closer to the ball bag at second base with the throw.

I liked the Red Sox because I idolized Ted Williams, the greatest ever. On their last trip in, I said to him, "I'd like to have something to remember you by." He took off his hat and handed it to me without a word. I remember sitting next to him in the dugout during the second game of a doubleheader, and he put his arm around me. He didn't like writers or fans who were always pressuring him, but there was an aura about him, and players treated him special. When he spoke, everyone listened. I'd get the key to the gate through the tunnel so Ted could leave the ballpark the back way and avoid fans, and I'd watch his silhouette walking across the field. He'd always greet me with "How're you doing, kid?" but once, instead of "kid," he said, "Thanks, Tommy," and I got chills.

Jimmy Piersall was really nice, a unique guy. I always brought him two orange Tru-ades and a big cup filled with ice. He put his locker next to Scott's and mine, and he'd play with us, box around while doing blow-by-blow narration and calling himself Carmen Basilio.

Billy Pierce and Nellie Fox were two fine guys with the White Sox. Pierce would talk pitching with me, and Fox was always polite, but always chewing and spitting, like Harvey Kuenn of the Tigers. Jim Rivera was always playing crazy tricks—shaving cream, hotfoots, handful of rocks and pebbles and dirt in cuffs or pockets. I saw him shake up a beer can and put it in the cooler as a practical joke on whoever drew it. I decided to try that one myself on the Yankees. No one took that can until finally Enos Slaughter did. He was all dressed up in a dark blue suit for some special occasion, and he got soaked and furious.

Crump used to let us spend Friday night at the ballpark before a Saturday day game. We'd sleep on trainer's tables, use the whirlpool, check out the equipment, and use the field in the morning. We felt we were part of Griffith Stadium. But I wasn't cocky enough to confess to Slaughter.

The Yankees were the '58 champs, and I was always excited when they came to town. The place hummed, they were class, they even brought their own visiting batboy uniforms. I sometimes had to sign autographs to get back to the locker room when I was wearing that uniform. In b.p. Mantle would line the paint off the wall, and the players would cheer me shagging flies. I always bought the best equipment I could, and I slept with my super Rawlings glove. Mantle tried it and said, "That's a really good glove, wanna trade?" I refused, even when he offered his glove plus twenty bucks. He and Berra were the worst about signing balls. I practiced their signatures for hours and signed hundreds of balls for them.

I saw Mantle hit one out of Griffith off Chuck Stobb, almost as far as one Williams hit over the highest part of the wall in dead center. You know, one of our chores was bringing notes to players from girls in the stands. I usually discarded them. But I remember Mantle during a rain delay, checking out the crowd under the stands from the training room, and sending me with a note to a blonde—"See you after the game—#7." I gave it to the wrong girl, but I told Mantle, "Yeah, that's the one." Of all the Yankees I guess I had the highest regard for Gil McDougald, and my daughter Deni is named for Denise McDougald.

We'd hitchhike from Silver Spring to the bus line and then transfer to get to the Stadium. In '59, with Bill Turner as head batboy, I worked on the home side under Fred Baxter. He was gruff and hard on us, but he got uniforms for us for road trips. The club wouldn't pay for that—we paid our own way, but I got to shag in Comiskey Park, and I met Mel Ott and got his autograph. Washington lost eighteen straight games on that trip, and Julio Becquer told me I was bad luck. I never got over that, never even knew if he meant it.

We went to the All-Star Game in Pittsburgh, too. Scotty wrote the Pirates p.r. guy and arranged to meet him outside the ballpark. We took an overnight train from D.C. to Pittsburgh and got onto the field, without passes, without seats, just walking around in street clothes but wearing our Senators caps. We had our picture taken with Hank Aaron, and with Vada Pinson and Frank Robinson in their Reds uniforms. And we saw Eddie Mathews hit a home run and Willie Mays triple home Aaron for the win.

That was the year Harmon Killebrew came up. He had trouble fielding and he struck out a lot, but he was a genuine, good person. On the Senators side the batboys had our lockers separate, but Harmon would come in to talk. He'd drink an occasional beer but would never leave the locker room with one. At the time I didn't realize Mormons are not supposed to drink at all. But he was a most considerate man. It was a thrill to see him hit some tape-measure jobs off Herb Score, who otherwise dominated the Senators.

Camilo Pascual was a favorite, a good friend who'd play catch with me. He had a fine fast ball and the best curve in baseball. He taught me how to throw a curve and encouraged me that I should be a major-leaguer. Whitey Herzog was another who said I was a fine player and should pursue it. Pedro Ramos was a fun-loving guy. He'd have me squeeze his hand as hard as I could. I admired his cowboy boots with a big eagle on the front, and he bought me a new pair. I wore them every day, everywhere, for years, until I finally buried them toes up in the desert. Those are the kind of souvenirs that matter to me. I think collectors' attitudes about memorabilia are comical. My cards are all personally signed to me by players, dogeared, and therefore supposedly worthless, but invaluable to me.

Dick Hyde and Herb Plews were other players I remember on that club. And Albie Pearson, the only one smaller than me. Clint (Scrap Iron) Courtney was there. He was having problems throwing the ball back to pitchers, and he worked several times with me to overcome that. The Senators were all afraid of batting against Ryne Duren, but not Courtney—he'd grit his teeth and stand in. And Bob Allison was there, a fine athlete, hardnosed and businesslike. He was nice, but more into himself than most. I admired his physique, but he got irked when I asked if he lifted weights. "I'm not a fairy," he said, "not musclebound—I got these muscles working on the farm."

That was the most fun time of my life. I was taught about baseball, but I also learned about being independent and about working hard. I think there was more camaraderie then. The guys were good to each other. There was some smoking and chewing, but I never saw any drugs or alcohol abuse.

At the end of my senior year at Montgomery Blair High School I finally got to pitch and won, with many strikeouts. Then I was 9-1 at Montgomery College and a Junior College All-America. I went to Arizona State in '63, and in '64 we were the No. 1 team all season but didn't win the College World Series. I was third or fourth pitcher in the rotation and went 5-1. Summers I played with the Federal Storage teams, and then I was signed by Lew Krausse for the Kansas City A's. I was 5-4 my first year in the Appalachian League, all four losses against the Johnson City Yankees, with Bobby Murcer homering twice off me. After my second year at Shelby, N.C., my manager Wes Ferrell got fired and the new manager was not partial to me. By then my arm was shot anyway, I had married Dotty, and it was time to begin my career as teacher and coach.

*Tom MacDougal taught junior high and high
school in Las Vegas, Nevada, and Mesa, Arizona, and coached baseball and basketball.
Still teaching, he now concentrates his coaching on his children, Denise, Molly, and Mike.*

CLUB HOUSE
PLAYERS ONLY

Batboys enjoy special access, but it's all in the line of duty. Stan Strull toted the bats for the Brooklyn Dodgers during spring training in Vero Beach, Florida in 1951.

Batboys across the generations: Tommie Ferguson, with the Boston Braves in 1946 (previous page). Hank Le Bost, a Dodgers' batboy in 1915, visits the Mets' dugout (above). Washington Senators batboys Jim Ryan, Billy Turner and Bob Farmer before a game in the late 1950s (right). On the closing day of the 1950 season, Dodgers batboy Stan Strull met with his successor, Charlie Di Giovanna, who was the visiting team's batboy on that day (following page). Di Giovanna worked for the Dodgers until his death in 1958, after which Coronet magazine started a batboy award in his honor.

Chicago Cubs batboy Billy Philips went head-to-head with Stan Musial in advertisements that ran in Sport *magazine in July of 1955. Musial plugged Rawlings gloves, and Philips checked in two pages later for Wilson. Musial went on to the Hall of Fame, while Philips became a commodities broker.*

Batboys and ballplayers go together like ball and glove. As the visiting team batboy for the Senators in 1957 and '58, Tom MacDougal met many of baseball's most prominent statesmen, such as Mickey Mantle (left, top) and, with brother Scotty, Ted Williams (left, bottom). Roy McKertcher worked with the Giants when Willie Mays towered over the game (above), and Tony Atlas hooked up with Nolan Ryan when they were Angels (right). Jay Mazzone, the Orioles' visiting team batboy, posed with Dodgers great Sandy Koufax before a 1966 World Series game (following page).

Scotty MacDougal . . . .

My brothers and I all hung around the ballpark. Bobby, the oldest, filled in briefly as a clubby, Tom and I were both batboys, and Dennis would often tag along. I was real small but even at ten I could shag flies, and the players loved me.

We grew up in the Four Corners area of Silver Spring, went to Pine Crest Elementary and Eastern Junior High. As a batboy I was a star in our neighborhood. I always knew where the camera was, where the TV cameras were, and I played to the audience whenever I could.

Fred Baxter, the equipment manager, was a crusty guy. He liked to drive with no pants on and sleep naked on a kitchen table. When the players were out of town he'd mark up their tabs, or he'd have the batboys do it. But he wouldn't pay us till the end of the season. We did get two balls per game, and we'd stash them on the emergency cot in the trainer's room. But once, when a player got hurt and the balls rolled off the cot, we got in trouble. It was part of our pay but, officially, according to Fred, they were "stolen." Jay Ryan was one batboy who'd carry his balls out of the stadium in a locked metal box.

Fred loved it when Rocky Colavito tried the old bat-stretcher trick on me. I fell for it because I'd heard of a hat-stretcher, and so I went looking for the bat-stretcher. Colavito, Larry Doby, and Minnie Minoso helped make the Indians the best tipping team. The best tipper in the game was Ted Williams, always a buck per day when few players tipped a buck for a series. He was a great guy, distorted by the press which played up and played on his anger. He was excited about history, and he'd spend afternoons at the museums, but he never forgot us.

Minoso was a great guy. In Cleveland, an hour and a half after a game, I saw him signing autographs for two hundred people in the parking lot. He'd take me and Tom out for Mexican food. Ten years later, I happened to be in Mexico, just traveling with a friend, when I saw a pink Cadillac in Mazatlan. I took off after it, my friend must have thought I was crazy, and I finally found it parked at a restaurant. Sure enough it was Minoso's. I was twenty-five, had grown from 5'6" to 6'5" since I'd seen him, but when I went up and introduced myself and asked if he remembered me, he said, "Sure, how's your brother?"

The club wouldn't pay for us to go on a road trip, but we went to Cleveland, Chicago, and Detroit. Doc Lentz, the trainer, looked after us. We happened to be in Cleveland when

Jimmy Hoffa's daughter had a big hotel wedding. Roy Sievers and Pete Ramos went, told us about the limos lined up for all the mob guys. It was on that trip that Jim Kaat arrived in the Show for the first time. He was nineteen and real shy. I was sent to the gate to show him into the visiting clubhouse, and we were best buddies from then on.

There were a lot of memorable people. I thought Billy Pierce was a great human being, concerned for the general welfare of people. Harmon Killebrew was another great human being. He'd personally answer all letters and sign all pictures. Every time I passed him he'd say, "Scotty-y-y." Jim Piersall wouldn't dress with his team—he had a locker over near the batboys. He was a nervous wreck before every game, and in batting practice when we were shagging flies he'd call for every ball within possible reach. Billy Martin and Cookie Lavagetto were two guys who'd visit with you for hours in the clubhouse after games. Once Lavagetto asked me who to start, and I said to change the lineup. "Who should I use?" he said. I came up with one suggestion—Reno Bertoia. That shows how much I knew.

They used to have fashion shows at the Touchdown Club, and sometimes I'd get to escort players' wives. You know, Vic Power was a great guy and well-educated, but he was harassed because he was a black player with a white wife. There was a lot of racial prejudice. The blacks' lockers in the visiting clubhouse were all crammed together. Same for the Cubans on the Senators. Players would all leave tickets at the gate for friends, but they'd always forget to leave them for Ramos. "Fuck 'em," he'd say, "I'll pay for 'em myself"—and he did. He used to have a different woman with him every night, but because his accent was so thick sometimes I had to make the phone call for him. I remember him saying to Mickey Mantle, "I'm going to strike you out, and I'm only going to throw you fast balls." And he did, a couple of times every game, but then Mantle started hitting some 485-foot homers off him.

It was Camilo Pascual, though, who had the great season in '59 for the lowly Senators. Second to Jim Bunning in strikeouts, e.r.a. leader among starters, six shut-outs, and seventeen wins. I have balls from wins sixteen and seventeen.

As a batboy I learned the importance of hard work and perseverance. Sports is a great teacher of discipline. I played on championship basketball teams in junior high and high school, then some at Arizona State and Cal State Northridge. But by my senior year in college a course project had turned into a successful business venture, the Morgan Day Camps, and my playing career as an entrepreneur had begun.

Scotty MacDougal's business triumphs include a tax office, an antique furniture store, a chain of antique-reproduction stores in southern California, a window factory in Maryland, and multi-level marketing of Nu-Skin products. Now in Dallas he's back in retail, producing indoor amusement facilities with his American Leisure Enterprises.

THE SIXTIES 60

The Sixties

If ever baseball could be said to be isolated from the culture at large it was during the Sixties. The clubhouse and the dugout seemed to be virtually immune to the divisiveness, turmoil, enormous conflicts of values, and cataclysmic events taking place in the country and the world. The ballpark could be treasured as a safe haven outside time and current events, or it could be travestied as an archaic ostrich with its head buried in the sands of tradition.

The batboys' memories of those times feature the persistence of the manners and mores of the past. What seems to surprise them, in retrospect, is the absence of relevance, the way war and assassination failed to intrude into their isolated world. On the rare occasions when current events would be mentioned, the attitudes expressed would consistently champion the status quo, the conservative, the hawkish. In memory, baseball people are perceived to have been generally grateful that they did not have to be actively involved. And yet an awareness of the civil rights movement is implicit in the prominence of Frank Robinson, in the cause of integration in the clubhouse and in the arrival of black batboys in Major League uniforms.

Besides the conscious maintenance of tradition, what dominates the batboys' reminiscences are impressions of some of the monumental players of the time. Snapshots of Mays, Mantle, Maris, Koufax, Aaron, Martin, Yaz, and Maz stand out in these memory books, along with the emerging enigma of Reggie Jackson.

BOBBY RECKER ....

My family's trucking company, Recker Transfer, specialized in transporting theatrical and sporting equipment from railroad facilities to theaters, arenas, and stadiums around Pittsburgh. I used to help load and unload equipment and that's how I got to know the Pirates equipment manager, who gave me a job in the clubhouse. After three years as a clubby, I became Pirates batboy in '59 and stayed on through the summer of '62. So I was there for the All-Star Game in '59 and the World Series in '60.

Stan Musial was probably the nicest guy I met. He was nice and friendly to everybody, tipped everybody, remembered you. But it wasn't just ballplayers I met. In 1960, because the Pirates were hot and winning, famous people dropped by all the time. It was the place to be or the thing to do, I guess, and I remember meeting Bing Crosby, Bob Hope, the Three Stooges, Arnold Palmer, and Jeff Chandler.

Batboys are usually taken for granted. When there was a thirtieth anniversary reunion of the 1960 championship team at Three Rivers I wasn't invited, but if you look at the team picture of that year, there I am on the front row between Joe Christopher and Roberto Clemente. At the time, though, I felt like a part of the club. They gave me a one-seventh share of the World Series money, about $1,500.

I'm still friendly with Bill Mazeroski, Hal Smith, and Bill Virdon. When I see Willie Stargell he always acknowledges me, and we're on a first-name basis. Don Hoak was another friend—I'll always remember that he asked me to drive his 1961 Ford Thunderbird back to Pittsburgh from spring training in Fort Myers. That was kind of special.

The craziest guy on that team was Dick Stuart. On a team that had a lot of straight, conservative guys, he was flashy, had a lot of California and Hollywood in him. The manager, Danny Murtaugh, was always ready to have some fun too. Reporters were his favorite target. He'd have tobacco chew in his mouth and spit it right on their shoes from about six, maybe seven feet away. He was very accurate. They had a lot of fun because they were winning. When you win, bad things just don't seem to happen.

I was embarrassed a few times on the field. Catching foul balls after they rolled off the screen behind home plate, I tripped a couple of times and fell on my face. Once I was pushing the wheelbarrow with the bats in them and I ran over first base and the bats went flying. And once, when I was just starting, I remember it was in a game against the Cardinals, I grabbed a ball when it was still in play. The umpire and the batter were getting on me, but Murtaugh told them I didn't know what I'd done and to leave me alone.

I had a feeling that something special was happening in 1960, and I collected as many souvenirs as I could—autographed pictures, a Roberto Clemente glove, lots of bats. The following year I mentioned to one of the groundskeepers I knew that I'd love to have the 1960 pennant that hung on the flagpole. He said nothing, but, after the last home game, he took it down and gave it to me. Joe Brown, the general manager, found out about it, though, and made me give it back. I couldn't blame him.

They took me on a few trips and I made my first airplane flight with that team. What sends chills up and down my spine every time I think about it is walking onto the field at Yankee Stadium for the third game of the 1960 World Series. You grow up watching the Dodgers and Yankees play in Yankee Stadium and then to be there, that's a special feeling and one I'll never forget.

Back in Pittsburgh, when Maz hit the home run to win the Series, I was kneeling in the on-deck circle next to Dick Stuart. I looked around and saw thousands of people coming down to the field and right at me. I grabbed every piece of equipment I could and ran for the clubhouse as fast as I could. It was scary.

The whole batboy experience was very valuable to me. When you're in a spot like that, you just automatically grow up. It's an adult world, and you learn to act like an adult. You learn what to say, when to say it, and—most important in some ways—what not to say.

Bob Recker has coordinated the logistics of international tours for the Ice Capades, among other traveling shows, and is leading a campaign to establish a Professional Skating Hall of Fame in Pittsburgh.

JIM MERRITT ....

In 1961, when I was a senior at Edgewood High School in West Covina, Kenny Myers offered me the chance to be the visiting team batboy for the Dodgers until graduation. I got to suit up in a Dodgers uniform and pitch five to ten minutes of easy batting practice, then ten or fifteen minutes in a simulated game. I also threw a lot of batting practice for Charlie Neal, who was rehabilitating a knee, and Frank Howard, who wasn't getting much playing time.

The Pirates were a playful bunch, with Dick Groat, Bill Mazeroski, and Smoky Burgess always looking for hotfoot opportunities or trying to spit tobacco juice on shoes in the dugout. I have two vivid memories from those days on the field as batboy. One is being about five feet away when Leo Durocher and Augie Donatelli had a kicking contest. The other is seeing Willie Mays playing center field—the right fielder loses the ball in the sun, Willie races over and makes the catch on the foul line thirty feet behind the right fielder, whirls in one motion, and throws out the runner at the plate.

I was shining the shoes of players I later played with and against—Frank Howard, Ron Fairly, Sandy Koufax, Don Drysdale, Frank Robinson, Kenny Boyer, Maz. I got kidded some about that, but never seriously teased.

Graduation night I signed and spent the rest of the summer with the Dodgers rookie team, working with Eddie Roebuck and Ray Boone. After the season I spent a week on Santa Catalina with the Lefebvre brothers at their dad's camp. Then I was drafted by the Twins in the spring of '62, pitched against Sparky Anderson in Daytona, and eight years later was playing for him in Cincinnati. In the '65 World Series, the Twins against the Dodgers, I was playing against my old friend Jim Lefebvre.

As a player, I always took extra time to acknowledge the batboys. From my own experience I knew that most players take them for granted.

Jim Merritt pitched eleven seasons in the majors, for the Twins, Reds, and Rangers. He lives in Desert Hot Springs, California, and is a sales rep for a printing firm.

RENE LACHEMANN ································

I was the Dodgers batboy in '60 and '61, ballboy in '62. I got the job through Lefty Phillips, the Dodgers scout who signed me. He'd signed my brothers Billy and Marcel who were already playing semipro ball. I worked with Jim Merritt and Doug Anderson, Sparky's nephew, and played with both of them on the Dodgers Rookie team in '62.

We were paid five bucks a game, ten for double-headers, plus two tickets per game. Then there was a quarter share of playoff money. I did OK, had a red and white Corvette when I was sixteen. We used to liberate balls, too, a few at a time. But when Lefty Phillips caught me with a gym bag in my locker loaded up with balls, I got quite a lecture from him. On road trips, the players passed the hat for us in lieu of a per diem, and they were a generous bunch—Sandy Koufax, Don Drysdale, Duke Snider, Maury Wills, John Roseboro, and especially Gil Hodges.

As ballboy I looked out for the umpires. I got their clothes pressed, even took their white shirts home for Mom to launder. (She's Swiss; my dad was a chef at the Biltmore.) The umps loved it, especially Al Barlick, the best I've seen. They all tipped me five bucks a game, except Mel Steiner, who gave only two and also took home whatever beer was left. When Barlick asked me some direct questions I told him straight answers, and he set Steiner straight pretty quick.

They played the usual tricks on kids, sending them for the key to the batter's box, a bag of knuckle balls or bad curve balls, but not on me. The hardest job was unpacking visiting teams with the clubhouse guys under Jim Muhey. There was a kid named O'Malley who was always goofing off, drinking the umps' drinks, and I decided to teach him a lesson. I pissed in a 7-Up bottle for him to drink, but it was Muhey that grabbed the bottle. "Don't drink that!" I yelled, but too late. "Tastes like piss," he said. And I said, "It is."

With that lousy Coliseum field, we had to do the shoes with wire brush, saddle soap, and buff. And sometimes the whole staff was Senator Griffin, Nobe Kawano, and me. It was odd to be playing with and against players whose shoes I'd shined as a batboy. In the minors, Stan Williams and Ron Perranoski, whose typical response was "must be getting old, facing a fucking batboy." Then Phil Ortega, Pete Richert, Frank Howard, and Ken McMullen. When I played against Ken in '65 he said, "What the hell are you doing on the field, you should be in the clubhouse shining shoes."

I'll never forget the silence in the clubhouse after the '62 playoffs. A brighter memory is from June that season when Koufax no-hit the Mets. I'm not usually a souvenir collector but I got one of those game balls and came into the clubhouse for Koufax's signature. He was surrounded by media people for interviews but he looked over, saw me, and said, "What do you want, Lach?" "Just wanted you to sign the ball, but I'll get you later." He stops the interview and says, "I'll do it now." He was the classiest guy.

It was always fun. One day in the dugout the other batboy and I were laughing at something but we got caught in a *Sports Illustrated* picture of Vada Pinson swinging at the plate. The Reds were beating the Dodgers in a crucial series, and we got called on the carpet for enjoying it. A worse day for me was the one time I didn't wear a cup in my uniform, and a foul off Joe Christopher's bat hit me. I had to be treated on the field and then assisted to the clubhouse.

As a batboy I learned to chew tobacco, drink, and got my sex education. But it was a good preparation for a career in baseball, because I learned to relate to batboys, clubhouse guys, and umpires, as well as players.

Rene Lachemann has remained in baseball as player, coach, and manager. He is now manager of the Florida Marlins, and his brother Marcel is on his coaching staff.

JIMMY LEFEBVRE......................................

I was visiting team batboy at the Coliseum for the Dodgers for part of the 1961 season. I was in Morningside High School, and I played on the same American Legion team that produced Sparky Anderson, Billy Consolo, and Billy Lachemann. I got the job through Rene Lachemann when my brother Gilly had to quit because he was going out for football.

I was signed by Lefty Phillips and Kenny Myers. As a batboy I got to take infield, and Dick Schofield said, "Hey, you can play." Later he became my roommate. After seeing me take ground balls, Don Zimmer said, "Kid, you wanna sign a contract, I'll sign you right now." "I already signed," I told him.

The Pirates were the hardest team to clean up the clubhouse after. They came out early to the ballpark, they all chewed tobacco, and they sat around playing cards and spitting on the floor. There was a stream of tobacco juice running down the floor. Smoky Burgess—I thought he was a trainer, a roly-poly guy with his gut hanging over. Then he put his uniform on—it surprised me that he was a player, and then with a bat in his hands he was an artist. They had a rookie pitcher named Alvin O'Neal McBean, who'd sit in the dugout with towels wrapped around his shoes so they wouldn't spit tobacco on them.

Players usually don't remember visiting batboys. There were no tips. I did it just to be around big-league players. I didn't know what second-guessing was. I was just in awe of their hitting, running, fielding a ground ball—it's a beautiful art. In '63 I came back to help the visiting clubhouse guys unpack for the World Series. To hold Mickey Mantle's shoes, with No. 7, was a special thrill.

My main impression was of absolute professionalism. They talked baseball, nothing else. One lesson I learned quickly was never take the bat out of a hitter's hand—if he strikes out or pops up, let him take it back to the dugout, throw his batting helmet, whatever, and then pick it up. I remember Hank Aaron after going 0 for 4, saying, "Tomorrow, somebody will pay."

Another lesson I learned from Gene Mauch, who was managing Philadelphia. Late in the season, the Phils beat the Dodgers like 15-0, and they come larkin' into the clubhouse. Mauch shuts them up and delivers a tirade. "I been tellin' you all year you could do it," he says, and plenty more along with that.

My experience as a batboy is very useful to me as a manager. I am very well aware of what a good clubhouse is and isn't.

Jim Lefebvre has remained in baseball as player, coach, and manager. At this writing he is third base coach and hitting instructor for the Oakland A's.

GILLY LEFEBVRE ....

My dad, Benny Lefebvre, was the director of parks at the Rancho La Cienega playground in Los Angeles, which had four baseball diamonds over near Dorsey High School. There were three Lefebvre sons and six Lachemann boys, and Dad told us we'd all have careers in baseball. And he was pretty nearly right. Two Lachemanns played in the majors, three seasons each, and have stayed on, coaching and managing. My brother Jimmy had the best career as a player and still as a manager. Tippy, Jimmy's twin, is a pitching instructor at UCLA. I'm eleven months younger and I never got higher than the Florida State League, but I enjoy coaching now at the high school level.

Marcel Lachemann and I were signed together by Lefty Phillips and Ken Myers for the Dodgers. It was customary at that time for high school kids to be signed and put in some time as batboys. In fact it was Jim Merritt, later a Reds pitcher, who broke me in as batboy. And two of the funniest things I remember as batboy had to do with Rene Lachemann, who was a real cocky kid. One was seeing him chase the geese on the field for Goose Day, and the other was seeing him get hit in the balls by a foul ball.

I batboyed on the visiting side for three seasons, through '61, and my worst moment came late that last season when Cincy came in for a crucial series. Vada Pinson was on second base late in the game. The batter singles and lays the bat down right on the plate. I know there will be a play and I ease around Johnny Roseboro to pull the bat away just as the throw is coming in. Roseboro shies at my shadow, loses the ball, and Vada scores. He tells me, "Appreciate it," and the Reds clinched the pennant that game. But Roseboro said to me, "Don't feel bad—you did the right thing."

My boss in the clubhouse was Jim Muhey, one of the great storytellers in the game, along with Dick Stuart and Stan Musial. He hated Curt Flood, complained that he always played his radio too loud, and he'd throw wet towels over the locker at him. One of our chores was to bring cards from girls with their names and numbers on them down to the clubhouse for players—Orlando Cepeda was the most popular—but if Muhey was mad at a player he'd hold those cards.

The great stars were usually nice guys, like Mays and Musial. Ron Santo spent time talking with me and gave me hitting lessons. Hank Aaron would come out early to the ballpark and sit around playing cards with me. But once on the field, after he struck out, he went bananas when I tried to take his bat.

Batters would often ask batboys in the on-deck circle what the pitchers were throwing. One day Joe Torre says to me, "What's he have?" "Just heat," I say, and he goes up and strikes out. When he came out for his next at-bat, I said, "What happened?" He didn't laugh, struck out three times that game.

There was no regular pay for batboys on the visiting side then, just four tickets and two balls per game plus broken bats. There were tips, of course, and I learned how to hustle. One good payday was fifty bucks for posing with Ernie Banks for a milk ad for billboards. Even better was a Gillette commercial that Rene and I did with Don Drysdale in a studio. Rene was catching a Drysdale pitch and I was firing back another ball. That one ran for a long time on TV.

That was one advantage to working in L.A. We had an annual Hollywood Stars Day at the ballpark, and we were kept busy getting balls signed by players for the stars and by the stars for the players. I enjoyed meeting people like Ed (Kookie) Byrnes of "77 Sunset Strip." And I'll never forget the night when I was out on a date and was greeted by the cast of "The Untouchables," whom I'd met at the ballpark. I was impressed, even if my date wasn't.

Gilly Lefebvre has a law degree and business experience, coached and taught government and social studies in high schools, and now works at Juvenile Hall in Orange County.

Rich Eberle ....

I was going to DePaul High School when I applied for a job with the Cubs by sending a composition to Yosh Kawano, the equipment manager. As soon as I got the job, I learned at school what "connections" were. There'd be a problem with a teacher and I'd be sent to the principal, who'd be waiting with his sleeves rolled up. But when I said the magic word "batboy" he'd listen to my explanation and say, "By the way, can you get me some tickets?"

There were no washing machines in the clubhouse at Wrigley then. It was part of our job to take the uniforms to and from the laundramat at Newport and Clark. Yosh had one rule for us: use your common sense. And he used to let us make extra money by selling cracked bats—for as much as five bucks each, some signed balls, and used balls—till someone reported it upstairs and we had to stop.

Ron Santo was my guy. I got him hot dogs and hamburgers from outside the ballpark, until Leo Durocher caught him. "I hope that sandwich tastes good," he says, "because it costs you $150." Another time, in Houston, Santo met the current Miss Texas. He sent me to deliver a message to her in the stands, but she was sitting next to Don Kessinger's wife, so I kept him out of trouble by not delivering it.

When I started in '65, the Cubs were doing their rotation experiment of management, but then Leo took over. Another time in Houston, I remember that the umps were getting on him and the press was bugging him too, and I saw him rip the telephone out of the wall in the dugout and throw it at the umpire. But what I remember most clearly is that it wasn't done in rage but was all calculated and deliberate.

Of those players, I remember George Altman as a real gentleman; Fergie Jenkins as a character, a nut, but with real affinity for us kids; and Dick Ellsworth, who'd invite us to his house for a barbecue, saying, "Just walk around my new sod and talk for a while."

I may see two to five gaves a year now.

Rich Eberle, who has been a developer and a cabinet maker who rehabilitated old buildings near Wrigley Field, is now a social worker earning his Master's in counseling.

Phil Cline ....

Up to 1965, DePaul Academy used to supply all of Yosh Kawano's clubhouse kids for the Cubs. I had a friend there, but the school was closing, so when Yosh hired me we started a St. Benedict's tradition.

I was playing some ball in high school, third base and first base, and it was a kid's dream to be around Ernie Banks, Ron Santo, and Billy Williams. My second year Curt Simmons came over, and then Robin Roberts late in the season. It was amazing how well they all treated us kids. Joe Amalfitano was a father figure type, and Dick Ellsworth was like a big brother. But I guess we were closest to the younger players. Ken Holtzman was just a few years older. Fergie Jenkins was a rookie—I was there when he pitched his first game, a shutout, winning 1-0 on his own home run.

The rookies sometimes treated batboys as sounding boards. My best example is Byron Browne, a young outfielder who used to lend me his Olds 442 to drive to school when he was on the road. One day in Wrigley he slid so far short of the bag that he never got there, stopped two feet short and was tagged out. Leo was going nuts in the dugout, and the players were trying to keep from laughing, their hands covering their mouths. Byron sits down next to me, and quietly asks, "Was it that bad?" I didn't know what to do but I finally had to say, "Well, yeah, it was."

Durocher was just starting as manager there, and I learned more about baseball from him than anything else. One day he gave Ellsworth the sign to hit an opponent, in retaliation for the last inning. Ellsworth threw a strike. Leo went to the mound and lifted him. He was somewhat distant from the kids, but when we went on a road trip to Houston, Atlanta, Cincinnati, and Pittsburgh, he put the arm on the players to pitch in for expense money for us. We also got $30 per diem meal money.

Our regular pay was $500, which we got at the end of the summer. But the tips were good—Santo, Williams, Glenn Beckert were good for a hundred each, but Banks was $10. Then we'd make a few extra bucks by selling cracked bats to fans—with Yosh's connivance, but someone in the front office spotted a transaction one day, and after that all cracked bats stayed in the clubhouse.

Yosh was a taskmaster but we were very close to him. Rich Eberle and I used to fool around with him all the time, squealing on each other to Yosh and then making faces behind his back while he chewed the other one out. The Wrigleys didn't even have washers and dryers in the clubhouse, so we had to tote giant laundry loads three blocks to the laundramat.

Yosh taught us a good lesson, that hard work really makes a difference. I also learned that baseball is not just a game but a profession, that a pitcher who got a sunburn and had to miss a start got fined. But I have to say that I appreciate the experience more in retrospect than I did at the time.

Lt. Cline is with the Gang Investigation
Section, Organized Crime Division, of the
Chicago police.

GUS THAM . . . .

I was in the eighth grade when I started working for Red Adams as a clubby in the Giants visiting clubhouse in '63, then was visiting batboy in '65. That was a great place to be. When the Mets came to town, Red and Casey Stengel would talk for hours. The kids would sit on the floor around them and just listen. Even though we couldn't understand most of what they said, it was still funny and fascinating.

From '65 through '67, through my years at St. Ignatius, I was Giants batboy, then went off to Prescott College in Arizona. When I showed up at spring training in '68 I got hell from Gaylord Perry because I had let my hair grow long at college. Gaylord had taken me under his wing in the clubhouse, even gave me a game ball from his no-hitter, signed by him and catcher Dick Dietz. I used to play catch with Dietz before games—he'd throw away his mitt and catch my hardest throws bare-handed.

The Giants were contenders in those years, with Mays, McCovey, and Marichal. It was an exciting time. The dugout is really alive in a pennant race, everything is meaningful. Among coaches and managers, I found Alvin Dark to be a hard man to know. Herman Franks was interesting, always on top of situations. Cookie Lavagetto always had time for the kids. And Wes Westrum was another nice man.

Twice I made the game stories in the papers. Once, in Los Angeles, I collided with catcher Jeff Torborg when I was running to pick up a bat, getting me a subheadline next day: "Batboy only injury in Giant loss." The other time was during the famous confrontation between Marichal and Roseboro. I was right up close for it. I knew somehow that something was going to happen, and then when it did I had an adrenaline rush. There was no time for forethought, and I jumped right in. I was the one who took the bat from Juan. Gene Moreno of the grounds crew, who always took care of the kids, grabbed me and pulled me out of the melee. Next day the papers called me a hero.

When my brother Brad started working, it was a great opportunity to be with him. I mean, not just sleep in the same room like most brothers, but suit up together, do a job together. When it was over, especially in the first few years after, it was difficult to sit in the stands as a fan.

Baseball is its own little island. I learned lessons of common sense, maturity, how to carry yourself, how to be a man and have fun doing it. Of course I'd want my sons to be batboys. If every kid in America could be a batboy, America would be a better place.

To be able to reflect on Major League adolescent experiences is something very few can do. What keeps coming to mind is the relationships that were built with the marginal players—the guys that were on the bench waiting for their shot at stardom. You get closer with them because you sit and talk, watch the game, and fool around while the starters are out there doing it. Some are only there a short time, but others you get to know well. These are the guys who usually were the most sincere, and in many cases more knowledgeable on the finer points of the game—basically many of these were future coaches of the game.

After six months as a teacher, and more than twenty years as an air-freight truckdriver, Gus Tham is earning his Master's in Rehabilitation Counseling at San Francisco State University.

BRAD THAM ....

My brother Gus, four-and-a-half years older, was already working for the Giants when I started as a clubby on the visiting side in '65. Then I was batboy in '67 and '68 and stayed on for another four seasons as ballboy. Murph, who took over as visiting clubhouse manager, practically raised us.

I got to watch and be around the greatest player of all time, Willie Mays. I was there for McCovey's MVP year, I was there for Gaylord Perry's no-hitter followed by Ray Washburn's the next day, and I was there for Bobby Bonds' grand slam in his first game. I saw Marichal, Cepeda, Hart, Koufax, Drysdale, Gibson, Brock, Banks, Clemente, and Aaron, and I especially remember Pete Rose, because of the way he'd stop and talk with the batboys.

It all taught me a different perspective on the game. I learned that the umpires are truly a rare breed, constantly on the road. I learned to analyze hitters, to think innings ahead, and it makes the game more enjoyable. And I learned that the d.h. is just not baseball.

I can tell you about one funny incident. One morning I'm sitting in the dugout in the rain before a game with the Braves when I see their traveling secretary, Donald Davidson, an abrasive foul-mouthed midget, walking across the field. There was a new security guard named Mark there, and I say to him, "Get that kid off the field." Mark goes after him, and when Davidson figures out what happened he yells at me, "I'm gonna get you fired, I'm gonna talk to your boss, I'll talk to Mr. Stoneham." Well, I just laughed, didn't think anything about it, until Eddie Logan tells me he got a call from Chub Feeney, and they had to keep me under wraps all weekend till the Braves left town.

I made lifelong friends with the guys I batboyed with. Especially Bob Fenech. We still play golf and softball and travel together to the Super Bowl.

Brad Tham is a business representative of the
Teamsters Union in San Francisco.

BOB FENECH....................................

My dad, Sam Fenech, played for the PCL Oakland Oaks and knew Red Adams as a trainer. So when Red came to the Giants, I had an in. It was Red who hired Mike Murphy as batboy in '58. I worked from '66-'68, two years as visiting batboy under Murph and the third year as ballboy and umpires' attendant.

Mike Murphy is a great unsung hero to me. He promotes baseball better than anyone in the game. He's constantly getting balls and bats for sick kids, and he's always there when needed. I still see him two or three times a week.

As a kid I was a fanatic Giants fan. I remember the '62 World Series, when I played hooky from school, and Red let me into the park early. At 12, to be walking through the tunnel with the players was a great thrill. I idolized the players then, but my attitude changed as a batboy.

In fact, my first few weeks marked the biggest change in my life. I learned a lot of new words, and I learned, being around players every day, that they're only human. On Opening Day in '66, versus the Cubs, I was ballboying down the line, and the first time I returned a foul I could hear Durocher screaming, "Get rid of that fucking ball." He had the foulest mouth I ever heard, with a command voice, but he was really good-natured.

We used to have fun with Willie Davis before games. He'd play pepper with us kids, but he only wanted to bat. He'd say, "Catch ten balls in a row and you can bat," but if we got up to eight, he'd smash one by. In two full seasons I never got to bat. But in the clubhouse the Pirates were the most fun, always a happy bunch with their radios going—especially Stargell.

I was the only one who would warm up with Willie Mays ten or fifteen minutes before a game, because he loved to throw hard then. By the way, I'm the answer to a trivia question: Who is the only player to catch a fly ball off Willie Mays and a TD pass from Marty Domres? It was during b.p. for one and in touch football in the service for the other.

Kneeling with them in the on-deck circle, I used to ask players to name the toughest pitchers they'd faced. No surprises—the consensus was Koufax and Gibson. One day in the on-deck circle, Ron Hunt of the Mets said, "Get me another bat, I don't like this one." He didn't have another bat in the dugout, so I raced to the clubhouse and back, but not before he got to the plate and hit a home run. In the dugout, he complained to me, "Where the hell was that bat?" and then he used the new one next time up.

Sometimes we'd spend the night in the trainer's room, playing cards and drinking beer. Once, after a getaway day game, Murph was out on a date, and we were supposed to wait for Cincy to come in from L.A. to unpack them. So we decided to have dates in ourselves while we waited. Well, the Dodger game ran long, extra innings, and by 2 a.m. we'd had too much beer and had passed out. The Dodgers' equipment arrived at 5 a.m., but no matter how hard they hammered at the door they got no response. It wasn't till Murph arrived at 8 that we could be roused and start to unpack.

I met a lot of good people—Gus and Brad Tham and Rich Pieretti, son of Marino Pieretti who pitched six years in the American League. Pieretti and I used to work four or five innings each and then trade places. It was a great time.

Bob Fenech, after graduating from San Jose
State, has been for two decades a police officer
at the San Francisco International Airport.

ROGER HAILEY ....

Mostly I remember the fun and games, except for one awful minute. I was in the on-deck circle as batboy for the visiting Orioles when Ken Tatum's fastball hit Paul Blair in the face. Ken was a promising young pitcher, and he was never the same after that, although Blair hardly slowed down for the next ten years.

I was an Angels batboy for five or six seasons in the Sixties, helped out in the Dodgers clubhouse, too. Tommie Ferguson hired me and he was like a father figure to me. I was twenty years old when the team was coming off a road trip, and Fergie said to me, right there in LAX, "You can handle the visiting clubhouse job, can't you?" So I stayed on in baseball for another six seasons, the last four as equipment manager for the Angels. The best testament from those years came from Mickey Mantle, who told me, "You make the best hot dogs in the American League."

It was a lot of fun, a great time of my life. In the Angels clubhouse, Jim Fregosi, Bobby Knoop, and Buck Rodgers took me under their wing. It's interesting that those are the guys from that club who stayed in the game as coaches and managers.

I remember the hilarity before games, the hotfoots, the lighted newspapers burning in someone's hands, Bob Uecker entertaining everybody.

My moment of fame came when the Angels still played in the Dodgers' ballpark. During a downpour that flooded the dugouts, I was practically up to my neck in the water, trying to get equipment back into the clubhouse. They took my picture, and the caption in next day's *Examiner* had the "batboy swimming to save the bats."

Of course, as the oldest son of a famous writer, I was used to being close to fame. When my father came to the ballpark, "Welcome Arthur Hailey" lit up the scoreboard. But fame's a relative thing. Once, flying back from Detroit, I made friends with Mike Love of the Beach Boys. I left tickets for them all at the ballpark for the next home game, and when they came, both Fergie and Mr. Autry said, "Who are those guys?"

When I left baseball after the '72 season, I was burnt out. At first I didn't even want to see any games. Now I'll go occasionally.

The son of the author of Airport *is a supervisor for American Airlines in Nashville.*

JERRY RISCH

I worked my first game for the Cardinals in '66, suiting up in a Pirates uniform—it was John Logan's—and wearing No. 23. Butch Yatkeman ran the clubhouse, and we all learned to do things Butch's way. When Whitey Herzog left, I thought of a "Butchism" he'd often repeat—"the only people who are irreplaceable are the ones in the graveyard."

Of all the players I've seen come through here, I'd say Roger Maris was the nicest guy, quiet, a fine fundamental player. We lost a fine man when he died.

My favorite batboy story is about Sean Roarty, the son of a Busch executive who was to start working for us when he was 13. His first day in the clubhouse Jerry Reuss gave him a chew, and Sean spent the whole game in the bathroom, puking, and we had to suit up the regular kid. Later Sean became a good batboy. He used to sprint to the plate for the bat, and the players loved it. He's an exec in the Anheuser office in Chicago now.

My brother Jeff over there still works in the clubhouse part-time, but he won't even talk to you—he's of the Butch Yatkeman-Buddy Bates school of clubbies. As for my son, I don't want him to be a batboy. I don't want him exposed to the language he'd hear. He'd grow up too fast in the clubhouse.

Jerry Risch is visiting clubhouse manager for
the Cardinals.

MIKE DOYLE ....

When I was in the eighth grade, the principal, who was quite a baseball fan, urged all of us to enter an essay contest—the Pepsi Batboy Contest—250 words or less on why we wanted to be a batboy for the Milwaukee Braves. There were twelve winners, and at the first game we were all introduced over the p.a. like a starting lineup.

Going through the tunnel from the clubhouse to the field was an emergence into a bigger-than-life closeness to the game. The Braves were playing the Cubs, and as I stood there, just a nervous kid, Ernie Banks put his arm around me to calm me. I'll never forget that, not just the gesture but his sensitivity to my needs. Ron Santo was with that club, too, an exceptional person. I admired his consistency, the fact that he never took his own emotions out on others.

Through three seasons I worked for the Braves, up to their last game in Milwaukee, against the Dodgers. Hank Aaron is the one player that stands out in my mind from those years, a real class act. I remember Sandy Koufax, too. I warmed him up once and forgot to put a sponge in my mitt—what a sore hand I had! We had fun in lots of ways in the clubhouse, like racing to shine shoes. I remember that the liquid polish came in containers similar to the pine tar containers, and one day one of the kids polished the Giants' shoes with pinetar. They ended up all glued together, and I can still hear the Alou brothers swearing in Spanish when they found them.

But baseball hadn't left Milwaukee. The White Sox would play a dozen home games in Milwaukee, and I'd take care of the visiting clubhouse. I remember that one game against the Twins drew a record crowd at City Stadium. So when the Brewers came I continued to work at the ballpark, as assistant to clubhouse manager Jim Ksicinski. (I was also working as a waterboy when the Green Bay Packers played home games in Milwaukee.) When Fergie [Tommie Ferguson] came back to Milwaukee with the Brewers, I had the chance to work under two of the most wonderful people in the world. Jim and I have maintained our friendship ever since. And Fergie really understood batboys. It was he who arranged road trips for the kids, and I got to visit every American League ballpark.

I had the chance to meet some memorable personalities. Reggie Jackson, for example, who was very intense—he'd take his frustration out in the clubhouse. And Billy Martin, one of the most genuine people I've ever known. He always treated us clubhouse staff well, and he never held grudges. Then there was Mike Kekich—what a prankster. He took a player's jacket once and the mascot, Bernie Brewer, found it on top of the scoreboard.

I continued to work at the ballpark through the '73 season, when I was already in the seminary, two years before I was ordained. I learned some valuable lessons as a batboy, lessons about how people handle pressure and challenges, lessons about the variety of reactions to winning and losing. I saw all the fragileness of being human, and I was always bothered by violations of sacredness in relationships.

After ten years as a diocesan priest, Mike
Doyle pursued a career in radio and TV. He is
now Senior Producer for "Today's Life
Choices" at Golden Dome Productions at
Notre Dame.

MARK MCKENZIE ....

I substituted for a friend in the Twins clubhouse a few times during the '68 season, then was visiting batboy for two years. So for the first ALCS I was the Orioles batboy when they clinched. They were a great group of professionals. They were in town for only the one day to finish the playoff, but Brooks Robinson collected twenty bucks from each player and coach for the clubhouse guys before joining the celebration.

Earlier in the season, I had been in the on-deck circle with Frank Robinson, who asked me about Tommy Hall's pitching. "He's got a fastball, slider, curve, and straight change," I said, "and his curve breaks away." "But he's a lefthander!" he said. I was embarrassed, but I forgot about it, until after the game when I was summoned to kangaroo court. There was Frank with his wig and gavel. But Don Buford got me off with a thumbs up verdict.

I did better with Reggie Jackson. I told him that Jerry Koosman likes to throw a slow curve, then follow it with a slower curve. Reggie went to the plate and froze on the slow curve for a strike and a 2-2 count. Then he just sat back and waited and hit the slower curve into the seats.

But I was already Reggie's friend. I had read in a *Sports Illustrated* cover story on him that he was a trivia buff. So as soon as the A's came to town, I challenged him with a trivia question: Who's the Yankees all-time home run leader with how many? He started to blow me off, but I persisted. Sal Bando, Catfish Hunter, and Blue Moon Odom were all there, going "Oh, no," wondering who this sixteen-year-old kid was. So Reggie gave the obvious answer—Babe Ruth, 714. Except that he forgot that 55 of those home runs were not hit as a Yankee.

He was impressed at getting caught with the trick question, and he told me to sit down with him. "I'll never forget your name," he said to me, and he hasn't. We became such good friends that he was godfather to my daughter. He was present at her christening and then, when she died at two, he dedicated his 500th home run to her. When our twin sons were born the following year, Reggie, at his own request, became their godfather.

The Red Sox were a good bunch to work for, with Yaz and Reggie Smith and Gary Peters. So were the Tigers, with Al Kaline, Bill Freehan, and Norm Cash. On getaway day Cash always checked with Jim Wiesner, our clubhouse manager, to make sure that none of the Tigers had stiffed him.

I remember Rod Carew as a kid, pouty and ready to quit. Coach Posedel said to him,

"Babe Ruth died and they continued to play the game—don't blow it." I think he listened, because through the years I've known him as one of the finest guys I've met.

I remember Lou Piniella as a rookie, a great guy and playful. He knocked my hat off with a knuckleball once. But his temper was awesome. Once, then he struck out to end an inning, I was working the foul line and tossed him a ball between innings like I'm supposed to. He took it and threw it out over the upper deck.

Then there was Billy Martin's temper. In '69, at the end of the season, with the division already clinched, the Twins were playing the Mariners and Don Mincher hit a home run. Martin demanded to see the bat, because he thought it was corked. I had already stuck it back in the No. 5 slot in the batrack, so I grabbed all the No. 5 bats. Billy called me a liar and a cheater, and Jim Wiesner had to convince him not to fire me.

Next to my parents, Wiesner was the most influential person in my life. He helped to raise me. Baseball teaches how to win and lose in life. It teaches you a sense of responsibility and a work ethic. You grow up faster in the clubhouse, and it teaches you a sense of loyalty.

Mark McKenzie has been a stonemason, now deals in sports collectibles and licensed apparel, still manages the visiting clubhouse for the Minnesota Vikings, and coaches baseball at Minnetonka High School, wearing No. 8 on his uniform in honor of his boyhood idol, Carl Yastrzemski.

THAD MUMFORD ....

I don't know anyone else who got a job as batboy the way I did. Even though I grew up in Washington, it was a Yankee batboy I intended to be, and nothing else would do. I bombarded them with letter, and whenever they came to Washington I'd manage to harass Michael Burke in his box. I even invented a fraudulent history for myself, that I was a student at Erasmus Hall in Brooklyn, instead of Western—now Duke Ellington—High in the District. On December 14, 1967 I got the letter offering me the job. I believe I was the first black batboy in the Major Leagues.

I was a high school senior, so I had to take some liberties to be in New York in April. My parents didn't approve, but I managed to keep it up till May 6, in part because I persuaded Colonel Stallings' secretary not to take any calls from Dr. Mumford. But he finally got through, on a day that I was suited up and ready for the Indians, and I was called into the office, still in uniform. Colonel Stallings said, "I don't want to see you here till you graduate." So I missed a few weeks of the season.

Then in September it happened again. I was to start college at Hampton Institute. My folks drove me down to school. I waved goodbye to them, and as soon as their car turned the corner I was on my way to the bus-stop to get back to New York. It was during the High Holidays, and I was homeless for a night in New York, broke because I'd had my pocket shaved from my pants. But when I got to the ballpark I borrowed five bucks from Hawk Harrelson of the Red Sox.

I lasted till the final weekend of the season, a four-game series with the Indians again, as it happened. They had a home run contest before the game, featuring Mickey Mantle and the Samoan, Tony Solaita, and I was shagging in center field. I happened to make a great catch in front of the monuments, and of course it was featured on TV. My cousins saw it, called my father, and he showed up by the fifth inning of the second game. Sudden Sam McDowell was in the visiting clubhouse, where I had dressed, when I got word to come up to the office. "From what I hear," he said, "you should take everything with you." By the next season I had transferred to Fordham and I was able to work a full schedule.

I never liked working on the visiting side, helping players who were playing against the Yankees. They must have sensed it—I can remember Earl Wilson of the Tigers snarling at me, "Gimme those stirrups." And when Frank Fernandez hit the foul pole for a home run for New York against Washington I must have celebrated, because Ted Williams kicked me off the bench.

I was shocked at the kind of language used by people like Mantle and Pete Sheehy. Sheehy was still in charge of the pecking order in the clubhouse, and he was always trying to hang hangers from players' pants before they went onto the field. I saw and heard a lot of things, but I was determined not to be another Jim Bouton. I believed in the *omerta*, the code of silence.

For two years I was one huge goosebump. Imagine having Mantle throw you knuckleballs on the Yankee Stadium field. Or meeting Joe DiMaggio when he visited. I sat on the bench in the dugout with him in '68, and of course I had to ask, "What were you thinking when Gionfriddo made that catch in the '47 Series and you kicked the dirt?" He gave a little smile and just said, "Oh, shit."

Reggie Jackson always joked with me, when I'd come back to visit after I'd become a TV writer, saying, "When are you gonna put me on the show?" But in August of 1969, when I mentioned to him that my grandfather was in a hospital in D.C., Reggie and Paul Casanova took the time to visit him and spend an hour talking baseball with him.

I was supposed to be majoring in Art History at Fordham, but I was writing jokes instead of papers. I had gotten on as a page at NBC—about the same way I got on as a Yankees batboy—and when I was assigned to the "Tonight Show" I got my first view of writers. Back in high school I had sent some material to Norm Crosby and gotten a two-page letter back. Now I got a boost from Marshall Brickman, after harassing him, and critiques from Hank Bradford, and in '71 I could leave Fordham for a job with the Electric Company.

After moving to the West Coast I was able to play baseball, right field for the Pasadena team in a semipro league, and visit the ballparks and clubhouses often. But though I worked on "Bay City Blues," with its minor-league baseball theme, I've never used my baseball experience in my work.

As TV writer and producer, Thad Mumford has credits on "Maude," "MASH," "Different World," "Baghdad Cafe," and others; he wrote the "Second Generation" episode of "Roots"; and as of this writing he is developing properties for HBO.

BOB SCHERR....................................

My family was very close to Milt Pappas and his wife, and he basically helped me get the batboy job. The Orioles had a vacancy, Milt put a word in, I was interviewed, and I got the job. It was 1964, I was fifteen, in the ninth grade at Pimlico Junior High. Pappas was my best friend on the team, and in '66 he was traded for Frank Robinson.

I was so upset about it I was gonna quit because I missed Milt, but I had mixed emotions because it was a pretty good trade and I thought we might have a shot at winning the pennant that year. So I stuck around, and we won the pennant. It was Frank Robinson that did it. That trade almost made me leave, but at the same time it kept me there. I knew '66 would be my last year, I'd had enough. As much fun as it was, it was a lot of hard work, and I decided I'd give it one more year. I really wanted to be with the first pennant-winning Orioles team.

I'll never forget my first week as a batboy. I started on the visiting side, and for my first Opening Day I was wearing the uniform of the defending American League champion New York Yankees. That was a bigger thrill than wearing an O's uniform. That was a great Yankee team, with Mickey Mantle, Roger Maris, Bill Skowron, Tony Kubek, Bobby Richardson, Tom Tresh. They were champions and Yogi Berra was in his first game as manager. He didn't say anything to me. I really don't recall anything clearly. I was in such awe my judgment is probably very clouded.

After that three-game series, the Boston Red Sox came in for the first night game of the season. I'm kneeling in the on-deck circle on the first-base side and a foul ball is hit over my head. Norm Siebern, the O's first baseman, and John Orsino, the O's catcher, are running in my direction. I'm looking up and don't know what to do, holding the lead bat. This never happened to me before—I look up, can't see the ball, it gets lost in the lights. I got scared, panicked, dropped the lead bat, and ran toward the visitors dugout. Siebern just about caught the ball, but tripped over the bat I had left there, dropped the ball, and was charged with an error.

He was OK, nice about it, didn't say a word. But Orsino started screaming and hollering and cussing at me, right on the field. I was scared to death. When I ran across him later on in the game, he mumbled a couple of cuss words at me again. A month later, when I got the chance to move over to the home side I was scared to take the job. But Orsino never said another word. Either he didn't remember the incident or didn't realize I was the same kid who was the visiting batboy at the time.

My favorite guys on the team were Pappas, Siebern—a terrific guy, Brooks Robinson, Robin Roberts—a real gentleman, Steve Barber, and Wally Bunker—a nineteen-year-old kid who won nineteen games his rookie year. I was friendly with him, and then the following year Curt Blefary became my best friend on the team.

Boog Powell was another terrific guy. He was always drinking beer after games. After every single ball game, we were always trying to get out of there. We'd have to clean shoes till 1 or 2 a.m., but there were three guys you could never get out of the clubhouse—Boog Powell, Jackie Brandt, and Jerry Adair. Those three would sit there and drink beer for hours after every game. Adair went on to be a coach, but he died at fifty of lung cancer.

He was a chain smoker. So was Blefary. Probably half the club were smokers. That surprised me, and the beer in the clubhouse. Ballplayers smoked during the game, in between innings. They'd come in, down the tunnel. They weren't allowed to smoke in the dugout because fans could see. They sold cigarettes in the clubhouse, all the players had credit with the clubhouse manager, but the beer was free, I believe. There'd be a table in the tunnel with fifteen or twenty packs of cigarettes. Blefary would have a special corner of the table for his.

I was shocked that so many smoked and drank. It was like meeting celebrities. When they're celebrities you don't really know them. They have this halo over them. You don't even look at them as people. They're larger than life. When you get to meet them you find out they pull their pants up the same way you do. They're just human beings, have all the faults we have, the same problems we have, the same language we use. That shocked me too. I heard nothing but four-letter words. The halo was off when I got to meet them as people. And I liked certain players and didn't like certain players.

I was scared to death of the manager, Hank Bauer. I never talked to him in three years, other than "Yes, sir." I never told him until a twenty-year reunion in 1986. "What do you mean?" he said. I told him I was scared, first, of his voice, that deep gravel voice, and second that he was very tough-looking. He just laughed and we had a nice talk.

I remember that late in the '64 season we went into Chicago in first place and lost three of four. Steve Barber, having a horrible year after winning twenty games the year before, lost the second game of the double-header, and on the plane coming home he got into a fight with the pitching coach, Harry (The Cat) Brecheen. Brecheen, he's a little skinny guy, started throwing punches at Barber, who was a big hefty guy, and players were grabbing both of them.

There were reporters on the plane, and when everything settled down Bauer walked down the aisle of the plane telling everybody to forget what they saw. I heard him leaning over to different people saying, "You didn't see anything, did you?" I knew he'd come to me. I was scared, though he'd always been nice to me. I heard him coming down, I watched him when he leaned over and put his nose in each reporter's nose, and I know he's gonna get to me. Sure enough, he leaned in my face and said, "You didn't see anything, boy, did you?" I said, "No sir, not a thing." I was scared to death, but no one else broke that story either.

Another almost fight, Hank Bauer and Jerry Adair, just before the trading deadline in June of '66. Davey Johnson had come up and beat out Adair for the second base job. Adair was upset about being used strictly as a pinch hitter, so he and Bauer didn't get along. The last month he wasn't even sitting out in the dugout during games, he was in the clubhouse. When Bauer was looking for him to pinch hit that day he couldn't find him and sent Jim Palmer up instead.

At the end of that inning, I was going to the bathroom in the clubhouse and I could hear Bauer screaming from the tunnel, "Where is Adair?" Bauer came in screaming, then they were screaming at each other, they had their hands on each other, shoving, and I felt awfully intimidated. But no fists were thrown and next day Adair was traded to the White Sox, which may have been what he wanted, for Eddie Fisher, the knuckleball pitcher. The O's won the pennant, and Fisher was part of it.

Another White Sox pitcher I remember was John Buzhardt. He was fast but wild. During one game I was kneeling in the on-deck circle, holding the lead bat with my right hand, not paying attention while he was warming up, looking back toward the dugout, waiting for the O's batters to come up. All of a sudden I got hit on the hand. He smashed my finger. I couldn't believe he threw the ball that far away from home plate. The O's trainer came out and froze it. The finger was broken, and I missed a couple of games.

In '65, when Blefary was my buddy, I went on a road trip to Detroit and Cleveland. I had my own room, so he asked me to get into his bed for bed-check, to put the covers over my head. Bauer was pretty lenient, but they still did bed-checks. I think Billy Hunter may have done it. Blefary wanted to go out past curfew, so I did what he asked. Someone did come in, unlock the door, I pulled the covers over my head, and then they went out immediately. Another time Blefary asked me to pitch to him for extra batting practice. I drilled him in the ribs, and he chased me around the bases. I started running and he came after me. I'm glad we were good friends.

I wasn't much of a ballplayer, but I was pretty vain. I wore glasses, but never during a ballgame. There were embarrassing moments because I didn't wear them. When a pop foul came off the screen, the batboy was supposed to run over and catch the ball. One Sunday afternoon, with the game on national TV, the ball comes off the screen, I missed it, and it hit me on the head. They showed me on TV getting hit in the head and Chuck Thompson said something about it on the radio. That year the visiting batboy was Jay Mazzone. Jay didn't have hands, he had hooks. Very embarrassing, when Jay ran and caught balls in his hooks, and I was missing half of them. My vision was real bad, couldn't see those balls coming off the screen. I dreaded having to catch those balls. I'd catch half, and Jay was catching every one of them.

I got to meet a lot of celebrities—Hubert Humphrey, Frank Sinatra, Mia Farrow. Milton Berle sat right behind me one game and kept throwing peanuts at me. On the way to the World Series in Los Angeles in '66, Eddie Watt asked me if I wanted to meet Ann-Margret.

He said he went to school with her in Iowa, he was gonna see her and talk to her, and would I like a date with her. I said, "Yeah." He's telling me this on the bus going from the hotel to the stadium, and all the players are hearing it. Everyone on the bus is getting into it, saying, "Get him a date."

We get to the ballpark at 10 a.m, and I'm so excited I can't see straight, because of Ann-Margret, not the game. She's there. Watt walks over to her, starts talking to her. I'm watching this, he looks back at me, I start waving, and she waves. I'm thinking I've got a date with Ann-Margret, he walks backs, tells me it's all lined up. I know now I never had a date with her, and I never saw her again. But after the game, all the players started kidding me and razzing me. But that was it. The O's swept the Dodgers, but I didn't score.

Whenever I was on the road, Chuck Thompson would always announce to my parents on the air that I was having a good time. I thought the world of him, he was terrific. Bill O'Donnell too. When I started doing stats I always sat next to Phil Jackman of the *Sun*, who was official scorer, and we'd always have a ball—he's a funny guy. Then in the '69 Series I did stats for NBC. Right after I was introduced to Curt Gowdy, he said to me, "Hey, kid, run and get me a hot dog," so I wasn't big on him, didn't like him very much.

It's always good for a kid to work, but being a batboy is a great experience. It's terrific to get to see all the home games, to travel, and to have the glamor along with the hard work, the responsibility, and the sense of independence. I also learned to take advantage of every free moment, to study on the run, to utilize time profitably. I did my homework between innings. I could do my job on the field and at the same time say something over in my head that I had to memorize. That helped me through high school, college, and law school.

Bob Scherr is an attorney, with offices in Baltimore and Glen Burnie, has run for Congress as a Republican, and has hosted talk shows on local radio and television.

Jay Mazzone ....

My hands were badly burned when I was two and had to be amputated. When I was old enough, my dad helped design these hooks for me so that I could play football and baseball. I've always liked a challenge, to see what I can do for myself, and as a kid it helped me to be sure of myself to play sports.

I played in an 8-10 league in Baltimore and then in the 11-12 league. It was all organized by Mary Dobkin. There's been a movie done on her life. Jean Stapleton played the part. Anyway, they had a Mary Dobkin Day at Memorial Stadium. Brooks Robinson and some other Orioles had been involved, donating bats and equipment to the organization. Anyway, part of the festivities were that there were two Honorary Batboys for the day, chosen by the kids themselves. I got the second-most votes so I was visiting batboy for the day. That was in 1965.

You know, it was every kid's dream to be out there on the field during a real game. We were in our Little League uniforms, helping out the regular batboys, and got to meet all the players. Then, through the Junior Oriole organization I was chosen to be an Orioles batboy for another day.

During the winter, my mom and dad and I were talking about how nice it would be for me to be a batboy all the time, and Mom said, "Why don't you ask, write them a letter?" So I did, reminding them who I was and that I had been there and that I'd love to be Orioles batboy. They wrote back, saying it was up to the batboys when they would leave, that Bobby Scherr was returning next season, but the batboy for the visiting team was going into the service and leaving for boot camp, and would I care to do that. Of course I wrote back that I'd sure like that.

I was the batboy for the visiting team in 1966, which was a great year for the Orioles. It was kinda tough sitting there watching the Orioles have such a great year and working on the visiting side not being able to root for the Orioles. But I got to work the last game Sandy Koufax pitched in his career, in the World Series, and I had my picture taken with him that day.

Another honor I had was being chosen as American League batboy for the All-Star Game in St. Louis. That was the first, and as far as I know the only, time that was done—normally, wherever the game was, the batboy who was there worked the game. That game was played in 105 degree heat, ten innings. I was probably the only one in uniform to last the whole game. But there was one game in Baltimore I remember when it was 120 degrees in the ballpark. People in the stands were dropping like flies, they were changing ballplayers every couple of innings and stuff, and I passed out in the eighth.

In '67 Bobby Scherr retired and I went over to the Orioles side and stayed there until '73. Frank Robinson was more or less the real leader of the ballclub. I came to the club the same year he did and left the same year he did, too, but he was always a leader-type person. Back then there was not a real mixing of blacks and whites and he kind of led the way, seeing that everybody got along and that there was no contention in the clubhouse.

He led all that with the kangaroo court. He and I hit it off pretty good and so he decided to feel me out and see how I felt about different things. Nobody was really asking me to do too much in the clubhouse, and he broke the ice by fining me in kangaroo court for not voting on an issue, whatever it was, because he couldn't tell whether I was thumbs up or thumbs down. That broke the ice for the rest of the ballplayers. They figured I wasn't self-conscious, and so they didn't have a problem after that asking me to go get a soda or glass of ice or whatever. Frank and Jimmy Tyler, the equipment manager, must have had this cooked up before, because they took me into the back where they had made up a big cardboard hand with thumbs sticking out on it. They taped it to my hand and then I could vote.

Brooks Robinson and his wife and his kids are the Ozzie and Harriet type of people. Always were and always will be. It doesn't matter where or when you run into them, it is always the same. You never heard him say anything bad about anybody.

Guys like Curt Blefary and Moe Drabowsky were the practical jokers. They kept a lot of spirit in the club, always trying to outdo each other with their practical jokes. Elrod Hendricks just wanted to explain everything to you, why catchers do this, why players do that. He even liked to share things with fans. He spent a lot of time on batting and just wanted to share that with anybody who wanted to talk with him.

They were all great guys. I didn't really have a problem with anybody, except one ballplayer that not too many people really cared for a lot. He didn't stay long—he just had an ego problem. He thought that everything he did was absolutely the best, and he finally figured out that he wasn't the all-star he thought he was. I don't know where he ended up.

I don't really keep track too much of baseball per se. It's a hassle to go to the ballpark. I know Frank and Elrod are still there, but they're the only ones I knew that are still with the organization. I might take the kids to a couple of games a year, but I don't go into the clubhouse. You know, I have more fun going down and watching my son play Little League than going out to the ballpark anymore.

Jay Mazzone is a heavy equipment operator
for a utility and road construction company in
Maryland.

Bob Elder ....

In my senior year of high school I had to make a choice between playing ball and being the Angels batboy. I was a shortstop and pitched some, and I planned on playing college ball. But I chose batboy.

It may have helped my game. I played at Golden West Junior College and then Cal State-Fullerton. Summer of my junior year I hit .300 as a shortstop in the Northwest League. The Pirates, Mets, and Angels expressed some interest. A popped rotator cuff ended that dream, but I hung on in baseball, doing some coaching at Fullerton, and working baseball camps, until I got started in broadcasting.

The batboy job was great. I remember standing in line with a couple of hundred kids to be interviewed in a trailer—before the club had even moved to Anaheim. And I still don't know why John FitzPatrick, Jr. and Tommie Ferguson chose me. I often got to take second infield, and you know we always played for cokes—whoever made the error had to buy. Jose Cardenal was usually at third and Chuck Hinton at first. I only lost one time, and I remember once Hinton saying, "I ain't buying no fucking batboy a Coke."

Hinton was very nice to me though, was one of the players who took me under his wing. Clyde Wright and Rick Reichardt, too—I took care of their apartment when they were on the road. Rigney was always nice to me—years later, we'd exchange greetings ("Rig!"—"Bobby!")—but he'd never let me take b.p. More than anyone else, Jim Fregosi looked after me. He took me on a trip to Palm Springs, took me to a golf tournament I'll never forget, and even gave me his glove. I wore his number, eleven, all through high school and college.

The high point was working the right field line in the '67 All-Star Game. I had pitched seven innings two days before and had a sore arm, but I didn't think about it through fifteen innings, playing catch with people like Clemente and Conigliaro. That was the game with Dick Allen, Brooks Robinson, and Tony Perez scoring the only runs on homers while twelve pitchers struck out a total of thirty, including six by Fergie Jenkins.

That was the first time I'd seen Rod Carew. I learned later that he was the most misunderstood player in the game—battered childhood, bad marriage, and all that. But that day Fregosi had passed around two dozen balls to be signed, and I remember Harmon Killebrew handing them to Carew, who didn't want to be bothered, and saying, "Sign 'em—now."

Some of the signing was always done by batboys. Mantle said, after I had signed the team picture for him, "You're a better signature guy than the guy I got in New York." And my Rigney signature was letter-perfect.

I learned a lot of lessons, not all of them good. I saw a lot of pill-popping. I'd see someone like Yaz finish a six-pack before getting his uniform off after a game. On a road trip once in Washington I was hung over after being out drinking the night before, and Fergie wouldn't let me suit up. I had to go to trainer Freddy Federico to get something for it. But I guess it's all part of growing up. I learned about travel, about teamwork, and about responsibility. I guess I didn't learn much about politics or current events. My mom used to say, "If the world came to an end, you'd have to learn about it from the sports page."

Bob Elder has been sports coordinator for KEZY AM and FM in Anaheim, is now Vice-President and General Manager of the Anaheim Bullfrogs, reigning champs of the international roller hockey league.

LEONARD GARCIA ....

I wrote the Angels a letter in 1965, asking for an interview. I was hired along with Bob Elder, now sports director at KEZY, and Mike Collins, who went on to play two years for the Dodgers on their rookie league team and is now with the Orange County Police doing drug prevention work with kids.

I was batboy in '66 and '67, assistant clubhouse manager in '68 before doing my National Guard service, then got back into baseball in '72. That was in Davenport, Iowa, as trainer for the Quad Cities team in the Angels organization. I knew I had to try it, to get it out of my system, even at $450 a month and with a pregnant wife. But I never looked back, seven years with the AA club in Salt Lake City, three with AAA Edmonton.

When I started, the first player I met was Bobby Knoop. I had a silly smile of awe on my face then, but never again—except for when I met Mickey Mantle. That was a good veteran team, with Joe Adcock and Norm Siebern. Young guys were Jose Cardenal, who used to give me clothes, and Rick Reichardt, who had me use his apartment when they were on the road. And I was close to a Mexican pitcher named Jorge Rubio—I almost cried when he got sent down. Remember when the A's went to white shoes with their uniforms? Knoop and Jim Fregosi took infield wearing golf shoes. Only two guys gave me a hard time, both pitchers—one who later became a friend and another who we later learned was struggling with a drinking problem.

I went on one road trip in '66, to Chicago, Minnesota, D.C., and New York. And it seemed that everywhere we went we saw prodigious home runs—by Harmon Killebrew in Minnesota, Frank Howard in Washington, and Mantle in New York. In '67 the whole season was exciting because we were in a pennant race till near the end. In the final series, we beat Detroit, and Boston won it.

Ours was a fun clubhouse. We played a game called sani-ball or clubhouse ball. We all did some of the players' signatures. I did Cardenal's and I did Fregosi's on two dozen balls before I realized I was misspelling his name. Bob Elder did Mantle's, by the way, and that Hall of Fame ball in Anaheim Stadium is forged. Speaking of forgeries, the Aurelio Rodriguez rookie card in the Topps series has my picture on it—Rodriguez was sick the day they took them.

There was always music in the clubhouse, not hard rock but stuff like the Zhivago theme and the Lettermen, with just a little soul music starting to come in. Despite momentous events in the country and the world at that time, serious matters were not discussed in the clubhouse. You try to stay in this fantasy world as long as you can.

Leonard Garcia was equipment manager for the California Angels for several years before moving to Mesa in 1993 to handle the club's minor league facilities.

BILL BUSH ....

I actually started out at eleven or twelve as water boy for Santa Ana Junior College. The student equipment manager there was Bob Hassenjaeger—he's still with the Angels in charge of video—and he brought me on at Dodger Stadium where I finished the '65 season as visiting batboy. I was head batboy for the Angels in '66 and again in '67 until I started college.

You mature rapidly in the clubhouse. You get to see players as what they really are—human beings. But at first it was with total disbelief at the profanity I heard in general, but especially from people like Mantle and Maris. Maris was a great guy, by the way, and Mantle gave me a bat he used in the All-Star Game in '67.

Bobby Knoop was a player who became a friend. Don Mincher took me under his wing and so did coach Don Heffner. Moose Skowron was another one who was good to me, and so was pitcher Jim McGlothlin. Some others were not so great. I won't name them, but there was one jerk of a pitcher who'd criticize one of his best fielders, another guy who was a paranoid whiner, and a guy who was so rude we suspected he had an alcohol problem.

I saw that an adversarial relationship with the press was common. Tongue-in-cheek remarks were often taken out of context, and guys would pick up the paper say, "Let's see what I said yesterday." It was a fun clubhouse, though. Bob Elder, who's in radio now, was another clubby, along with Fred Mueller, who at 16 already had the body image of Babe Ruth. We invented the game of sani-ball, played with a sanitary wrapped with tape. We're having an old-timers' sani-ball game pretty soon.

I was embarrassed a couple of times on the field. One day Joe Adcock, who finished his long career as an Angel, lined a foul down the left field line but it was called fair. I had the best view of it and shook my head no at the call. The ump didn't see me do that but Adcock did and chewed me out about it later. The other time was during the All-Star Game, when Tony Oliva threw his bat and Orlando Cepeda picked it up at first base. When I ran out to get it, Cepeda teased me with it, embarrassing me on national TV.

I was probably the only college pitcher who never played high school ball. I learned as a batboy under pitching coaches Marv Grissom and Bob Lemon and from veteran pitchers like Lew Burdette, Curt Simmons, and Jack Sanford, who all pitched for California late in their careers. Sometimes I got to throw b.p. when a coach was hurting, and I always focused on mechanics when I was watching. That experience helped me later on. I was a Business and Journalism major at San Diego State, but I went back for a teaching credential. And for two years I was a teacher and coach in a country village in Australia.

When the All-Star Game came back to Anaheim in 1989, I took my seven-year-old son. I got the impression that the players are not as approachable as they used to be, that the clubhouse isn't as loose and friendly. Still, I'd sure want my son to have the chance I had to be a batboy.

Bill Bush is now involved in insurance and
investments.

FRED MUELLER ....

I was seventeen, a student at Anaheim High, when Leonard Garcia got me the job. I was the world's lousiest ballplayer, and that was the best job I ever had—part of '65, '66, and half of '67.

I learned right away that baseball players were just great big boys. Unpacking them when they got back from road trips, there would be much evidence of their womanizing. And yet, with people like DiMaggio and Pee Wee Reese and Sandy Koufax passing through, I was still in awe of them—and I still am.

I enjoyed road trips to Washington, Cleveland, and Detroit, especially old, old Tiger Stadium, which just reeks of baseball. Just recently, I went back into the clubhouse in Anaheim for the first time in twenty years, and it felt great that Jimmy Reese and Bobby Knoop both recognized me and called me "Fred."

The one incident I'll never forget happened when I was ballboy down the right field line for a game against the White Sox. I'm daydreaming, just sitting there eating sunflower seeds, when a ball is hit toward me. Acting on reflex, I half stand up, stick out my glove, and make the catch. Their manager was Eddie Stanky, and he jumps up from the dugout and just glares at me. And then the ump says, "What did you think, you were on TV?"

Fred Mueller is in the printing business,
supervising the graphics and typesetting of a
computer room.

EDDIE BAXTER ....

I was the Washington Senators batboy from '67 through '71. My father was the equipment manager. I was named for Eddie Yost. I was around the clubhouse a long time before actually working there. I was nine when Camilo Pascual gave me a uniform with my number on it, and I can remember putting out cigarettes on Frank Howard's chest.

At Walter Johnson High School, I played the outfield, was all-county as a sophomore. But the high point of my playing career came during an intra-squad game at spring training in Pompano. I was sixteen, and I hit a bases-loaded single off Bob Priddy. I struck out the next five times, all on curves.

Gil Hodges was a quiet man, kept to himself. But Ted Williams motivated hitters by talking—he was an educator, preached a philosophy of hitting, always stood behind the backstop during batting practice.

Tim Cullen was always giving batboys hotfoots. I remember he and Eddie Brinkman nailed Pete Broberg's shoes to the concrete floor in the clubhouse. I also remember Joe Coleman and Eddie on the road using their duck callers in the hotels. It was fun, being on the road in Boston and New York, and getting to go out with Brinkman and Howard.

In Boston I got invited to a cookout at Dick Bosman's. There wasn't a lot of drinking, just beer. Paul Casanova, Horacio Pina, and Joe Grzenda were all good guys. Casanova and Aurelio Rodriguez were among the good tippers, Johnny Roseboro was generous too, and Frank Howard would give you twenty bucks for a ride to the airport. Denny McLain never gave a tip. He'd never even say thank you for taking care of his car.

A few other people stand out in my memory. Nellie Fox, who was very smart, and I think should have had a shot at managing. Frank Kreutzer, a rebellious hothead, who was very vocal about the treatment he was getting. And Mike Epstein, who was usually reading some book—there were lots of books around—or the *Wall Street Journal*.

It was an interesting time. Vietnam was followed very closely in the clubhouse. The attitudes were anti-demonstrator, but we were all glad we weren't there.

*Eddie Baxter is a mailman in Montgomery
County, Maryland.*

FRANK COPPENBARGER ....

The Giants had a farm team, the Commodores, in Decatur, Illinois, where I grew up, and I used to walk past the ballpark every day on my way to Little League practice. I started out as a batboy when I was ten years old, still in grade school, in 1967. My dad bought me my uniform, with No. 10 on it.

A few good players passed through on their way to the majors—Gary Matthews, John Montefusco, Steve Ontiveros, and Don Hahn. But this was a typical minor-league operation, with the general manager sitting in the stands to chase down foul balls. He'd throw them back to me on the field and I'd put them back in play. One night he tossed one down toward me at the same time there was a wild pitch, and the two balls ended up two feet from each other, both in play, or neither. Tough ruling.

The biggest night of the year in Decatur was G.E. night, a big promotion to attract a crowd from the plant, with lots of specials and prizes. My cousin from Sacramento was visiting that week, and he'd collected about fifty tickets for the drawing. I was the one picking the winners from the barrel, and the grand prize went to my cousin. It was supposed to be a stereo set along with free delivery, but when they found out it was going to Sacramento they changed their minds about delivery.

The team folded my senior year in high school, and for two years while I went to Milliken College my only contact with baseball was an occasional visit to Danville, eighty miles away. But in '77, I got back in the clubhouse with a job at Davenport, Iowa, with the Angels' Quad Cities club, with Ned Berger, now the Angels trainer, and manager Chuck Cottier, now a Cubs coach. Al Unser had been the manager at Davenport, and his house had a batting cage and a pitching machine. His sons Larry and Jerry worked as clubhouse kids, and their brother Del played in the majors and is now minor league director for the Phillies.

After that first season in Davenport, I went to the Instructional League in Arizona for the Angels at $300 a month for three months as a clubhouse guy, and next season moved up to Salinas in the California League with Cottier as manager. At spring training with the Angels in '79 I was promised the AAA Salt Lake job, but it fell through when Cottier went to the Mets as third base coach. So it was back to Illinois, where I got a year-round job with the Cardinals' AAA club, doing ticket sales and advertising in the off-season.

One time at the annual exhibition game with the Cards in Springfield, I mentioned to Butch Yatkeman that I would like a Major League clubhouse job. Then in '81, during the strike, manager Whitey Herzog and g.m. Lee Thomas were in Springfield almost every night, and there was a job waiting for me in Butch's clubhouse, but I had to stay on in Springfield until the settlement. Butch is a hero to me, and I had the thrills of being on hand in '82 when he threw out the first ball and when the Cardinals gave him his special day. In 1990, Lee Thomas, as g.m. of the Phillies, brought Nick Leyva in as manager and me as equipment manager.

Frank Coppenbarger is equipment manager for the Philadelphia Phillies.

DON DEASON ....

I was a ballboy for the Cardinals in '67-'68, batboy in '69-'70. My brother was a friend of Jerry Gibson, the batboy who wrote a book about it. During the second home series in '67, I got to replace another kid. Butch Yatkeman gave me a two-week tryout to see if I exhibited the boy-scout attributes he looked for.

I went to Central High and lived in a neighborhood near the old ballpark. At fourteen I was impressed with the large size of the Sportsman's Park clubhouse and the smallness of myself. I was scared, meek, and shy. Warned by Butch, I managed to avoid the initiation tricks and the kidders. Still, the level of needling surprised me.

Dressing the first night, I got my socks on backwards and Curt Flood told me how to do it. I liked him. He'd go out of his way to give us kids a ride home after a late or rain-delayed game. Rich Allen was always good to clubhouse kids, too. And Roger Maris was the nicest person in the world. He never asked kids to do anything we weren't supposed to, he always tipped, and he talked with us not at us.

In '67 and '68 we were in the World Series. My quarter share of about $2,500 bought me a car and helped pay for school. Believe me, I counted up the cost when Flood failed to catch that fly ball against the Tigers.

Jack Lamabe took me under his wing, also Johnny Romano. On my first trip, a twelve-day West Coast jaunt, I tried to pay for myself at a lunch counter in San Francisco. Romano stopped me, said, "Don't reach for a check unless you're ready to pay for everyone." Lamabe would play cards with me in his room, and he really helped me through a personal crisis.

Once I wrecked Lou Brock's Dodge Daytona in the parking lot. I had just got my license, and I smashed his front end into the wall. After debating with myself I told him about it, very sheepishly. Brock just laughed. "Don," he said, "I own the dealership—don't worry about it."

One day during batting practice I was carrying a bucket of balls from behind second base, being careful of batted balls, but a throw to first from Ron Santo hit me in the head and knocked me cold. I spent the game in the umpire's room. The only other game I missed was on the road in L.A. when I spent the day at Disneyland and got fined in the clubhouse court next day.

I liked umpire Tom Gorman and happy-go-lucky Augie Donatelli. I got in trouble once with Al Barlick. Mike Shannon, just back in the lineup, lined a ball down the left-field line that was called foul. Taking the bat back from me, he asked me and I told him it looked fair. Barlick yelled, "Who do you think you are? I'm gonna have your job!"

I played soccer in my senior year in high school and then at the University of Missouri, St. Louis. We won the Division II NCAA championship in 1973. I was a reserve goalkeeper behind a three-time All-America. That was a fun experience. But I owe my success today to what I learned at the ballpark, namely, what it takes to win regarding personality, self-management, self-motivation. For example, Tim McCarver, Shannon, Bob Gibson, Brock, Phil Gagliano—they've all done well outside baseball.

I only saw a handful of games in the '70s, started back in '80, and now share season tickets. In recent years I've bumped into Orlando Cepeda—who taught me to tie a tie, Joe Torre, and Bill White, all away from the ballpark. They all remembered me, by name.

Don Deason is sales manager of Sun
Microsystems, a computer company.

ROCKY MAUNAKEA ....

My three brothers and I all worked in the clubhouse. Michael, Randy, and Stevie. I was the first. My stepfather is the A's equipment manager, Frank Ciensczyk. I remember when I started, Billy Martin gave him hell after one of my first games, because as visiting batboy—Martin was managing the Twins—I congratulated Dick Green of the A's for a home run.

Those '69 A's were a bunch of crankers—Catfish Hunter, Paul Lindblad, Dave Duncan, Sal Bando, Curt Blefary, Rick Monday. I was their favorite. They stuck me in a garbage can, taped it shut, and played crank with me. They sent me for the key to the batter's box and a left-handed screwdriver. They also helped teach me right from wrong.

It's like you're around a lot of big brothers. Guys like Mickey Mantle, Al Kaline, Denny McLain, show you the way. The Robinsons, Brooks and Frank, too. A lot of people don't understand Reggie Jackson. He could be grouchy, but he'd sit down and talk with you, too. He could be aggressive and then come back and be sweet.

You could make up to $400 in tips on the visiting side. Trips? Well, I went to Anaheim. Charlie Finley didn't like to take batboys on the road. The new owner is much better about that. You know what I remember best? I was eleven or twelve, just starting as a ballboy on the A's side, and I was throwing a ball back but I threw a curve. Some fan reaches over and intercepts. I had to learn to throw straight.

Rocky Maunakea is a mover of office furniture.

MIKE PIERALDI ....

I was the last of the counterculture batboys. Well, maybe I was the first counterculture batboy. I was never crazy about baseball—I liked going to games, but not playing. I had long hair and leftish political views, I was fifteen, and all I wanted was to go to Berkeley. And there I was in the visiting clubhouse of the Oakland A's in 1968. My first game in uniform as a batboy was May 8th. Remember that? Catfish Hunter's perfect game against the Twins.

I felt unique in the clubhouse, politically isolated. Players would talk about their views occasionally. One day I came to work wearing my high school jersey, but I had put a peace sign on it. Frank Howard was at the ballpark early and said, pointing at my shirt, "You know what that's about, right there? Don't wear it around here."

When Kent State happened I wore a black armband, and someone said, "Are you in sympathy with those people?" I said yeah, and he said, "Well, they all shoulda been shot." When Bobby Kennedy was killed the team was on the road, and when they came back nobody talked about it—or about politics at all.

That was Mantle's last year, Reggie's second, and Curt Flood was starting his litigation. Mantle and others taught me about strength and inner character, achieved and maintained at great cost—that's what being a pro player was all about. It was the biggest thrill to see Mantle up close, kneeling in the on-deck circle with him. I saw him hobbling on bad knees but giving his all to baseball. It showed me the stresses, the pressures; it was not fun. I learned to do my best, give my best shot, that trying and failing is better than not trying. And I learned to set goals. I thought of myself as the Abby Hoffman of baseball, but I learned healthy attitudes from the players—to them it wasn't a game but their life.

A "Reggie rule" evolved among batboys—I remember passing it along to Dennis Bekius: If he strikes out, keep your eyes open and be ready to duck. One day in '69, I wasn't concentrating, probably looking at some girl in the stands, the bat flew by me, just missed me by inches. My folks were there, almost stopped breathing. Another time a foul off Ken McMullen's bat just missed me in the on-deck circle.

Certain players stand out in my memory. Yaz—a dignified, classy man, intensely interested in his game, which I found to be common among the top players. Frank Howard—friendly, would talk to me about personal things. Dave Nelson—very friendly, talked with me, always called me by name. Brooks—played catch with me, sprained my thumb with his knuckleball. Killebrew—no talk at all, not surly, just quiet.

And the great ones I got a chance to meet in the clubhouse. DiMag, who'd always say, "How're you doing, young man?" Ted Williams, who came into the clubhouse early one day, and we all stood at attention. Leo Durocher. Don Larsen. I have an Ernie Banks story. The Cubs were playing an exhibition game with the A's before the '69 season, and I was in terrible shape from a party the night before. Banks noticed how I looked and said, "How're you doing, son? I can play two today." With Jenkins pitching against Hunter, I was hoping it would be a game of ninety minutes and gone. But with the score tied 1-1 late in the game, Banks came in the dugout, smiled at me, and said, "Extra innings, young man."

Another time, after a night of partying and experimenting with drugs the night before, I looked and felt awful. I was moaning to my fellow clubby and Rick Reichardt overheard. He looked at me very seriously, took it all in, and said, "Son, please don't kill yourself. That stuff's no good."

Another guy who was very friendly and tried to help me was the White Sox trainer, Charlie Saad. I was a skinny kid who had to tape an oversize uniform together, must have looked like Ducky Medwick. When Charlie saw that, on their next trip into Oakland, he brought along some smaller uniform pants for me.

The equipment manager, Frank Ciensczyk, was a major influence on me. He made me keep my grades up and taught me the discipline of work. He'd give a pre-season speech to all the kids, warning us about the language we'd hear, that players will sometimes be testy, but that they're here to work, not play at being heroes, and that our job is to stay out of their way and help them when needed. And then at the Labor Day weekend in '68, he made sure all twelve kids on the staff got their road trip—it was my first—to Anaheim and Disneyland.

Baseball taught me some of the ironies of life. I could see the deep depression of a player sent down to the minors. In '72, I was watching the World Series on TV, Oakland at Cincy, and Curt Gowdy said, "Look, even the A's batboy has longer hair." It was my brother, Ron, who was not politically radical or anything but had adopted the team's style.

At the time I thought being a batboy would make me popular with the girls, but socially it just gave me a little notoriety at school. Obviously, baseball gave me more important lessons than that. Now, I see maybe one game each home stand.

Mike Pieraldi eventually graduated from
Berkeley, and now supervises a claims office
for Farmer's Insurance.

THE SEVENTIES

THE SEVENTIES

You would think that the more venerable of the clubhouse initiation traditions would die out after half a century, that batboys would no longer be fooled by orders to fetch the key to the batter's box, a bucket of steam, or a bag of knuckleballs. The fact that these rituals persist is testimony to the enduring characteristics of batboys' attitudes. They enter filled with awe, they are shocked by some of what they find but are determined to serve the players, they discover as they quickly mature the humanness of the players, and they are singled out to form privileged relationships with a few genuine baseball people.

The position of batboy, however, does undergo some change through the decade. Baseball's anti-trust exemption notwithstanding, by the end of the Seventies all Major League batboys are earning at least the minimum hourly wage rather than a per-game salary. For many, it thus seems to be an entry-level job in a business rather than an apprenticeship in a sporting fraternity. In this way it reflects a growing perception in the clubhouse that baseball is moving from its traditional status as national pastime to its realistic function as part of the entertainment industry.

The broadened and intensified media attention to ballplayers, the whole process of creating and projecting public images for athletes, has an interesting effect in the clubhouse. The batboys are now more often blessed with a private experience of the players that is at odds with the public view. Their insider's vantage is all the more cherished because, rather than merely illuminating dark corners, it actually contradicts commonly accepted rumors broadcast by media.

What you see in the papers and on the field, what you hear on broadcasts and interviews, are distortions or taken out of context.

No one can know or understand a Steve Carlton, an Eddie Murray, a Billy Martin, a Jim Palmer, a Carl Yastrzemski, or a Gaylord Perry like the batboys who see their better natures on a day-to-day basis. Some public perceptions are confirmed—the consistent goodness of Brooks Robinson, the flakiness of Sparky Lyle, the professionalism of Nolan Ryan—but nothing pleases an old batboy more than to tell how the guys you thought were bad guys were good guys after all. And meanwhile, the legend of Reggie Jackson expands to its contradictory extremes.

DENNIS LIBORIO ....

I used to deliver laundry from the dry cleaners to Fenway Park and help Don FitzPatrick, the equipment man, carry it into the clubhouse. Then he'd let me go into the stands to watch the games. At the end of June in 1969, when he needed to hire someone to work in the visiting clubhouse, he asked me and I jumped at the chance. From the first minute I walked into that clubhouse I was thinking I wanted to make it a career.

I worked there until late in the '71 season, when I moved over to the home side. Wearing the visitors' uniforms was sort of like being in the minor leagues. But when I got to put on that white uniform, with Red Sox written on it, it was a great thrill. I had always been a fan, and the greatest moment was being in the stands when the Sox beat the Twins to clinch at least a tie for the pennant in '67. I haven't matched that feeling since.

You know, if the Sox are in first place in July, there's pennant fever in Boston. The greatest disappointment was the strike season of '72, when we lost to the Tigers by half a game. We had just lost a tough game on Sunday in Baltimore, when a Bobby Grich home run beat Luis Tiant 1-0, and we were ending the season on Tuesday night in Detroit, the winner going to the playoffs. Even the players were nervous that night. We were all butterflies. I was shagging flies in batting practice alongside pitcher Don Newhauser, and I remember calling him off, yelling "I got it, I got it" on a ball that went twenty yards over my head. They went crazy after that game in Detroit. I think we had to wait three hours after the game before we could get out of the ballpark.

In the visiting clubhouse, it seemed that every club that came in had a couple of guys who would be good to us and fool around with us, like flamboyant Ken Harrelson who had been traded to the Indians, Lou Piniella who was still with Kansas City and would enjoy being with others of Italian extraction like Vince Orlando and me, and Billy Hunter, a coach with the Orioles. Except the Yankees. They were the strangest team, always seemed to have their noses in the air, and all we cared about in Boston was beating the Yankees and getting them out of Fenway. Among the managers, I remember that Earl Weaver would rant and rave at players but have no time for us kids, while Billy Martin always had time for us— he was one of the nicest guys.

Eddie Kasko was the Boston manager, and he was real low-key. The Red Sox clubhouse was loose, mostly because of Carl Yastrzemski and Reggie Smith. They were serious about baseball, were always talking hitting, but they also played jokes on everybody. I remember when they got Luis Aparicio one time in the airport coming home from Minnesota. Luis always dressed very well and expensively—while Yaz would wear any old thing—and he gets up from his seat to put on his jacket and the sleeve falls away. Then the other sleeve too. They had cut them, and instead of a fancy jacket he was left with a ragged vest.

Yaz and Reggie looked out for me when I went on road trips, and so did Doug Griffin and Marty Pattin. They never played any tricks on me, but there was a clubby in Boston they'd get on. We called him Crazy Pat, a schoolteacher in his late twenties, who'd do anything Reggie or Yaz told him, no matter how disgusting or ridiculous. And they'd keep thinking of new things because they loved hearing him holler and moan.

I think Boston has the greatest fans. Whenever I'd run out to catch a foul ball off the screen, they'd make this noise as the ball came rolling down, and then if I missed it they'd boo, but if I caught it there'd be silence. I'd always look up to the box after making that catch and see Mr. Yawkey watching me. "Well," he'd say to me later, "I see old stone-fingers is getting better."

Mr. Yawkey worked out every day on the field with us. A guy would hit pepper at us from home plate and we'd line up at the screen. I'd protect Mr. Yawkey to the right of him, Vince Orlando to the left of him, and another kid to the left of Vinnie. I'd be wearing a first-baseman's mitt and a batting helmet—like Dick Allen—and Mr. Yawkey had a Ty Cobb model glove about the size of his hand. We'd get to the ballpark between ten and eleven, but sometimes it would be after three before he'd get down to the field for his pepper game. Then every month he'd give us fifty to a hundred dollars for playing with him. He'd also give us bonuses for road trips.

I left after the '73 season, which was when Reggie Smith was traded, but he and I kept in touch. When he was with the Dodgers in '77 he suggested I come to Philadelphia for their playoff with the Phillies so that he could introduce me to their equipment manager, Nobe Kawano. I did, and Nobe said he wanted to hire me as his assistant, would call me in two weeks. It was a Sunday night and I was at a Bruins game when the call came, and I was soon on my way to L.A. After two years there, the opening for equipment manager came up in Houston, and Nobe told me I had to go for it. So three times I was in the right place at the right time for a job in a baseball clubhouse.

Back when I started, baseball was fun for everybody, including the players. Guys today still treat you nice, but don't seem to have the fun they used to. I started as a batboy and now I hire batboys. I enjoy seeing the good kids come back to visit, and I appreciate it when they call to see how things are going—even years after they worked in the clubhouse. I love it in Houston—the climate, National League baseball—but I still follow the Bruins. I wouldn't want to be anywhere but the Astros clubhouse.

Dennis Liborio is equipment manager of the
Houston Astros.

Rick LaCivita ....

I used to play summer ball with Johnny Boggs, and in 1970 I was visiting batboy for the Washington Senators.

In my very first game I was there to shake Harmon Killebrew's hand after he hit a tremendous home run on Opening Day. Harmon was so pumped up he broke my hand shaking it.

I remember Boog Powell in the clubhouse, with a standing order for a six-pack before the game and another one after.

I guess the high point of my clubhouse career was having Mickey Mantle give me a hotfoot. And on the field, I remember an incident involving a ball Frank Howard hit down the line, with everyone from an usher to owner Bob Short getting into the act.

For me, being a batboy was the thrill of a lifetime, a dream come true.

Rick LaCivita rose from Harvard second baseman in two College World Series to producer of "Monday Night Baseball" on ABC and then Major League Baseball on CBS.

JOHNNY BOGGS ....

I was a ballboy in Ted Williams' first year as manager of the Senators, 1969. My most vivid memories come from the post-seasons of '77, '78, and '81. I was twenty-four and already married when I went down to Philadelphia and suited up for the Dodgers. I got to play pepper with Pete Rose, who called me "the banker batboy"—which I was, I was working for a bank at the time—and he promised me one of his bats. He came through, too.

It was exhilarating, a fantasy, and it brings you back down in time to be living out fantasies. When Dusty Baker was hit in the arm by a pitch, while play was stopped and the trainer was looking at him, I leisurely stood at home plate alongside Thurman Munson, gazing out at the monuments in center field of Yankee Stadium and just fantasying.

It was chilly in the Stadium for the '78 Series, and Jay Johnstone insisted I wear a warmup jacket on the field. So I'm shagging flies for batting practice when I see Dodgers equipment manager Nobe Kawano waving at me. I go, "Me?" And he goes, "Yeah, you." It turns out I had Alejandro Pena's jacket on, and he was looking all over for it. I sheepishly gave it back to him, but I'm not sure that Latin understood—or believed—my apology.

A bigger embarrassment was to come. In the stadium bullpen I warmed up Joe Beckwith, who was coming off an injury and was throwing easy. I borrowed a cup and chest protector, but no jock. After a few minutes I was sweating profusely—after all, I was used to sitting at a desk all day—and my Achilles tendons felt like Turkish taffy from squatting.

Now Jerry Reuss and Ron Perranoski arrive, and Ron says, "How's the new bullpen catcher?" "Oh, he can handle it," Beckwith says, so Ron asks me to warm up Jerry a little. I say OK—I'm not gonna say no to Perranoski. Well, it was a different story from Beckwith. I gave Reuss a low inside target and the first two pitches find the glove. But the third pitch gets away, I couldn't move in time, and it hits my mask and takes it right off. Reuss and Perranoski break up, while the Stadium fans looking into the bullpen go crazy, yelling at me, wondering if I'm gonna start for the Dodgers tonight.

John Boggs is, among other ventures, the
agent for Tony Gwynn, and still has—like his
client—"great enthusiasm for the game."

John Mitchell ....

I was a ballboy for the Senators their last two years, '70-'71. I didn't get the job through my father, who had been a batboy in the Forties, but because at Walter Johnson High School I was a teammate of Eddie Baxter, whose father was equipment manager. We were paid eight bucks a night plus souvenirs.

I was there when Ron Luciano threw Frank Howard out of a game the first time to start their feud. Howard took a metal folding chair and tore it apart with his bare hands. I once rode with him out to the airport to take an early plane. A cop stopped him on Constitution Avenue for turning left where there was no left turn. He'd get stopped thirty or forty times a year, he said, and he never got a ticket. He tipped me ten bucks for the ride and driving his car back. Denny McLain, who had the biggest salary, never tipped at all.

Ted Williams had an office off the main locker room and always had his blinds drawn. One batboy tried peeking through the blinds one time, and Williams came up behind him and said, "Is that s.o.b. still in there?" I remember that he threatened to fine anyone he caught playing golf during the season a thousand dollars.

Locker room topics are the same at every level. Any time you bent over with Eddie Brinkman around, you'd get a bat poked in your rear. Paul Casanova, who was hazy on his English, smoked expensive Cuban cigars. He thought that a security guard, a guy they called "Seize-All," was taking them, so he wound tape around the box, then spent a week trying to get it off so he could have a smoke.

Aurelio Rodriguez told me he was in the country on his brother's visa, "got me five extra years." Joe Grzenda told me how he threw a spitball—it was K-Y jelly on his shirt, but the trick was to keep the wet stuff on the clear part of the ball. Curt Flood told me nothing. He kept totally to himself, and when he left he left suddenly, leaving his locker full of personal things.

Tim Cullen was a nice guy and Mike Epstein a real nice guy. Ballboying down the right field line once, near the gravel pit, I saw Mike dive for a foul ball, miss it, and get an ovation. He got up and said to me, "I tripped myself on my new long mitt."

One night Bob Short came into the locker room with Hubert Humphrey, who shook hands with everyone. I was so excited to shake his hand I didn't realize my hand was covered with shoe black from shining the players' shoes.

The experience took some of the gloss off the life of a Major League ballplayer. I've not since thought of an athlete as an idol. I'll go to a couple of Orioles games a year now. But Harmon Killebrew—Dick Bosman says he hit the longest ball—he's my hero, and I had my picture taken with him when he was back for an old-timer's game.

John Mitchell, after several years with Prince George's County, is now Operations Director of Encore Marketing International.

BRIAN PRILAMAN ....

In 1971, when I was 17, I was visiting team batboy for the Padres, so I was on the field when the Giants clinched the division over the Dodgers on the last day of the season. That was the team with Mays, McCovey, Marichal, Gaylord Perry, Bobby Bonds, and Chris Speier as a rookie, and I got to experience the thrill of a locker-room celebration.

I remember a twi-night doubleheader against Houston, twice delayed by fog, that ended at 3 a.m. when Jimmy Wynn lost a ball in the fog.

The players that stand out are the ones who get a bad rap in the media but are super in the clubhouse, like Steve Carlton and Dick Allen. Or George Foster, who always had a big friendly smile, treated us kids good, and played pepper with me.

I played high school ball, pitched one year at San Diego City College, but my playing career ended when I got to go to spring training as assistant clubhouse manager. Then I moved through the ranks, as visiting clubhouse manager, and now equipment manager.

Kids can lose their innocence pretty fast in the clubhouse. That's why I maintain a set of guidelines for batboys, including rules of appearance, procedure, and behavior.

As equipment manager for the San Diego Padres, Brian Prilaman runs a tight ship.

BUDDY BATES ....

Starting in '68 I was hanging around the Cardinals clubhouse with my friend Don Deason, and I worked a little part-time. Finally in '69, Butch Yatkeman got tired of me bugging him and hired me full-time. I was fifteen, a sophomore in high school.

I was too clumsy to be a ballplayer. Jerry Gibson, who batboyed with me and then wrote a book about it, had the most athletic ability of any of us kids, and he was the smartest kid, too. I was batboy through '71, then hung on as a gofer for a couple of years, worked with Jerry Risch in the visiting clubhouse, and moved over to the home side when Butch retired.

Not too many funny things happen when Butch is around. The same goes for Whitey Herzog. Whitey was able to maintain discipline and be a friend. He relaxed some rules, like curfew, but tightened up others to maintain the focus on baseball.

I never realized the game was so complex and detailed when I began. But now, when I'm asked for interviews, I just say, "People don't want to hear from a clean-up man, they want to hear from a clean-up hitter."

Buddy Bates is the St. Louis Cardinals equip-
ment manager.

ROY FIRESTONE ....

I was fifteen years old in 1971 when I got to be a batboy in spring training for the Orioles. I just showed up at Miami Stadium, home of the Marlins and the Baby O's, asked for the job, and was hired by Clay Reed to start the next day.

Now I wasn't an athletic kid—just a fan and collector—but I was a showbiz kid. So right away my mother and I had to rehearse the drive to the Stadium for the next morning, to get the timing down. And then for thirty-five or forty consecutive games I worked with the team, traveled on the buses with them. I had to play hooky from school to do it—it was like running away to join the circus.

That first day I didn't even know how to put the uniform on, what went first, and where the sanitaries went. Marcelino Lopez, that big Cuban lefty, was next to me in the clubhouse and showed me how, after telling me, "You no do this this way." And then I slid and fell on the concrete ramp going up to the field for the first time because I didn't know how to run in spikes.

That was a great Orioles team, with Buford, Grich, Dave May, Cuellar, and Blair. One of my regular jobs was to run out for ribs for Boog. I never got tips, but lots of equipment came my way.

I was a kid comedian working Miami Beach clubs, and I'd do a ten-minute shtick for the players before workouts. I did impressions of Nixon, Earl Weaver, etcetera. Palmer and Boog were the best audience, but most of them loved it. Frank [Robinson] didn't really approve of the shtick, but he gives grudging approval now.

One day [trainer] Ralph Salvon walks up and says, "Are you our new batboy?" Yes. "And you're the one that tries to be a comedian?" Yeah. "Well, you're the worst fucking batboy we've ever had. You got a lot of smarts, kid, but you're a terrible batboy."

I was, too. One day I picked up a passed ball still in play. The Senators catcher Jim French screamed at me, Earl Weaver screamed at me, the whole crowd screamed at me. But I loved it all, came back for another spring season in '72. My next job was as counselor at Bob Griese's football camp, where I got to meet Larry Csonka. But the most decent and pleasant guy of all was Brooks Robinson, who went out of his way to ask me to play pepper with him. My son is named Andrew Brooks.

I'll never forget one day on the bus, passing all these low-lying Florida ponds along the coastline, when we see a huge alligator. Curt Motton, a reserve outfielder, a rural southern black from Darnell, Louisiana, starts telling bayou tales about gators, building up to the big one that goes, "Saw a gator eat a horse once." And that's all Pete Richert, who's from Floral Park, New York, can take. "Cuz, there's no way an alligator can eat a horse," he says. Motton sits there a while, giving it some thought, and finally says, "Hm, maybe not, but he can try."

A couple of springs ago, I went to Arizona to perform for the Orioles Dream Game, doing stand-up again for Palmer and Boog—a most pleasurable experience. Got lots of color shots with the boys in uniform. It's the greatest feeling in the world to go back in the clubhouse and hear the laughter, Blair's high-pitched cackle, and hear Boog tell tall tales.

A reaffirming sense came over me, a wave. It's all about the game, the interaction and fraternity of men, being themselves in the clubhouse, away from fans and media, locked in on their reality. (When the press is around, it's always a performance.) But now the players are getting *my* autograph on *their* ball, and somehow that doesn't feel right or good.

Roy Firestone is host of ESPN's daily "Up Close" show.

FRED TYLER ....

We lived two blocks from the ballpark, and I used to help out in the clubhouse, unpaid, until I finally got to suit up for the White Sox in '73 when I was eleven. I wore number 88, worked part-time for four years, and then regularly till '79. I was also ballboy for the Colts for five or six years.

My dad, Ernie, Sr., was working in the stands when a ballboy at the screen picked up a passed ball still in play. He offered to take over that job on a two-week trial basis and hasn't heard from them since, passed the 2,600 consecutive-game mark in '92. My mom was French—Dad met her in North Africa during the war—and she cooked and catered the post-game meals in the clubhouse from '75 to '83. And five of their six sons were batboys at one time or another. I came after Ernie, Jr., whom I idolized—I couldn't get over hearing Brooks and Frank Robinson call him "Ernie."

I approached the batboy job as a job, not as a baseball or Orioles fan. I never thought it was my place to talk to hitters about pitchers or anything like that. They'd yell, "Hey, number 88," and I'd run to see what they wanted. But there were exceptions, like Thurman Munson, who liked to talk personally with the kids, and I enjoyed playing catch with him. When he died, I went to New York for the pre-game memorial, but I was only fifteen and I think the impact would have been greater a couple of years later. Dick Howser was another who made it a point to come back and talk. And I always looked forward to Hank Aaron's visits.

Reggie Jackson was one of the nicest guys in baseball. He remembered me through my whole career, from a little kid on, and he was happy for me when I got the clubhouse job. He was with New York then, and he took the time to shake hands with me and wish me well. Whatever anyone else says, to me he was always congenial.

Fred Tyler is visiting clubhouse manager for
Oriole Park at Camden Yards.

NEIL CASHEN ....

My grandparents lived one block from Memorial Stadium, and I visited them often. I used to play stickball there with young Ernie Tyler, and in 1968, when we were 12, I got to help him shine shoes in the visiting clubhouse for a buck a night. The next three years I was a batboy on the visiting side.

In 1972, I replaced Jay Mazzone as Orioles batboy, but I almost didn't get the job because of the name Cashen. With my Uncle Frank as general manager there was the fear of a nepotism charge, so the name on my uniform was changed from Cashen to Neil.

You see a lot of things and learn about people in the clubhouse. I remember seeing a Kansas City outfielder break down in the clubhouse and get placed on injured reserve. I saw Lew Krausse of the A's, after getting hammered by the O's, pour lighter fluid on his uniform and burn it. I saw Earl Wilson throw a stool and overturn a table, and Dave McNally kick over the cooler and the catcher's trunk and throw his uniform up into the lights. Lou Piniella was another one with a terrible temper. He'd yell at us for nothing, so one day when someone tossed a glove on getaway day that knocked a coke all over his suit we all had a big laugh.

It's not all fun and games. You see great mental anguish, too. Jim Fuller, for example. We all pulled for him—he used to let me drive his V.W. Rabbit. He was a phenom who never quite made it, moved up and down from the minors for several seasons. Jim Palmer had some tough years to get through, when everyone in Baltimore was getting on him. But he was my idol and the player I was closest to.

Brooks Robinson was likeable but kind of a loner. He was a de facto leader but not actively so. He and Boog Powell took me out for a beer one day on a road trip. Earl Weaver seemed very distant to me. He'd walk by as if I wasn't there, and I was sure he didn't like me. Then one day in Detroit he took me out to dinner, to Mario's Restaurant, and said to me, "How come you never asked my daughter out?"

Of all the people I met in baseball, Reggie Jackson makes the top ten list of those I have no affinity for. I was there when he ended his holdout and helicoptered into the park after a game for b.p. He was always playing mental games, even with a fourteen-year-old kid. He

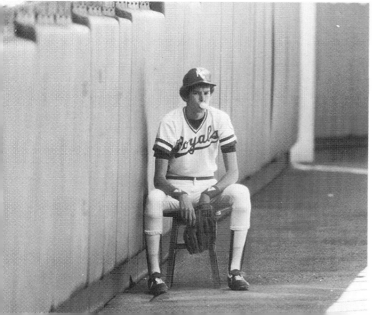

Guarding the line isn't the most exciting job in the world. Steve Winship (left) worked on his bubble-blowing skills during a Royals game in the early 1980s. Later in the decade, without gum and having stayed up all night unpacking the team's gear after a road trip before going to school, Wes Patterson dozed off during the third inning of a game.

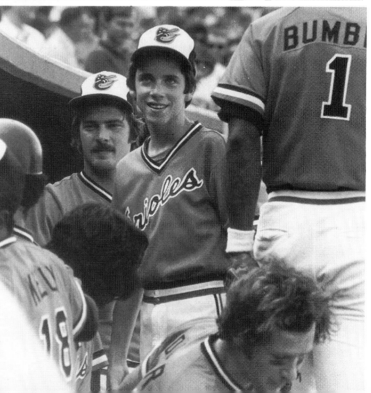

Despite the differences in age, income, and fame, batboys are "one of the guys" when they're around the players, and are often barely distinguishable from them. On the previous page, Tony Atlas granted an interview to Jim Hill of CBS for a Game of the Week broadcast (above). George Catloth looked like he belonged in the Washington dugout in the 1930s (left). Outfielder George Case, wearing the jacket, is in the background. Kevin Cashen mixed well with the Orioles in the late 1970s (right). Dennis Cashen joined White Sox catcher Carlton Fisk in the on-deck circle (above). Patrick Quinlan greeted Willie McCovey after a home run (right).

Luckpiece in Flesh for Cleveland Indians

Young Freddie Wiseman, pictured above with his particular hero, Hal Trosky, is Cleveland's luckpiece in the flesh. Since the youngster has been taken along with the club to act as batboy, the Indians have driven right up into the first division and are now right on the heels of the leading New York Yankees. The above photo was snapped recently in Boston.

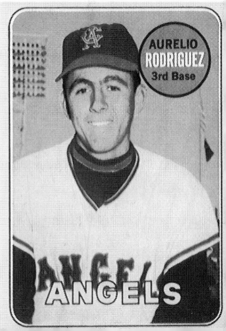

Sometimes batboys make news. In 1936, Fred Weisman (previous page) took a road trip with the Cleveland Indians and his hero, Hal Trosky, and was dubbed a good luck charm in the newspaper—which misspelled his name. In the 1957 World Series, batboy Chad Blossfield (No. 4), who had shined the shoes Milwaukee's Nippy Jones wore in the game, retrieved the ball from the backstop for umpire Augie Donatelli, who changed his call when the polish stain proved the pitch had hit Jones in the foot—much to Yogi Berra's dismay (above). California Angels infielder Aurelio Rodriguez was sick the day a Topps photographer showed up to take photos for baseball cards, so batboy Leonard Garcia (right) filled in—making the card worth a few extra dollars today.

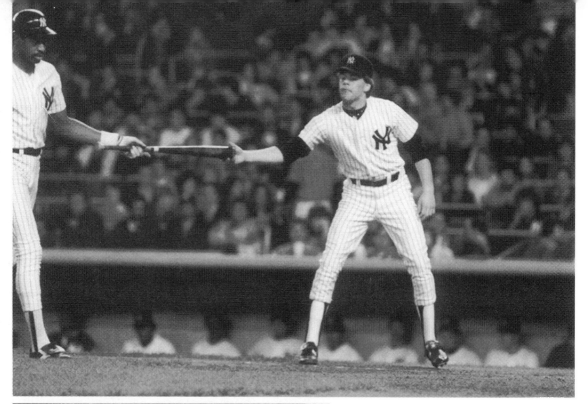

A batboy's work is never done. New York Yankees batboy Merritt Riley takes the bat from Dave Winfield (above) after an unsuccessful turn at the plate. Mike Macko of the Texas Rangers plays soft-toss with a batter fighting to get out of a slump (left). On the following page, Washington Senators batboy Jim Ryan provides clean towels for the locker room, takes a break after packing a trunk for a road trip, carries catcher's equipment to the field, and empties a bag of balls (with Bob Farmer) for batting practice.

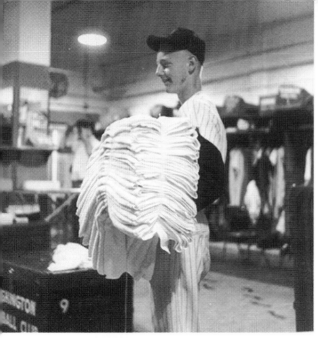

Batboys have plenty of chances to meet celebrities. Tommie Ferguson had a cigar ready for Groucho Marx (above) when the legendary comedian stopped by the Los Angeles Angels training camp in 1961. Ferguson had become traveling secretary by then. Paul Greco rubbed shoulders with hockey great Wayne Gretzky (above, right) in the early 1980s. Mike Macko was part of a group of Texas Rangers who visited the White House when Ronald Reagan presided (center, right). Washington batboy Jim Ryan got Dwight Eisenhower's signature on a couple of balls on Opening Day in 1958 at Griffith Stadium, as Senators owner Calvin Griffith looked on.

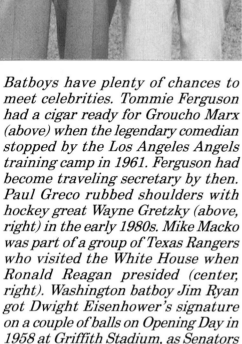

was a chameleon, would go from being the nicest guy to being really ignorant and using people and his position. For example, as a Puma rep, he had tennis shoes to give to us but would play games about it, and he always had a demeaning attitude, would order us around.

I guess my moment of fame came, not from suiting up for playoff and World Series games, but for something that happened in the clubhouse. A kid had gotten inside somehow after a game and snatched a couple of bats. I saw him leaving and without thinking took off after him. He shut a glass door and my arm slammed through it and I was cut pretty badly. Earl Williams and Elrod Hendricks tended to me and got me to the hospital for stitches. Next day, though, when I showed up with my arm all taped, it was Boog who posed with me for the picture that made the newspapers.

I learned that celebrities are normal people doing normal things, but have a lot of talent. I learned how to carry myself, how to be professional—partly from those who didn't. I go to maybe four or five games a year now, though I'm very active in rotisserie leagues. When you sit in the dugout and the clubhouse for over six years, there's a level of intensity of your involvement in the game, when Robinson is "Brooksie" and Palmer is "Cakes," so that when you're up in the stands, even though you see the intricacies, you don't appreciate it because the involvement and the intensity are missing.

Neil Cashen, an MBA from Loyola, is Comp-troller of PHH Fleet America.

Michael Cashen ....

My job with the Orioles had nothing to do with Uncle J. Frank being g.m. I was just following my brother Neil into the clubhouse, where I helped out during the 1970 and '71 seasons. Then I was visiting batboy in '72, a clubby for the O's in '73-'74, and finally O's batboy in '75-'76.

It's the relationships with the people that are really important. Baseball players had a kind of mythos about them for me when they were in uniform, but when they took the uniform off they were just people. Like Tommy Davis, a very personable guy, or Jim Fuller, who I used to play tennis doubles with, or Tony Muser and Ross Grimsley, who became good friends.

Pitcher Bob Reynolds was always kidding around, once threw me into the whirlpool just for grins. Jim Palmer was another good friend. I helped him move and even landscape his home in Phoenix. On one road trip I remember he took me to see a Woody Allen movie, Love and Death.

Reggie Jackson was the exception. He was doomed to fail with Baltimore fans because of the holdout, and he was very standoffish with us. I was in the on-deck circle when he got hit in the jaw with a fastball. It was the most horrible thing I ever saw. I helped him into the locker room, and he already looked like he had swallowed a grapefruit.

You see funny things, strange things. Once in the dugout, I didn't realize that Billy Hunter was using a Coke cup for a spittoon, so when I took a taste of what I thought was Coke and gagged, they all laughed. Once Alvin Dark got tossed out of a game and kicked the ice bucket so hard he thought he broke his toe and sent me running for the trainer. Another time a pitcher after a bad outing went right into the shower with his uniform and spikes still on, then poured lighter fluid on them and burnt them right in the shower room.

Mike Cuellar would only travel in a blue suit, but nobody laughed. I had to take all the players' superstitions seriously because they did themselves. I had to remember who wanted the bat handed to them inside or outside the circle, or whether we'd be kneeling or standing.

It was always fun to meet famous people in the clubhouse. I met Lee Majors and Roy Clark. Joe DiMaggio passed through and handed me a buck, saying, "Buy yourself a big cigar." I saved that dollar bill and framed it. But it was fun away from the ballpark, too. Like driving Doug DeCinces' or Kenny Singleton's van to California after the season. Or picking up Paul Blair's girlfriend to drive her to the park from Columbia. Or escorting DeCinces' wife and Dave Duncan's wife to the America concert at Loyola when their husbands were on the road. We were pretty close to the DeCinces family—my sister Maureen babysat for them. Or driving Bobby Grich's Porsche, which I got to do every year he was in Baltimore. Later, though, when he came back as an Angel, he had sort of changed, gotten bitter or something. His message to me was, "Don't rush into getting married."

When I traveled to Oakland for the '74 playoffs, I was 16 and it was my first plane flight. I'll never forget staying in the same hotel as Mr. Finley's pet donkey. On the road in Texas, Don Baylor took me to Nieman-Marcus in Dallas. I saw a thousand-dollar sport coat and said to him, "It's definitely not Hecht's." That was my favorite trip—New York, Rochester, Cleveland, Texas. In Cleveland I was taken to an all-black disco club by Baylor, Kenny Singleton, and Earl Williams. What a thrill. There was no fear in me, not in the company of those three, but in the whole place there were only four white faces, three women and me. On the whole, the best lessons I learned in the clubhouse were the positive ones about race relations.

Michael Cashen, MBA from University of Baltimore, is Telecommunications Manager for PHH Fleet America.

Steve Maunakea ....

I got to be batboy for the A's, like my brothers, through our stepfather, Frank Ciensczyk, the equipment manager. The Burrell brothers were there around the same time. Chris was a batboy, Lewis a clubby, but Stan just played around in the dugout. Whatever M.C. Hammer says now, he was never a batboy. Frank even ran him out of the clubhouse. But he used to call me Charlie Brown, he'd do the Michael Jackson moonwalk, he'd dance for Vida Blue, and he got close to Charlie Finley, who called him "honorary vice-president." I never even met Finley.

I played varsity ball at Balboa High School for three years, hit .500 my last two years. But I was a pitcher, with a 17-1 record including two championship games in the Trans-Bay League. Then I played at San Francisco City Jr. College and Skyline College, but never made it in the pros. On one road trip with the A's I got to pitch batting practice in Yankee Stadium. I felt chills to be where Ruth and DiMaggio played, butterflies. The fans are wild there, not like regular fans everywhere. I couldn't get the ball over the plate, think I hit a couple of guys.

The players had a hard road to get to where they were. Rickey Henderson, for one, seems cocky, selfish, and lackadaisical, but he's really not; he gets at it, one hundred percent. Catcher Jeff Newman was one who was an inspiration to me. Pitcher Rick Langford would sit down and talk—he taught me to throw a hard slider by pushing off with the thumb. And Mike Norris taught me to throw a screwball by choking up on the ball in my hand to get less power but more movement.

I saw Vida Blue burn his hat in the walkway when the umpire had him remove it, and then he threw it in the umps' room. Vida was a real nice man. I was sorry to see what happened to him, but you make your own destiny.

Billy Martin was the nicest man you ever wanted to see, out of uniform, real nice, but fiesty and competitive. You couldn't walk by him in the dugout when he was flashing signs. You had to walk around him.

Scary moments. Sheldon Mallory running into the right centerfield wall and breaking his teeth. Seeing something like that sends a jolt through your body. The scariest was standing three feet from trainer Joe Romo when Wayne Gross's bat split and a piece got Romo in the head, sending him to the hospital for stitches.

I learned from baseball to respect other people and what they own, to take nothing for granted, and to practice. I loved baseball. I still love it. I'd still play if I could. But I can't go to watch it. I may see three or four games a year, but it really hurts. I think about coaching sometimes, I'm confident in what I have to offer, but I like my job. It's good work, I have fun, and I'm around lots of sports fans.

Steve Maunakea is a machine operator in a bakery.

JEFF SIPOS ....

I can remember, as a kid, the thrill of coming to the ballpark, getting to the top of the ramp, and looking down to see this bright green field with a diamond cut into it. I still have programs from games I saw when I was in the fourth and fifth grades. It was the next best thing to playing. I loved playing, loved watching, and—being a Clevelander—loved getting frustrated by it, too.

I'd get a rush seeing baseball on TV, hearing Jimmy Dudley do the Indians games on radio, even spring training games. The Indians used to have essay contests to choose batboys. In 1970 I was a finalist, one of 25, and I got two season passes. My essay gave three reasons for wanting to be a batboy—to be an example to kids in the neighborhood, to be an example for my little brother, and because I needed the money—after two years they gave you a thousand dollars toward college education.

The next year, still hooked on baseball, I submitted the same essay—and won. I don't know how or why, but I think my name may have become familiar to some people on the club because I frequently wrote letters to the "Fans Sound Off" column in the *Plain Dealer*. So I was batboy on the visiting side in '71, home side in '72.

Opening Day '71 was with the Red Sox. Eddie Kasko was the manager, with Yaz, Reggie Smith, George Scott, Sparky Lyle in the bullpen, Aparicio, Petrocelli, Doug Griffin, Carlton Fisk, and Bob Montgomery. The Indians won three straight to open the season, two on pinch hits by Gomer Hodge of all people. I remember the frustration of Carl Yastrzemski in the clubhouse after the second loss. "We've got a good team," he said, "but we've got to get our pitchers to take it more seriously." I didn't care much for Yaz going in, based on the picture Jim Bouton painted of him in *Ball Four*, but changed when I got to know him. His loyalty to the Red Sox was rare.

Growing up, I had idolized players, Max Alvis, for example, and because I was lefty, Tito Francona and Jack Kralick. And that didn't change much when I came into the clubhouse. Mike Kekich is on my personal list of heroes, along with George Frazier, Mike Fischlin, and Jeff Torborg. Alex Johnson is one of my favorite people, a very private person who loved kids. Gaylord Perry is a favorite, and lefty Del Unser, and Chris Chambliss, a classy rookie who got on me for smoking. And there was Buddy Bell—I knew him as a shy, scared kid, and he became the most intense player I've ever seen and a good, good man. The Indians had to trade "Puff" Nettles, who was something—a true American original—because Buddy had to play third base.

What I enjoy most are the people in the game. It's a small world, a strange world—baseball. I think of Syd O'Brien, the Angels utility player, whose specialty was sitting on cakes—he'd come out of the shower and sit bare-ass in the cake. The psychology of the game baffles me sometimes, but it wasn't really a "game" then, and it's definitely not a game now—too much at stake. On my first road trip to Boston, the night before my birthday I fell in love with Fenway Park. But that night I got deathly ill on some Cantonese shrimp in Boston's Chinatown, but that didn't stop our manager, Ken Aspromonte, from fining me for missing b.p.

After high school I went to Bowling Green State University, graduating in '77. But I came back summers to work with the ground crew. And every year I'd spend two weeks at spring training. I couldn't get it out of my blood. In '81, when things were at their lowest in my life, I started hanging out in the clubhouse again, was hired in '83 as umps' attendant, and the next year became assistant equipment manager.

Jeff Sipos has moved from assistant to equipment manager as the Cleveland Indians move into their new ballpark.

MICKEY MORABITO ....

The law in New York City was that you had to be 17 to work at night, so I wrote a letter to George Stallings, Stadium Manager, and I started to work for the Yankees in '70 at $12 a game. Then another batboy filed suit, and I started earning minimum wage.

They'd hire six kids for a season. On the field, there'd be two ballboys down the foul lines, two batboys, one ballboy at the screen, and one on the phone to communicate lineup changes. We'd all rotate assignments, and of course all did the chores in the clubhouse. At first I was in awe of the lockers, the names. The kids dressed in back, in a kind of storage room behind the training room. But the awe wore off in a couple of days. Mike Kekich and Fritz Peterson were the first to be nice to me—those were not very good Yankee teams.

We used to play hockey in the locker room, with a wad of tape for a puck and the bottom end of bats for sticks. One time I stepped on Thurman Munson's hand, he ran to the trainer, and later the trainer scared me that I'd injured him so badly he'd be on the d.l.

You get a different picture of people in the clubhouse. Alex Johnson, for example, was difficult with the media, and they called him "curt" and "mean." But he was great to the kids and the clubhouse guys. In fact, he was Pete Sheehy's favorite. On my first road trip, to Washington, he sat with me on the plane, and he spent the whole time reading an electronics manual.

That turned out to be a very scary trip. It ended with the last game in RFK, with a riot and the game forfeited. I was throwing bats, helmets, and equipment down the stairs to the tunnel, where Sheehy was collecting them. Peterson and Gene Michael took care of me, getting me out of there in one piece.

I became a big umpire fan. I used to drive them downtown, take them out to dinner after games. In those days, after an argument, they'd walk to the opposite dugout between innings. Now they're more confrontative. One day I had the phone assignment and Bob Fishel called down from the press box to ask Jake O'Donnell, the third base ump, about a play for the official scorer. Frank Umont, a gruff crewcut guy, was working behind the plate. He says, "Where the hell you goin'?" I told him, and he says, "Goddamn it" and walks back, grabs the telephone by the dugout, and starts screaming at Fischel, "You guys are watchin' the game up there, do your job up there, and don't be askin' us for help."

By '74, I was finishing my degree at Hunter, student teaching, editing the student newspaper, and doing anything to stay in baseball—part-time p.r. at Shea, answering mail, working the scoreboard. When Lee MacPhail moved to the American League office and took Fischel with him, I moved up to assistant p.r. director under Marty Appel. Then when Appel left, in '76, George Steinbrenner gambled on a 24-year-old p.r. director—it was a good year for him, he won the pennant, and for me too.

At spring training in 1980, Billy Martin asked me to come to Oakland. "There *is* no front office," he said. Mr. Finley was trying to sell the team, and I had to be both p.r. director and traveling secretary. I never thought I'd root for anyone but the Yankees, but you see people move around so much, the concept of loyalty changes. I root for the A's now, and if I moved to another team I'd root for them. It's a very big business, part of the entertainment industry. I still enjoy the traveling—I'm a single man, I love spring training, and best of all I get to watch baseball every day.

Mickey Morabito is traveling secretary of the
Oakland A's.

MIKE WALLACE ....

I was the Texas Rangers batboy in '73. Whitey Herzog started the season as manager, and I worked with his son David. Another kid in our group was Vic Vandergriff, the son of the Arlington mayor who helped bring the team to Texas in '72.

Joe Macko was the equipment manager. He had gone to spring training as a player in 1950. When his son Steve made it up to the Cubs, their equipment manager, Yosh Kawano, gave him Joe's number 12 for his uniform. That's how tradition works in baseball. I knew Steve as a sixteen-year-old. You know, at Baylor, where he was All-American, he was the only college player I knew who used a wooden bat instead of aluminum. He was determined to develop the skills he'd need as a professional. It was tragic when he died.

I stayed on, working in the Rangers clubhouse through '79, until I got the job as visiting clubhouse manager. Then in '89 I became equipment manager for the Royals. Part of the fun is watching kids who hung around the clubhouse when they were young make it as Major League stars. The Alomars and Barry Bonds, I knew them as kids in Arlington.

Mike Wallace is equipment manager of the
Florida Marlins.

MARIO ALIOTO ....

My dad drove a truck for a linen company and had Candlestick on his route, so he got to know Mike Murphy and got a job for my brother Carl as batboy. I was always visiting him in the clubhouse, and finally Murph hired me—I got five dollars for sweeping out the room one day. I replaced Carl as visiting batboy in 1973, worked till I was 18 in 1979.

The first month I was there, the Mets came in and it was Willie Mays' last game. He didn't take batting practice and when he appeared on the field ten minutes before the game there was a tremendous ovation. Then he comes over to the dugout and asks me to play catch with him. I was so nervous, it felt like he was throwing two hundred miles an hour.

I loved to play catch with Charlie Hough, trying to field that knuckleball. But of all the players I played catch with, the only one to hit the target every time was Pete Rose.

It seemed like the pitchers were the best guys. They'd take time to talk with you while we were shagging flies in b.p. Maybe it's because they're only stressed every four or five days. It was Jim Barr who took up a collection for us kids on our road trips to L.A. But shortstop Johnny LeMaster was another good guy.

Candlestick Park was so cold you'd hang the towels in the dugout and they'd all blow off the hook. One day there was a power outage but they played anyway—against the Cubs, who were always fighting the Giants. Gary Matthews and George Mitterwald had a blood feud. Well, it was so dark that Don Kessinger lined one foul that nailed me standing at the bat rack. So I'm groping back to the clubhouse, to get taken care of, and the tunnel is pitch dark, when Dave Kingman lets out this yell. I don't think I've ever been so scared.

I used to love hearing what was yelled at the umps from the dugout. Doug Harvey was my favorite. He always had something pleasant to say. Kibler, too. But it was the clubhouse stuff that was the greatest, not what happened on the field. The smells of chewing tobacco and pine tar. Crazy Doug Rader, who should be a comedian. The Pirates were the caziest, with rowdy Manny Sanguillen. And the Mets—always in suit and tie.

At the end of the '79 season I started college at St. Mary's and I left the Giants for a few months, working as a bank teller. But I was homesick for the ballpark. Eddie Logan retired as equipment manager, and Murph moved over to the home side. Then Eddie Brinson, who was in line to manage the visiting clubhouse, was hit and killed by a drunk driver. They asked me to take over, and I did it for three years.

In college I was friendly with Von Hayes, who once traded me two bottles of Cabernet Sauvignon for my Phillies cap. A few years later he was playing for them. I got a degree in Business Administration and moved into the Giants front office. But you know, if I weren't married, I'd probably jump at the chance to go back to the clubhouse.

Mario Alioto is Director of Marketing for the
San Francisco Giants.

TIM BUZBEE...

It took me five years to get my foot in the door with the Angels. I kept writing letters to Harry Dalton, and in 1975, when I was 17, I was finally told to come to spring training in Palm Springs. I paid my own way, found equipment manager Mickey Shishido, and made myself useful in the clubhouse. I was paying my own keep, too, but it paid off because when there was an opening—one of the ballboys quit before the season started—I got hired. I worked the left field foul line in '75, then was home plate ballboy for four seasons, ending in '79 with the divisional championship team that lost to the Orioles in the ALCS. I got a 1/5 share of playoff money. My starting salary was $6.50 a game and I was getting $20 when I finished.

Batboying was like a dream. I'll never forget the feeling of running out to the mound with the game ball and rosin bag at the the start of a game in front of a sell-out crowd under the lights. I was awed.

Jerry Remy took me under his wing that first year. He nicknamed me Peanuts, then shortened it to Nuts. Jimmy Reese, whose own career dates back to Babe Ruth and the 1930 Yankees, was a grandfather type who took everybody under his wing. On road trips to New York, Boston, and Detroit it was trainer and traveling secretary Freddy Frederico who looked after me. Another good model as coach and friend was Grover Reisinger who was with the Angels one year. I spent two wonderful winter vacations at the Reisinger farm back in Missouri.

I got involved in a play once, in an exhibition game—against the Dodgers in the Freeway Series. Working home plate I picked up a passed ball rolling to the screen. Catcher Andy Etchebarren yells for the ball, I throw it to him, he throws to second, and the runner is called out. Walter Alston protested and the call was reversed. And I had no place to hide.

Probably the most exciting thing was Nolan Ryan's fourth no-hitter, June 1, 1975. He's a great guy, a competitor, a class act, and easy to talk to. His locker happened to be cater-corner to mine, and after the game in my locker I found a ball with "0" written on it. I never knew how it got there, but the next day in the paper I saw a picture of Ryan posing, holding up four balls marked the same way.

I had played some ball in high school, even played in our divisional championship game in Anaheim Stadium, and I played part of a season at Long Beach City College. But my job with the Angels didn't allow time to pursue it. Then I thought maybe I'd study to be a trainer, but turned to firefighting as a career. In 1984 I was officially badged as Fire Marshall for the Queen Mary.

I guess I got spoiled by being in the front row not hemmed in by the crowd, and I prefer to watch games on TV now. The money in baseball today has changed the game, overpowered other things. I still love it, though, and I coached my daughter's T-ball team when she was six.

Tim Buzbee's civilian job in firefighting, since 1990, has been to check plans for codes compliance.

JOHN PLEIN ....

I wrote a letter of application to the Padres and then was one of 25 interviewed in groups of five for five jobs. I was hired on April 6, 1976, to start the next day, an exhibition game against the A's. I was in Patrick Henry High School, but I got the message that I'd been hired while pumping gas at the Shell station.

I met my wife Cathy at the ballpark. She had season tickets, and for about a year all I did was answer her questions about the players. Finally she asked if there was anything wrong with her that I didn't ask her out, and I said I thought she was interested in players only. A few years later we were married.

I was the umps' attendant as well as batboy. You know an umpire's job is tougher than a player's. They're always on the road. Most of them are fat because of poor diet, but I fed them well—non-junk food. If they're sick, I took care of them, got the doctor, ran to fill prescriptions. As for the players, I always tried not to be a "green fly," their term for people who annoy them, get in their way. I always enjoyed pepper games, especially with Bob Davis and Willie Davis. I was pretty good at it, and when I played with the pitchers they'd get frustrated and embarrassed to be beaten by a batboy.

Doug Rader was one of the craziest guys, I mean fun crazy. He was a big Red Man chewer, and he teased me into trying it—this was in '78, I was 19. I kept a small chaw in my mouth for several innings, but I couldn't stand it and spat it out. But a couple of innings later I had to run to the bathroom, and I lost my lunch. Rader comes by and says, "Forgot to tell you, rookie, you're not supposed to swallow the juice."

Another time, he was visiting after his season as AAA manager was over, sitting on a metal folding chair in the photographers' section. He had two cups of beer, one in his hand and one on the ground. The guy next to him spits some tobacco juice in the cup on the ground, and then again, but when Rader finishes the first cup, he picks up the other and takes a sip. "I better tell you," the guy says, "I was spitting tobacco juice in that." Rader says, "I thought it tasted a little different," and drinks it all down, outgrossing the would-be gross-out artist.

Gaylord Perry was always good to the kids. On the road, he'd save me a seat next to him on the plane, and he'd take me to dinner at restaurants with no prices on the menus. In Chicago once he sent me to deliver a message to Herman Franks, who'd once told him he needed to develop another pitch. He coated a ball with vaseline and told me to throw it to Franks from about ten feet, saying, "This is from Gaylord"—and then run like hell. I did it, Franks was splattered, he cursed, and threw the ball over to the dugout where Perry was roaring with laughter.

In Pittsburgh on that same trip, Gaylord went into the clubhouse during the game and tied knots in my white cotton socks. I didn't say anything, but I got even in St. Louis by tying his sheer dress socks into tiny knots. I showered quickly after the game and I was already out of the clubhouse when I heard him bellow. He charged out after me, and chased me on foot all the way to the Breckenridge Hotel. The elevator just barely shut behind me, and I locked myself in my room. Well, he laid siege to my room and finally got someone else to persuade me he'd gone and I could come out for dinner. As soon as the lock turned he burst in, knocked me onto the bed, taking a bite out of my neck, saying, "I told you I'd get you." I look down and see that Gaylord is in his dress shoes but still without socks. We had big laughs all around.

When I started at Grossmont Junior College, I stayed on part-time with the ground crew, but I was lobbying to make the umpires' attendant a separate job. They did, in '81, and the job was mine.

John Plein's home is less than a mile from Jack Murphy Stadium so that he could commute easily between the two jobs he held simultaneously, as umpires' attendant for the Padres and in corporate advertising for the San Diego Union Leader. No longer with the paper, he is the proprietor of R&B Appraisers, but still serves the men in blue for the Padres.

TONY ATLAS......................................

I understand I was the only batboy ever hired this way. I played ball with the son of a scout for the Angels, and I asked him how to do it. He said you have to have pull, which is what I'd heard elsewhere. But in '76 I started writing a letter every week, first to the director of stadium operations and then, when I learned who was in charge, to the equipment manager, Mickey Shishido. They had over thirty letters from me before they finally gave me a call. They said they didn't need anyone, but if I was still interested next season to come down to spring training at Palm Springs. I did, they liked me, hired me for the visiting side where I worked for two years and then two years as the home batboy.

The biggest shock to me was all the smoking and beer-drinking in the clubhouse. I was disenchanted at first, disappointed. The image didn't match the reality. But it's just fantasy that they're not real people; you learn instead that they're kids who never grew up, who threw tantrums. And I learned that baseball was a business more than anything else, with an awful lot of politics. When it came to deciding who to release, who to keep, skill and talent didn't matter as much as the salary structure and even the value of cheerleading in the dugout and the clubhouse. I was there for the worst g.m. decision ever—Bavasi letting Nolan Ryan go for a million a year.

I got to know the two greatest players ever to play the game, Rod Carew and Carl Yastrzemski. Rod was still with the Twins in '78, and he kept his bats with him in the clubhouse. He yelled, "Hey, Mullion" (a baseball term for "ugly"), and when I turned around and said, "Yes, sir," everyone laughed. He was a real good guy, but he wanted things done now. When he came to the Angels he treated me like a son. I did yard work for him and washed his cars for pay, and when he had his hitting school I'd help out whenever he asked.

In '79, when Yaz came to town, I got to play catch between innings with one of my favorite players. I was so pumped up that I threw the first ball over his head. Yaz calmly walks back, picks it up, tosses it back. Then the second ball goes over his head. He picks it up, walks over to me, and says, calmly, but laughing, "You know, Tony, I'm an old man, if you wanna play catch, that's fine, and if you wanna throw the ball over my head and have me walk back to get it, that's fine too, but just let me know which one—I'm an old man and I don't like having to make adjustments."

My biggest embarrassment, though, was early in the '78 season. I was working the right field foul line, and Lyman Bostock hit a line drive against the Mariners. It was a couple of feet foul but was called fair, and I fielded the ball. There were 19,000 people there, and I was burning as I felt 38,000 eyes on me. I couldn't think of what to do, so I made the throw to second base. Perfect throw, one hop. Ump Dale Ford sent Bostock back to first. The Angels protested, and I got lectured. Grounds crewman Brian Nofziger said, "The best thing about it was he came up throwing." But he was wrong. The best thing was the one-time fantasy of coming into the clubhouse after a game and finding reporters waiting around my locker for interviews. For days after that the players hounded me, chased me around with a ball, making noises.

But I got to batboy for the All-Star Game in San Diego that first year, thanks to Billy Martin. I always took care of him when he came in, arranged for his rental car, got him his favorite Italian sausage and wine and pipe tobacco. He not only picked me as All-Star batboy, but saw to it that I got an All-Star ring.

When I started, I was a star-struck sixteen-year-old. I had written a little poem in school about Reggie Jackson, and I showed it to him. "Action Jackson is his name,/Bold adventure is his game,/On his way to the Hall of Fame." He liked it and left it tacked up in his locker. My boss Dave Howells saw it, ripped it down, and ripped into me: "You don't do that here, we're not fans." Next day he handed me a new poem: "Tony Atlas is his name,/Kissing ass is his game,/On his way to the Hall of Shame." I did a lot of favors for Reggie, ran a lot of errands for him. Once, for a Panasonic commercial, I flew his white uniform up to Oakland for him. I've been in his house and seen all his cars. And I'll tell you this—you either like him or you don't, but if you know him deep down he's a real good guy, often misunderstood.

You know, it's hard to play favorites on the home side, but some guys stand out. Bobby Grich, who sent me running to the bullpen for the key to the batter's box. Willie Davis and Larry Sherry, who got me with the oldest trick in the book—telling each other that a German chocolate cake in the clubhouse smelled funny, and then pushing my face in it when I went to check it out. Nolan Ryan and Don Baylor would always give you a pat on the back, and they were good tippers, too. Dan Ford was like a brother to me, the most loyal of all. I still see him socially, he lives ten miles away, and we have barbecues at each other's house. Rick Miller was like a friend. He treated me real well, he was a good tipper also, and we talked a lot about personal things, problems I experienced as a teen.

Some clear impressions remain of a few players on the visiting side. Lou Piniella—a crazy man, who tore things up and broke a coffee pot—a one-man assault team. Rusty Staub—a prima donna, a real jerk—what an idiot!—he had to have new sanitaries every day or he'd pout and cry. And Doc Ellis—he treated me worse than I've ever been treated in my life—he'd berate me, and everything he'd say to me was foul.

The job was important to me. I played ball in high school, but when I started junior college in '79 I decided that playing ball was not as important as working for the Angels. I think batboys are all disappointed players, wannabe players, and they like to be close to the action. We got to go on one road trip a year. The best for me was '79, when I had just turned

18, to Baltimore, Boston, and New York. Orioles batboy Kevin Cashen took me out with him, and I was shocked when a kid Kevin knew saw us in a club and called him a nigger-lover. Then it was worse in Boston. Carew had warned me not to get into it with fans there, because "East Coast attitudes are different." Sure enough, another batboy and I were walking to Fenway Park with Willie Mays Aikens when some guy threw a 7-Up bottle from a car at the other batboy, shouting "nigger-lover" at him. But New York I loved, bright lights, party life, bars with gorgeous women—it was an eye-opening experience.

Still, I wouldn't want my son to be a batboy, and not just because it would limit his ability to participate in baseball as a player. My mom wouldn't let me do it now if she had to make that choice again. She claims it changed my value system when I got close to the cars, the women, the money—that I grew up too fast from 15 to 19. And I wouldn't want my son to learn, as I did, to treat high school girls the way players treat women—often as objects but a hazard of being a groupie. As for me, it was the greatest experience of my life.

Tony Atlas has moved from Deputy Sheriff in Riverside County to a Deputy Marshall in Orange County. He earned his B.A. in Sociology from Cal State Fullerton in 1985 and is working toward a Masters in Public Administration at Kensington University.

MARK STOWE ....

My dad being equipment manager for the Reds, I got to work in the clubhouse during the playoffs in '73. Then, when I turned sixteen while I was at Elder High School, I was a regular ballboy—that was the '75 season—and the next year I was batboy. There's plus and minus working for Dad. It was easier to get the job and I knew how to deal with players, but it was harder because of the demands he made on me.

My first game as visiting batboy, Tom Seaver got me in the clubhouse, insisted that I go find some elbow grease to polish his shoes with. In the Cincinnati clubhouse, I found that the players who have lockers close to the batboys' lockers tend to get closer to them personally. George Foster's locker was next to mine, and he was always real good to me. So was Joe Morgan, who loaned me his Cadillac for my high school prom. And I'll never forget Ken Griffey, who ran over my toe scoring a run.

After graduating from the University of Cincinnati I returned to the clubhouse in '84—about the same time as Pete Rose returned to the Reds as playing manager. He was real intense during a game, sorta quiet. He said little on the bench, you didn't talk to him then or break his concentration. In the on-deck circle, he'd hand the donut to the batboy and tell him when he was gonna bunt. "Watch this," he'd say. But in the clubhouse he talked a lot more. He always made you want to hustle more. He'd compliment a batboy on hustle or point out what hustle was.

I got a 1/6 share of playoff money from the '75 series with the Pirates, and four of us divided a full share of the '76 World Series money. Money changes attitudes, I guess, but I remember as early as '76 that players would get money for signing balls. Players don't hang around the clubhouse after a game, rehash it, like they used to, like Buddy Bell. The young guys now either take off fast or they work out after a game—taking care of themselves.

Mark Stowe is assistant equipment manager
for the Cincinnati Reds.

Rick Merschbach ....

I was hired by the director of stadium operations in '76 and was the right field ballboy, then Reds batboy in '77, and home plate ballboy in '78. I subbed occasionally in '79, but by then I was well along in my studies in Criminal Justice and Law Enforcement.

Along with your parents and schools, baseball teaches you and supports your values. I really looked up to Johnny Bench and later Tom Seaver—a great guy—and equipment manager Bernie Stowe, and manager Sparky Anderson—what a super person.

Ken Griffey and George Foster had lockers close to mine, so I got to know them pretty well. Pat Zachary, too, and Bill Plummer, a super guy. Mike Lum was into magic. I took him to a magic shop in Cincinnati, and he taught me tricks at his house. When I dressed for my high school prom in the clubhouse, I took a lot of razzing from the players, led by Joe Morgan, but then I got to drive off in Morgan's car, a green Caddy with a white top.

The other thing I remember from the clubhouse was a nine-inch-high, briefcase-size, welded metal box kept in a back room. It had a sign that said, "Danger, Mongoose," had a lock on one side, and you could see a brown piece of what looked like an animal. It belonged to Bench, but he was quiet about it. He just liked to watch. Bernie would say, "Who's gonna feed the mongoose?" and someone might be tricked into doing it, and usually get real scared when a secret button was pushed and a fur tail would pop out.

I went to AstroWorld on a family vacation in '76 and batboyed when the Reds played in the Dome. Bill Plummer took us out to dinner, and we spent an evening with Bernie Stowe and some players. After that they all started calling me Tex. One of the best experiences of my life was going to New York for the World Series that year. I sat in the seat that every kid in the country would like to have, in the dugout. I got a 1/4 share, about $5,200.

Knee surgery ended my baseball career after my freshman year in college, and after that I focused on police work. I was on duty at Greater Cincinnati Airport in 1986, when Tommy Hume, pitcher-turned-announcer, spotted me in uniform and said, "Rick?" Same thing happened three years later, only I was working under cover at a concert, and it was Johnny Bench and his wife who saw me. "Rick?" Yes. Same guy, still taking care of them.

Rick Merschbach is a detective in the
Hamilton County Sheriff's office.

MAHENDRA NAIK ....

I was the first batboy for the Blue Jays, in 1977. I was born in Zambia, and when I moved to Toronto in 1972 I had a great interest in sports. I lived near Exhibition Stadium, and I'd ride my bike in to watch the Argonauts practice. One day I just went up and introduced myself to Peter Bavasi in the stands. They didn't even have a team name yet, it was just Metro Baseball, Ltd. After we talked for a couple of hours, he said, "Write me a letter. Maybe you can be a batboy." I did, and I was.

I batboyed for two-and-a-half years, then worked in the clubhouse for a while. I learned that professional athletes were no different from anyone, were a microcosm of society. Still, it was exciting to have a locker with my name on it right in the same room with the stars.

The team was very bad, so bad that the crowd cheered for me when I chased foul balls, chanting "Go! Go! Go!" It was embarrassing. The game should be the focal point—that's why I hate the Chicken and the wave. When we started in Toronto, they had horrible old bleachers where you couldn't see anything, and the fans were bored out of their trees.

I remember Opening Day, when the whole field was white with snow. Nobody knew what to do—half-an-hour before game time they didn't know whether to play, these so-called professionals. And I remember Earl Weaver removing his team from the field, forfeiting a game in 1979 because the crew wouldn't remove a tarp in the Jays bullpen.

I don't care what others say, Reggie Jackson was very friendly towards me. Rick Cerone, too. When he started with the Jays, his locker was next to mine, so I got to know him.

I share a set of season tickets now, at what I call Yuppie Stadium, it's so overpriced and loaded with marketing gimmicks. But I used to love weekend jaunts to Montreal and especially seeing games in Detroit, where you're so close to the action in the old ballpark.

If my little boy is interested in baseball, I'd push him to be a player, not a batboy. For me it was putting in a lot of hours with a lot of hardworking people. It was also being part of the game and having a high profile. I never tried to exploit the experience, though it appeared on my résumé and made a good conversation piece during job interviews.

Mahendra Naik, a graduate of the University of Toronto, is a CPA and financial consultant.

PATRICK QUINLAN ....

As a boy growing up in San Francisco I was always a baseball fan. I sneaked into Candlestick Park so many times I got familiar with the setup. I'd see maybe sixty games a year. From the time I was eleven I wrote letters trying to get a job, and I'd help out in and around the clubhouse whenever I could. Finally, a month after the end of the '75 season, I walked into the clubhouse, saw Ed Logan the equipment manager, and was hired.

I worked four seasons on the home side, '76 through '79. I loved being batboy, being around players who loved what they were doing. As early as January of '76 I'd be at the ballpark, working out with Bobby Bonds, Jim Davenport, and Kevin Bass. Randy Moffitt was a player I was close to—even before I was a batboy he was good to me. And then at last I was in uniform for Opening Day against the Padres.

I went through the usual initiation. They sent me for a bucket of frozen ropes. They sent me all over the ballpark for the key to the batter's box. Logan sent me to Moffitt, Moffitt to Mike Sadek, Sadek to the groundskeeper—that's clubhouse to dugout to bullpen to grounds crew and back before I figured it out.

Willie McCovey was a class act. I personally shined two pairs of shoes for him every day. And he kept me in Pumas, and gave me one of those orange T-shirts with "500 for 44" on them and my own name on it.

One Saturday in May I was sent over to the visiting clubhouse to get a line-up card, and there I met Willie Mays, who was a Mets coach at the time. We rapped for about twenty minutes, and then later, on the field we played pepper, I got to check his batting stance, and we ended up slapping five. That was sheer heaven. It was the greatest moment in my life.

I got to go on road trips to San Diego and Los Angeles. Later, when I moved to L.A. to work in restaurant management, I'd go to sixty Dodgers games a year. In '78 I got to go to spring training, driving my '65 Impala to Phoenix. Now, back in the Bay Area, with the sports bar, I still feel like I'm part of the game.

Patrick Quinlan has joined his brother in the
Flatiron Sports Bar in an 1883 building in
San Rafael, California.

RON PIERALDI ....

There was a family connection by marriage with Frank Ciensczyk, the A's equipment manager, which was how first my brother and then me got the job. I worked in the visiting clubhouse for the '70 and '71 seasons and then was an A's batboy for two World Series seasons. Now my dad, Lou, works for the club, seeing to the press area at the Stadium.

A few impressions from the visiting clubhouse: the White Sox—a nice bunch, Mickey Mantle—pretty shrewd, the O's—a loose bunch, the camaraderie on most of the teams, and Rocky Colavito—a real fun-loving guy. But most of my memories are from the home side.

I learned a lot from Dick Williams and Bill Posedel, which helped me when I played high school ball at Castro Valley High. But I went to UCSB and didn't play there. Williams interceded with Charlie Finley so that I could go on road trips. Finley was a smart businessman. He never talked to me. He didn't know people that he didn't need to know. But I got to Boston and Detroit, where I loved Fenway Park and Tigers Stadium, with the fans right on the field, so close you can smell the hot dogs in the stands from the playing field. And at Yankee Stadium, I was there for the ultimate Old-Timers Game—all that history.

Joe Rudi and Catfish Hunter were real generous. I was sitting next to Hunter when he was charting pitches one game, not paying attention, and I got hit on the inner thigh by a foul ball. Reggie Jackson took care of us real well. You either love him or you hate him, depending on whether he liked you or not. We got along. Some years later I went to a car show at the Cow Palace where he was showing one of his cars and taking questions from the crowd. I asked, "Are you still using that Adirondack 288RJ?"—meaning his bat, though the people must have thought it meant another car. Reggie made a big thing of it, introducing me to the crowd as an "award-winning batboy."

Rick Monday's kangaroo court kept things loose in the clubhouse. Rollie Fingers was your basic butt of jokes, like from Cucamonga, slow to react. He'd have a delayed reaction, laugh minutes later when he figured out a joke. Vida Blue started this ritual with me in '72—instead of placing the rosin bag and new ball on the mound, I'd walk out and hand them to him. Worked pretty good through '73.

Baseball taught me communication skills and broadened my horizons. I got paid $7.50 a game, but then three or four of us split a quarter World Series share, amounted to about $1,500. I have a picture of myself in the World Series parade, a car to myself with my name on the side. I was on top of the pinnacle at the time, so it's real hard to have anything negative to say about the experience.

I share a ticket package with my cousin, so I see lots of games. I see Joe Rudi around the Bay Area often. And not too long ago I ran into Mike Epstein. He said, "Look at you, Ronnie, how big you got!"

Ron Pieraldi is an inside salesman for a small electrical wholesaler.

PAT MCBRIDE.......................................

They called me "The Luckiest Boy in the World" in an article in *Scholastic Scope* magazine, because I worked in big-league clubhouses of baseball, football, and basketball. I got the job at first through an essay contest, and I worked for five dollars a game in 1969 for the fourteen games that the White Sox played in Milwaukee. In 1970, when a last-minute decision brought the Seattle team to Milwaukee, I was hired. I was the batboy in 1972 and had four other years working in the clubhouse.

In the football clubhouse—I worked the Packers games in Milwaukee—the intensity is extreme. I found it too unpleasant and quit that soon. The basketball clubhouse is more mature and businesslike, the players better dressed and serious. But the baseball clubhouse is relaxed, jocular, and loose. They razz anything even slightly intellectual, so that a bright guy like Steve Hovley took a constant ribbing. Baseball seems like a little boys' game.

I got sent for the key to the batter's box, I was the victim of a Moe Drabowsky hotfoot, and I got analgesic balm in my jock and had the toes cut out of my sanitaries. Like everybody else. On the Yankees, Mike Kekich and Fritz Peterson were constantly tricking each other, and then together they tied a waterbed mattress to the top of the scoreboard. And who could forget Sparky Lyle's butt on the sheetcake. He'd come out of the shower, with total aplomb, do a pirouette, and sit.

When I learned that players were just human beings, not idols, the balloon burst. I was shocked at first by the language and the smoking, in fact was crushed that Hank Aaron smoked. And yet I'd see the Governor and the Vice President act like kids when they were around Aaron and others. I remember the '75 All-Star Game, when Henry Kissinger was in the locker room, a baseball hat on crooked, his eyes glazed, looking around at Don Sutton, Steve Garvey, Pete Rose, Johnny Bench, Tony Perez, and Joe Morgan. Tug McGraw came up to him with a sandwich, said, "Baloney, Mr. Kissinger?" and everyone broke up.

Ted Williams was one of those legendary figures who was never left alone. He was gracious—until pushed too far. Once he was asked for batting tips by a kid with a bad eye, and he said, "What's your vision?" "20-400." "Try pitching," said T.W. Billy Martin was a bluntly honest man, like Williams, but always a gentleman and considerate in the clubhouse.

The Twins of that era were incredible athletes—Jim Kaat, Harmon Killebrew, and

Danny Thompson, who died of leukemia at 29. All three showed up at a clinic for my brother Tim. Kaat is an absolutely class triple-A person. He and Tommy John always seemed to have reached that middle ground between fear and relaxation. Dave Nelson of the Rangers and George Brett of the Royals are two others I admired.

On the road I remember Gus Gil, our utility infielder, taking me out to dinner. But I remember him best sliding into second base with a toothpick in his mouth. The White Sox trainer, Charlie Saad, was another guy who took me under his wing. Among the trainers I knew, though, it was Ernie Garber of the Milwaukee Bucks who was a major influence in my life.

I would deliver notes to women in the stands for the players and have to make small talk with them. I didn't appreciate that, nor ten-cent beer night on Saturdays in Milwaukee, especially when I was fielding foul balls down the line and would get my wool uniform soaked with beer from the stands. But one night, during a rain delay when I was delivering a message to the dugout, I tripped and slid across the tarp and got a standing ovation from the fans.

I always tried to appreciate what I had. I learned that hard work pays off. I'd see Alex Johnson, a guy with all the talent in the world, who never applied himself. But I was known as the "Charlie Hustle of batboys" and got positive feedback from the players. What I remember most from the experience is that life doesn't have to be miserable, that you could enjoy whatever it was that you did.

Dr. Pat McBride directs a program in heart disease and prevention for the Department of Family Medicine and Practice at the University of Wisconsin Medical School in Madison.

TONY MIGLIACCIO ....

My dad was a car salesman at the Selig dealership, and when my mom died when I was fifteen, my dad asked Bud Selig for a summer job for me. He thought I needed something to take my mind off things. So in February of '78 I was told to call Tommie Ferguson, and he asked me to come to the Stadium for an interview. I get there and Fergie is sitting in his office, his feet up on the desk, and a big cigar in his mouth. And in his high-pitched Boston accent he says, "Well, kid, ya wanna be a batboy?" "Sure," I said. "Here's what you do..." he says, and that was all that there was to it.

Opening Day was against the Orioles. My first shock was seeing Mark Belanger light up a cigarette. The novelty of being around players wears off quickly. You learn that if you cut them they bleed red just like everyone else. But they had fun with me, sending me for a bucket of steam or a box of curve balls, that kind of thing.

Gorman Thomas was the main prankster on that Brewers team, along with Charlie Moore and Rick Manning when he came over. It keeps guys loose to have stuff like that going on. When the Rangers came in, the first day Richie Zisk bet me ten bucks there would be between 30 and 50,000 people in the stands. There were under 30,000, but when I tried to collect, he says, "I said '30' not '30,000'." The second day he gets me on a similar bet, and on the third day he offers me a chance to win my twenty back. He says, "Pick the two biggest guys in the clubhouse and I bet I can lift all three at once." Well, there were some pretty big guys there—Jim Sundberg, Dock Ellis, Len Barker—and two of them get me down, get my arms and legs locked, rip off my pants, and pour tobacco, chew, shaving cream, soda, and ice on me. "Congratulations," Zisk says, "You're now a member of the Texas Rangers."

There were surprises with other visiting teams. Reggie Jackson was my idol as a kid, and then I was crushed to find him unfriendly in the clubhouse. He was just not a nice person, the word I'd use is "rotten." And then there was Cliff Johnson with the Yankees, who's supposed to be this big, ugly guy. Actually he was harmless. Collecting stuff for the valuables box, I asked him, "What's your number?" and he says, "Number 14 and don't you forget it," pointing his finger at me for emphasis. That was just his way. He didn't mean anything by it.

I was a catcher at Pius High School and I played two years at Central Arizona Junior College, where the coach is a Brewers scout. I wanted to play ball, but summers I'd come back to work in the clubhouse. I attended Arizona State briefly, transferred to University of Wisconsin at Milwaukee, and I was one semester short of my degree, October of '85, when Bob Sullivan, who ran the clubhouse, died suddenly at 43. Harry Dalton offered me the job. I was in the right place at the right time, so it was so long, college.

You know, most guys leave the game bitter, feeling they could play another season or have another job. Coop, for example, Cecil Cooper, a great guy, comes to the ballpark but won't come in the clubhouse. As a batboy I got to take one road trip a year, and I'd pick different cities. I learned a lot about growing up and being with people.

At 27, Tony Migliaccio was still the youngest
equipment manager in the Major Leagues.

MARK ANDERSEN ································

I was a school friend and contemporary of Kenny Bush, Jr., whose father was running the clubhouse then—in fact, our moms were good friends—and that's how I got the job. I was Phillies batboy from 1976-1980, started at $15 a game, then moved up to minimum hourly wage. I also got a 1/8 World Series share in 1980.

It's different in the clubhouse. Of course, you get to meet famous people—I met President Ford and ex-President Nixon. But I mean the hero on the field, like Mike Schmidt, may be so self-involved that he's less than a hero in the clubhouse. But a guy like Steve Carlton, not a media favorite, can be great in the clubhouse. He personally gave me a lot of help and moral support. Ron Reed was another player who acted as a kind of career counselor for me. And Jay Johnstone was good to me, had me tend his car when they were on the road, and I could use it for myself.

My most embarrassing moment came during a game against Montreal. A runner was trying to score from second on a single, and their pitcher, Steve Rogers, was backing up the plate. I'm retrieving the bat and I bump into him, so I get yelled at by one tough competitor. The next day I go over to him to apologize, and Steve Rogers says, "That's OK, you were just doing your job." That's a pro for you.

Mark Andersen is an assistant trainer for the
Philadelphia Phillies.

KEVIN CASHEN ....

My batboy years were '77-'79. I was a quiet rookie in '77, just like Eddie Murray. He was a shy guy who didn't deal well with the press. He was very close to his family in L.A., especially after one of his sisters died, and he was unhappy in Baltimore. In my second year, on a trip to L.A., he took me home for dinner, along with Lee May, Pat Kelly, Ken Singleton, and Al Bumbry. I was 16 but looked about 12, and there I was, a curiosity with five large black Major League players going to dinner at the Murray house in Watts. Eddie's five brothers and four sisters were there, and not one of them believed I'd never had ribs before.

Lee May was a big tipper, and Al Bumbry one of the most genuinely nice people you'll ever meet. Whenever anyone said "Ow" he'd say "What?", as if he heard "Al." Jim Palmer's a genuinely good person. He visited my sister Maureen in the hospital when she was injured. She's a fine athlete, you know—basketball at Mount St. Mary's, and she can beat all five of us brothers at golf. Doug DeCinces was another very nice guy, though he was always under a lot of pressure in Baltimore as Brooks Robinson's successor. And I'll never forget Larry Harlow, "the Hawk." I used to take care of his car, a T-top Monte Carlo, when he was on the road. The deal was that I could drive it as long as I washed it and kept the tank filled. When one of my friends ripped the top, I was really scared. But when I told him about it, he said, "Don't worry about it" and gave me a $200 tip for the season.

Reggie Jackson was the one guy I really didn't like. He made me feel like I was his personal servant, he was so into his own self-importance. All year, it was always, "Hey, kid."

I was always amazed, on the road, at the groupies hanging around the hotels. But there were great times. On my first trip, crazy Tony Muser and Rich Dauer and a few others took me out to Disneyland. We rode Space Mountain, and on the first hill, Muser yelled, "Kevin, duck!" as if I wasn't scared enough. Then, in Seattle, during the seventh inning stretch, Rick Dempsey caught the San Diego Chicken and stuck him in the bat basket I'd brought onto the field, and I not only got to wheel him into the bullpen but got on Mel Allen's "This Week in Baseball" doing it. It may have been on that trip that I had two beers on the plane, too much for my ninety pounds. I was stumbling when we landed, and Ken Singleton gave me a bad time about it.

During the World Series of '79, President Carter's box was right behind the batting circle, and I spent the whole game getting him to sign balls for the players. I treasure my A.L. Championship ring, but ever since we lost the Series to Pittsburgh I can't stand hearing "We Are Family." I treasure the whole experience. It helped me learn to deal with people, even prima donnas. It also looks great on a résumé. I'd have my son be a batboy in a minute. But I don't go to games much now—I don't know any of the players anymore.

Kevin Cashen, University of Baltimore MBA, is a commercial real estate lender at Signet Bank in Baltimore.

JOHN NELSON ....

I'm a clubhouse man, it's in my heart. From the day I started as a batboy for the Tigers in April 1979, I've known what I wanted—to be an equipment manager. I fell in love with the job. During my four years in the Air Force, I arranged my thirty-day leaves so that I could go to spring training. When I got married, I even went to spring training on my honeymoon.

I wasn't much of a ballplayer as a kid—just a little stickball in the streets. But when Jim Schmakel needed some kids, he called his old high school, St. Ladislaw's in Hamtramck, and I was one of the ten kids that Sister Cabrini picked for interviews. I must have impressed him in the interview, because he chose me for the job.

At first I was star-struck. But when players like Parrish and Whitaker say, "Call me Lance" and "Call me Lou," you feel at home. Gates Brown and Eddie Brinkman initiated me with the key to the batter's box routine, the length of frozen rope, and the bucket of curve balls. I fell for everything. Sparky Anderson made us all feel good by asking us about our personal lives. He's the greatest.

Kirk Gibson was another great guy to me. Not many people like him. He'd fire guys up by talking loud and being funny, but he'd get angry at himself and swear so that the crowd got on him. Jack Morris was quiet when he first came up, a funny guy, though, and he opened up as he matured. Jason Thompson was another quiet one—he didn't talk much at all, but he talked to me. Alan Trammell and Lou Whitaker are also quiet guys—they do their jobs and go home to their families.

Rusty Staub was unique. He always d.h.'ed when he was here, and he never wanted his bat in the bat-rack. If he grounded out I had to meet him at the third-base line with the bat—he had to have that bat in his hand. Steve Kemp was a throwback—always one of the last out of the locker room, always talking baseball. As for The Bird, Mark Fidrych, what I remember is Jack Billingham sitting on a stool reading the newspaper and The Bird setting fire to it.

In ten years there were only two Tigers I didn't get along with, and I won't tell you their names. One demanded I get him a hot dog during a game. It's strictly against the rules, and I wouldn't do it. He insisted and chewed me out when I refused, and afterwards he never talked to me.

After four years as batboy I took any job offered just to stay around the ballpark. I'd do whatever asked, and the title of Administrative Assistant to the Vice-President for   Office Operations meant only that I was still with the team. The one road trip a year as batboy was fine, but my favorite time was spring training, because I got to run the visiting side as clubhouse manager, to have some authority, and to meet great people like Kirby Puckett, Dave Parker, and Dwight Gooden. I've written letters with résumés to all potential expansion cities, hoping for an equipment manager's job. Of course I'd want my son to be a batboy, if he wanted to. My greatest fear is I'll have a son and he'll hate baseball.

Patience and persistence paid off for John Nelson, who in 1992 became Minor League Equipment and Clubhouse Manager for the Tigers.

THE EIGHTIES 80

THE EIGHTIES AND AFTER

Media coverage of baseball to the point of saturation has brought about some changes in the otherwise constant experience of batboys. In the clubhouse, for example, where once the visits of reporters were infrequent and brief, there now gathers, hours before a game, a cluster of media people who stand around talking mostly among themselves, perhaps deciding what the story of the day will be. And then, after every game, there descends a throng of microphone-wielders and note-takers to get the obligatory "quotes" and "bites" from players and others.

Indeed, so omniverous has become the appetite for first-hand witnessing of players and near-participants, that batboys themselves have been subjected to the heady experience of interviews—even on camera and live. Where once the only attention, and anonymous at that, would be the photo-op of shaking a home run hitter's hand at the plate, in the Eighties batboys would be asked to make World Series predictions on network TV telecasts and would lead a tickertape parade down Broadway carrying the Mets banner.

Still, these intrusions into the sacred precincts have barely altered the culture of the batboy's world or his traditional attitudes. He is still witness to and victim of the old-time pranks. His job description and the privileges that go with it remain virtually unchanged (we have Jimmy Triantas of the Orioles, Wes Patterson of the Royals, and Steve Friend of the Expos describing them in some detail here). Many batboys contrive to remain in the game somehow, though many still gravitate into law enforcement work. The reports of awe and disillusionment, thrill and embarrassment, surprising relationships and revealing personalities all persist, perpetuating the sense of tradition that pervades the clubhouse.

Yet there is a growing aura of nostalgia that accompanies the surviving attitudes of innocence and wonder. Perhaps that accounts for increased references to old-timers games. Batboys lament the atmosphere of "business" they feel as a strong presence in their world. They may admire the contemporary players in their suits, carrying their briefcases, and coming earlier to the ballpark to take greater care of their skills and their bodies. But they talk wistfully about the days when players stayed around longer after games, drinking their beer and talking baseball. That, after all, is what this enterprise is all about—talking baseball.

DENNIS CASHEN ....

I was the Orioles visiting batboy from '80-'82. In my very first game, Kansas City pitcher Rich Gale sent me to the bullpen to find the key to the pitcher's mound. I soon realized it was a joke and I was very embarrassed. But Gale was even more embarrassed—he apologized and gave me a T-shirt.

During the strike in '81, "Good Morning America" called to ask how the strike was affecting people other than players. They liked what I said and flew me to New York, sent me in a limo to the St. Moritz, then by limo to the studio in the morning. They also had an old black Yankee Stadium vendor and a young woman who played the organ at Comiskey.

I wasn't much in sympathy with the players, but I said, "Lock 'em in a room till they reach a solution." I thought there'd been too much breaking off and reporting back to teams. And it hurt me personally because it was before my last year in high school and I needed to make money for college. Later, ump Rich Garcia told me I'd done very well.

Reggie Jackson was affected, taken with himself, aware of his celebrity status. He wouldn't sign things—I tried to have players sign team pennants for me—and typified the new attitude of baseball as just business. Billy Martin, on the other hand, was unique, cordial, quiet, and reserved. He could be bizarre, like when he flipped over the table with the whole post-game spread after a loss, but he always asked me directions to a Catholic church and went to Mass on Sundays. Paul Molitor was a favorite player. My least favorite was Kirk Gibson, a bitter, angry man who was never satisfied. He must have had a terrible childhood. He'd throw his cleats at us if he didn't like the way we cleaned them.

The Blue Jays were an all-around nice team, especially Barry Bonnell and Garth Iorg. One time I took them and Danny Ainge—all three were practicing Mormons—in my mom's station wagon to one of the few movies they could see, not rated R, *The Empire Strikes Back*. But there was another guy on the team, one of the non-Mormon Latins, who had me deliver the key to his hotel room to some girl in the stands.

What baseball taught me, above all, was the work ethic.

An English major at Mt. St. Mary's, with a
minor in Communications, Dennis Cashen
now works for Davis Media Service.

BOBBY ALLDIS ....

I was in the tenth grade at Patrick Henry High School when I started with the Padres in '81, and I was a batboy through '85. The '84 season was the greatest, going on the road to Chicago and then the World Series. I have my ring, and I got a $750 share.

I got my initiation from umpire Lee Weyer, who sent me to find the key to the batter's box. Frank Pullen is the greatest ump there is. Dick Stello's great, too—we share a love of country music.

I was pretty close to Andy Hawkins, who once brought me snakeskin boots from Texas. I was sad when he left. Goose Gossage brought me cowboy boots, too, and Garry Templeton gave me lots of athletic shoes. Gossage was there on my first plane ride, to tease me and scare me, along with Steve Garvey and Graig Nettles. They locked me in the bathroom during some turbulence.

Eric Show and I used to play guitars together. He came to my house to teach me. He and Dave Dravecky and Mark Thurmond used to take me out to dinner with their wives. Tony Gwynn was a good guy, with a great attitude and work ethic. I guess I was closest to Tim Flannery. I'd take good care of him, get him his cup of coffee and Mountain Dew every day.

One day when I was working the visitors bullpen, I tried chewing tobacco, and I got so sick I couldn't continue. Otherwise it was fun working down the line, racing to beat fans to foul balls. The players loved it, kept score, me versus fans. That's how I met my wife. We have two boys and I hope they'll get to be batboys.

It seems like today's players don't care if they win. They care about themselves and bucks—stats and cash. But I love the game. That's why I've kept my job in the clubhouse video room since '86, even though I work full time at the paper.

Bobby Alldis worked in newspaper advertising from 5 a.m. to 1:30 p.m. so that he could be at the ballpark in time for his job with the Padres. Now working in a supermarket, he makes time to coach baseball for Patrick Henry High.

Tony Simokaitis ....

I wrote a letter to the Cardinals that equipment manager Buddy Bates liked, and then he and Frank Coppenbarger, his assistant, interviewed me, and I started working in '85. It was Buddy who gave me my nickname, "The Flea."

Right away I got sent for a dozen frozen ropes, and I knew I belonged. One of the first things Buddy taught me was to keep my mouth shut. "You don't say 'Good game' to a player, because then what do you say when he has a bad game?"

The best times were the victory celebrations. But I appreciated seeing a different side of the players from the fans. Like Tony Pena and Jose Oquendo. They're crazy. They'd play "burn-out"—throwing the ball as hard as possible until someone quits—with batboys at a distance of fifteen feet. And Neil Allen—the fans hate him, but he's really the nicest guy.

The Flea is now a Tiger at Mizzou.

CARL SCHNEIDER ....

I got my job with the Astros in '89 through Snuffy Ryza, who was already a batboy. Dennis Liborio hired me and looked after me ever since, including on a road trip to Chicago. He's the best boss I ever had.

If there was anything that surprised me, it was how normal everyone is. Sure, there was some teasing. Larry Andersen had a sore ankle and sent me for a bucket of steam. I didn't really know what to do, so he gave me instructions—"You can get it by carrying a bucket of water into the sauna."

The guys were all really nice to me. Rafael Ramirez and Eric Anthony would take me shopping at the mall, for example. But it wasn't just the Houston players. A guy like Kal Daniels would remember you from one road trip to the next. "Man," he'd say to me, "you gained some weight."

Carl Schneider is a student at San Jacinto College, exploring careers in the medical field.

STEVE (STRETCH) WINSHIP ....

My dad is a Royal Lancer, selling season tickets for Ewing Kauffman, and his travel agency owns a suite at the ballpark. My first job was shagging balls in the stands during batting practice, from 3:30 till 6 at $5 a day. That was in '78. In '79 and half of '80 I was in the visiting clubhouse. From then through '84 I was a ballboy down the left field line. Occasionally I'd sub as a batboy, but I'd found my home, my niche at the ballpark, down that line.

I can remember as a kid going out to Municipal Stadium. I was always a fan, and Lou Piniella and Amos Otis were favorites. Then I became an even bigger fan—the job was a dream. I felt very fortunate to have friendships among my heroes and idols, to have the thrill of shagging b.p. flies off the bat of George Brett, to take throws at first from Brett, U. L. Washington, and Frank White. And I got to enjoy the game from one of the best seats in the house.

In my first game as visiting batboy, the first batter was Lou Whitaker. I was so in awe I had to watch the ball he hit, so I was late running out to get the bat and I couldn't find it—the umpire was holding it. Then I was slow running out to get the Tigers relief pitcher's warmup jacket when he came in, so he gave it to Richie Hebner, who shoved it into my stomach and said, "I'm playing third base—do I have to be batboy, too?"

I was also embarrassed when I hustled to pick up a bat thrown on a long fly to left. I was returning to the dugout when I realized that everyone was yelling at me, and I turned to see the batter and the ump posed waiting at the plate—the ball had been foul and out of play. I guess it was not too long after that that Amos Otis sent me for the key to the batter's box so he could take some early b.p. He sent me to manager Dick Howser, who sent me to the dugout to look for it and then to someone in the grounds crew, who sent me to groundskeeper George Toma out near the bullpen, who sent me back to Brett in the clubhouse. Brett said I'd better change from spikes to tennis shoes and go up to general manager John Schuerholz's office upstairs on the fifth level to ask for duplicates. Fortunately, he wasn't there, so I went back to Otis and Brett, who sent me back to Howser, who finally told me the truth.

Once I was set working down the line I had a lot more confidence in what I was doing. I used to try to make good plays on foul balls, which was why Rocky Colavito started calling me "Stretch." The name stuck. Once, Jim Rice lined a shot just foul down the line. I took four running steps and made a headlong dive, sliding on my stomach with the ball in the webbing of my glove. It was the press box consensus play of the game.

Howser and Colavito would call errors on me if I misplayed a ball, waving white towels at me from the dugout. I'd try to get even by calling managerial misplays on them. Once, the third base ump called time, pointing to the dugout where the manager and coach were waving towels. It's the only time a game was stopped for the signal of a ballboy's error.

My relationship with Dick Howser was especially close. When Jim Frey was manager, he lived in a townhouse next to my dad's in Lakewood. When Frey went to the Cubs, Dick and Nancy Howser moved in there, so we were neighbors through my batboy and college years. But I had met Dick the day after he signed as manager in '81. He came out to the ballpark early, walked out of the tunnel and right away introduced himself to me and another batboy. By '86 we were so close that I was the Howsers' guest at the All-Star Game in Houston. That was the last game he managed before his brain tumor was diagnosed. After that I'd often spend the night at their house if I could be of use. And I was one of those at his bedside at St. Luke's in '87 when he died. Nancy remains a friend, and I often sit with her at games when I'm not working the suite for my dad.

That's the suite where my dad introduced Darrell Porter to his wife Deanne. I became their go-between with messages, but Dad always jokes that he made her a millionaire. His comeback after rehabilitation is a bright spot for us. After the Royals swept the Yankees in the '80 ACLS—on Brett's homer off Goose Gossage, with the rest of the team drinking champagne, I had a special moment sharing grape juice with Darrell Porter.

Amos Otis and Gaylord Perry were both good friends. Amos gave no comments or interviews so he got a bad rap from the press, but he was always practical joking with me. My glove, the one I still use after years of warming up players and playing softball, is the same new Rawlings he gave me in spring training when I went with the Royal Lancers in 1980. During pitching changes, he liked to come over and take over my stool, flipping me his glove to take over in left field. Or he'd call me out into the field to tell me a joke, or tell me to give a ball to that little boy in the stands and maybe get a date with his sister.

Gaylord was another prankster, always teasing me, giving me a hard time. On the Sunday of my last game, he invited me to breakfast, and when we were done he started pulling presents out of a shopping bag, including one of his 300-win T-shirts and a signed ball. Finally, he said, "Here's what you'll remember most about these years," and handed me a *Playboy* magazine.

The year before, Gaylord was pitching against us for the Mariners, and I was ballboying at the screen. Amos was out injured, and he took a ball and scuffed it up by rubbing it against the concrete side of the dugout. Then he wrote an obscene message to umpire Steve Palermo about Gaylord and sent me out to him with the ball. Palermo—one of my favorite umps by the way—along with Rich Garcia, slipped it into his pouch without looking at it and later in the inning throws it out to Gaylord. He looks at it and laughs, but throws it out, so Amos sends another—and this time Palermo sees it first.

Next day I was back in my regular spot down the line and that's where Gaylord caught me, grabbed me in a bearhug, threw me down, and sat on me for my part in the prank. Amos saw it and sent me with another message to Gaylord: "How much longer are you planning to stay around?" So Gaylord took me down for a second fall. Later, while I was warming Willie Wilson up between innings, Gaylord stole my stool.

I got in trouble with Wilson once when I was interviewed by the *Independence Examiner*. They asked me to rate on a scale of 1-10 the left fielders I warmed up with. I called Willie my favorite because he throws easy, and when he read it he got mad at me. Rickey Henderson was the worst. He'd play burn-out from fifteen feet, and once he broke the webbing in my glove, but he didn't care. Jim Rice was one who always had a big smile for me and would ask about school and girlfriends, and he'd call me out into the field to give me sunflower seeds. Believe it or not, he threw a better knuckleball than Quisenberry. And I'll never forget Ruppert Jones, who struck out to end an inning one day, and when I threw him the ball in left field he took it and heaved it over the fence into the water display.

Quiz taught me to throw a knuckler and taught me the value of hard work. He'd throw 15-20 minutes every day. Once he asked me to come out early so he could work on his move to first. So I took his throws there for a while, and then he wanted to work on fielding bunts and throwing to first. After that he had me stand at the plate while he worked on control. And then, finally, I got to take some swings—ten minutes of b.p. from Dan Quisenberry.

I remember a four-game series with the Tigers that had a lot of long rain delays. After the last game, Sparky Anderson shook my hand and palmed me a $20 bill. "I don't need that," I said. "Go ahead," he insisted, and then said to my boss, "You have the best batboy in the league right there." He had a way of making you feel great.

I remember Jerry Terrell, a utility infielder who played all nine positions in one game. He was a very nice, kind person, who was in charge of the Sunday services in the clubhouse—ten or fifteen minutes of informal prayer and testimony. I think he was a positive influence on the team, and when he invited the kids to take part I did so.

I was aware that there were issues of drugs and race. I think that when they named Brett and Frank White as co-captains it proved there was a split. But I developed an understanding of the players' attitudes, especially toward the media, and I became sensitive to all the stress that's put on them. But the most memorable discoveries had to do with the game. Like when Bret Saberhagen was a rookie pitching against the Yankees, and I heard Howser in the dugout say, "Throw to first"—and he did! I was amazed to discover that coach Mike Ferraro was relaying signs to catcher Jim Sundberg, and I was thinking he was just picking his nose. Maybe that's why I'm still out at Royals Stadium for almost every game.

A tennis star at Graceland College in Iowa,
Steve Winship now handles accounting,
promotions, and advertising for Winship
Travel in Independence, Missouri.

MERRITT RILEY ....

I wrote a letter to the Yankees asking them how to become a batboy, and they turned it over to Joe D'Ambrosio, who had been a batboy from '76-'78 and then worked in the front office in p.r. He answered my letter and we struck up a friendship—he even came to my Confirmation party. Joe told me what to do, and I wrote to Pat Kelly, an ex-cop like my dad, who was stadium manager. He interviewed me on a snowy day in January in the Stadium. I met Pete Sheehy in the clubhouse, and I was hired. I was seventeen.

There was a snowstorm on the eve of Opening Day 1982, and I was sleepless with excitement. I got to the Stadium very early to watch helicopters and snowplows trying to get the field ready for the game with the Rangers.

Sheehy was like a shrine—he had batboyed for Babe Ruth. I was always nervous around him, though he was a hockey fan and liked me because I played hockey. He was very good at signing players' autographs on balls. But he was also like a kid in the clubhouse, playing tricks like letting ice cubes melt on your pants or putting our fingers in warm water while we were sleeping over in the clubhouse. When Ralph Salvon, the Orioles trainer, sent me to Pete for the bat-stretcher, he went along with it and sent me to the umpires' room for it.

We were a unit of six boys, rotating jobs as home and visiting batboy, ballboys, and inside clubby. I soon learned that most visiting players were businesslike before games, but like little kids after. They'd have two or three beers and go out on the town in New York. They'd load their sanitaries with beers for the bus back to the Hyatt. A few like Broadway plays, but more are soap opera fans and would want tickets to studios for taping sessions. But I was disillusioned by the revolving-door aspect to their professionalism. Like when I had just gotten to know Butch Wynegar and two weeks later he was gone.

Kent Hrbek and the rest of the Twins were like a softball team. They were pro wrestling fans and would watch it on TV for hours. One day after b.p. Herbie pulled my shirt up over my head and threw me to the ground, yelling, "Body slam!" He grabbed my Yankee cap, wore it into the shower after the game, and then all dressed up in a three-piece suit he was still wearing my destroyed Yankee cap.

The only time I really hung out with a player was when Ron Kittle, just twenty-two and with a pregnant wife back home, took me and another batboy to his hotel room, where we drank some beer and watched TV. Another memorable experience was driving Dave Collins to Boston after a Wednesday afternoon game. We had an off day on Thursday before the Red Sox series, but Dave was going up early to meet a stewardess. It was like talking intimately with an old friend. And I stayed on for the weekend. Dave was having a tough season and the fans were on him. Late in the season, when he hit an inside-the-park home run, I was right there to see him slide home and slam his helmet into the dirt in frustration, as if to say, "Take that!"

Sparky Anderson was a grandfather type manager. Doug Rader had a temper but was a great guy, one of the guys. La Russa was one of the guys, too—until the game starts—but he treats superstars like ordinary people. With John McNamara I remember the red stoneface. He was like Gene Mauch, nasty and intense—there was no small talk, forget about it. I learned to stay away from Earl Weaver, who was a nut like Billy Martin in the dugout. Martin was a ball of fire, intense and screaming in the dugout. You don't go near him during a game. He did a lot of drinking, but none of it was ever seen before games. He'd take a limo to the ballpark every day. Yet after a game late in the season, he'd sit in his office and shoot the breeze with me for half an hour and he gave me an autograph for my dad. The guy the players loved playing for was Yogi Berra. He never said much to me, but when we were posing for team pictures, he grabbed my hair and said, "Better get this cut."

Among the players, Don Mattingly is my all-time favorite, a team player and a classy guy who does a lot of work for underprivileged kids. George Brett is another really nice guy—I was in the middle of the pine tar incident, and I have the picture of it with everybody's signature. Dave Winfield is very businesslike, shows up in the clubhouse in a three-piece suit and carrying a briefcase. He's a really nice guy, but cheap as hell. He gave me a dozen balls for All-Star players' signatures. And when I completed the task by the end of the season, there wasn't even a tip for me. Most players are good tippers who hand out ten bucks to anyone for any little thing.

Reggie Jackson. In his first at-bat back in the Stadium as an Angel he hits a home run. Later in the clubhouse he was shouting, in exultation, words for Steinbrenner. Then, after the Saturday night game, when I was sleeping over in the clubhouse for the Sunday game, I was awakened by Pat Kelly, who was there to check Reggie's bats that he kept in his locker, for cork. He found no evidence, but Monday's *Daily News* cites "confidential source says Reggie corks bats." He was very tight with his bats, though, wouldn't give away broken ones. One day on the field a batboy tried to keep a splintered one, and Reggie took it away and brought it back to his locker. He was still moving stuff out of his New York apartment and I carried some trunks for him. As a tip he gave me that bat for my collection.

He signed my copy of his book, Reggie, for me: "To Merritt, very best wishes, all my best, Reggie Jackson." Yet when I approached him to sign a card while he was reading stats in the clubhouse, he took it and threw it on the floor. Everyone else signed. Still, he treated his teammates, from veterans to rookies, all alike. The batboys were all on a softball team at the time, and one day we were watching TV in the trainer's room after a morning game, when Reggie came in with Rod Carew, Doug DeCinces, and Bobby Grich and they all joked around with us like regular guys.

around with us like regular guys.

On the Fourth of July in '84, I batboyed for the Red Sox for Dave Righetti's no-hitter against them. I was pulling for it but hiding it—that was part of the experience of learning to be professional. I remember Steve Kemp in right field diving into the stands to backhand a foul ball and Wade Boggs striking out to end the game. Most of all I remember how you could hear a pin drop in the Red Sox clubhouse after the game.

I used to run to OTB to place bets for players like Lou Piniella and Mickey Rivers. Rivers was crazy, didn't give a damn about anything. I remember seeing his wife chase him around the parking lot in her car when he was still a Yankee. With the Rangers one day, Rader wanted to use him as a pinch runner. He wasn't on the bench, so Rader sent me to the clubhouse to get him. The clubhouse manager said to look in the stands, and that's where I found him, eating hot dogs and talking to a couple of girls. Another time he had a hot tip and sent a batboy to the track with everybody's money—but he sent him to the Meadowlands and the horse was running at Yonkers.

And then there was Mike Norris, an A's pitcher under Martin. We'd sort the laundry in three piles—uniforms, underclothes, and towels—and we'd found a bag of coke in his uniform pocket and thrown it in the garbage. Fifteen minutes later Norris runs in all nervous, says, "Where's my pants?" The equipment manager says, "Mike, it's in the garbage."

For three years I did nothing but live baseball. I was a celebrity among my friends, and it was a tough transition after. My one regret is that I didn't use the experience to open doors to possible careers in baseball. But even though I'm applying to the Police Academy I'm still considering going to umpire school. The umps all seem to love doing it, and Joe Brinkman and John Shulock especially made an impression on me.

Merritt Riley is a New York City Police Officer,
patrolling Brownsville.

PAUL GONOUD ·····································

My mother was a friend of a friend of Pat Kelly, stadium manager for the Yankees, and that's how I got to be a batboy on the visiting side for '81 and '82. They were my junior and senior years at Monsignor Scanlon High School, where I was a catcher and pitcher. I even played for the league championship in Yankee Stadium in '81, as a d.h.

I was in total awe of the players. I idolized the late Thurman Munson, so I hoped for Rick Cerone to be a good replacement and really expected to be overwhelmed by him. Instead he proved to be nonchalant, snobbish, and impressed with glamour. His relationship with me continued hot-and-cold for the two years.

I found myself rooting for individual favorites, even against the Yanks, like Kent Hrbek. I loved it when Herby beat the Yankees with a twelfth-inning home run. Another time, he grabbed the Yankees cap off my head in the clubhouse and kept it on while undressing, showering, and dressing. When he finally gave it back to me, all ruined, he said, "I hate the Yankees," and then he gave me the money for a new hat. Other Twins—Gaietti was a nut but born-again, and Viola was a sweetheart of a guy. You know, the most nerve-wracking thing for a batboy is picking out a new bat when the hitter cracks one. I'll never forget the day that Dave Engle cracked his and yelled at me, "Where's the fucking bat?!" Then he winked and smiled. They often use each other's bats anyway.

Buddy Bell was another favorite, one of the nicest guys I've ever met. He'd tip me thirty or forty bucks just to help keep an eye on his kids when they visited. Mickey Rivers was with the Rangers then. One day he comes in with a hot tip on a horse— some guy in the bleachers gave it to him, number two in the third race. Mickey gives the tip to clubhouse guys, players, everyone, and collects money and sends me out to the Meadowlands with several hundred bucks to bet it all on the nose. So I bet it, number two in the third, and he runs out. Turns out, the tip horse was running at Yonkers. Actually, it didn't matter, because the right horse ran third anyway.

Among the Yankees, Dave Winfield was always amiable—he'd go out of his way to say hello to clubhouse kids. Gossage, Nettles, and Piniella were always clowning around, but Randolph was quiet and Dent snobbish.

Cal Ripken, Jr. was a genuine all-American type. In one Orioles game, when I was ballboy down the left field line, he hit a line drive that bounced off the fence and knocked my hat off. The players all kidded me about it, and Dave Righetti ragged me. Once I overheard a shouting match, over the starting rotation, between Earl Weaver and Jim Palmer inside the manager's office. Another time, Weaver pulled the cloth out from under the postgame spread, rendering the food uneatable, saying, "These guys don't deserve to eat—they play like horseshit."

The Blue Jays were fun. I remember when they got fined for playing whiffleball in the clubhouse—Garth Iorg and Danny Ainge were playing naked. And they were great for tying knots in cleats and putting shaving cream on the phone.

Billy Martin managed the A's those two years. He was always nice and generous to me. Rollie Fingers was gone, to Milwaukee, but he was still flaky, always complaining. I remember Sal Bando saying, after Fingers followed him from Oakland to Milwaukee, "I can't believe I'm still with this guy—what a dick!" The thing I remember best about the A's was the day the sprinkler system flooded the clubhouse, and Dave McKay held the valve until help arrived.

It's Pete Vuckovich I remember best of the Brewers. I had lost a friend in a car accident, and he consoled me. He was very open, talking about his own driving escapades, about wearing two different shoes when pitching, about popping uppers, about spending a month during the offseason just hanging out and getting high with his wife. I don't know how much of that was true or whether he was just trying to take my mind off what had happened.

It was during a televised game against the Brewers that my mom and aunt and many friends saw me running something—a batting glove or a shin guard—out to a batter from the clubhouse and heard Phil Rizzuto say, "Here comes a pinch runner—hey, no, it's the batboy, but look at that kid move, he's fast, and big, too. The Yanks ought to sign him. Holy cow!"

Other players who stand out were Jim Rice, who was very nice, Wade Boggs too, and Yaz, who was very quiet but gave me a bat when he left. I worked the '81 World Series and found Terry Forster to be a nice guy. Dusty Baker took good care of us kids, but Garvey, Cey, and Lopes were all jerks. Another memorable guy was Bert Blyleven. He'd come up behind me in the on-deck circle and take my knees out. Once I was warming him up in the outfield and he pitched me a curve without warning me—it broke right down through my legs, and he said, "Wanna be a catcher?"

Reggie Jackson stands out above all. He was a very bad guy who thought the world revolved around him. He called everybody "Junior" and ordered us all to do this and do that. His first time back in the Stadium in '82 after signing with the Angels, he struck up a lengthy conversation in the on-deck circle, and asked me about what Guidry was throwing. I said, "I guarantee he's gonna throw you a lot of sliders." "Really?" he says, and goes up and hits a home run. "I hit a slider," he says later in the clubhouse. I told him "Nice game" and he's sitting there screaming at us kids, eating watermelon, drinking beer, and throwing cans against the wall like a barbarian.

On Sunday morning, when I was sleeping over in the clubhouse after a night game, the stadium manager and two others came in and kicked us kids out of the locker room. "Never say we were here," he told us—later we found out they were looking for Reggie's bats to see if they were loaded. And later that afternoon when we were packing his bag we couldn't miss seeing the rolling papers in his gear. To tell you the truth, I really enjoyed hearing about the Steinbrenner party in Oakland when Reggie and some of his friends were high and screaming profanities at Ginger Nettles until Graig took Reggie out in the hall and flattened him.

If there was any one lesson I learned from the whole batboy experience, it was the value of the work ethic.

Paul Gonoud is an accountant with Shearson
Lehman Hutton.

Paul Greco ....

I got the job with the Mets through my boyhood friend Mike Rufino. We've been close all our lives, we were neighbors, we played Little League together, went to St. Raymond's and then Iona, even got married around the same time. Mike's brother worked in the clubhouse as assistant equipment manager. Now my father, a retired police officer, works in the clubhouse.

Mike and I carried the Mets banner to lead the World Series parade in '86. My World Series ring is the same as the players', with my name on the side. It's a conversation piece, becomes a focus in job interviews, so you go from being nervous to relaxed baseball talk. As Keith Hernandez said, "When you win the World Series in New York, it's forever." When we went into Boston down two games I was interviewed live on Channel 7, and I said, "We're gonna jump all over Oil Can Boyd, no way he's gonna beat us." The Mets scored four in the first and made me look real good.

After the first year it was no big deal—the players were just people. Sure, some stood out. I was proud to see players like Lenny Dykstra and Wally Backman hustle—that was a good lesson for us to learn, that and learning to talk with people. I never saw anyone go at it the way those two did, with so many skills for the game. And I never saw anyone study pitchers so hard as Rusty Staub. He always carried two bags plus his own bat bag, and he had to have new sanitaries every night. We learned that whatever Rusty wants, Rusty gets, and that whatever Rusty says is right.

My memories include taking batting practice from Lee Mazzilli and Keith Miller, driving Juan Samuel's car with its tinted windows and Doc Gooden's pick-up, getting a Twins bag from Frank Viola and a Blue Jays bag from Jeff Musselman, seeing HoJo and Kevin Elster sleep with their bats on the road to break slumps, and seeing Roger McDowell the prankster at work. He'd throw firecrackers into the bathroom and give hotfoots. He used to put on a different mask in the clubhouse every day, and the WOR cameraman would zoom in on him early in the game. One day in Chicago he came out with his shirt on his legs and his pants over his head, so it looked like he was walking on his hands.

Among the umpires, Jerry Crawford used to tease us with the bats all the time, but he had a very short temper. And Doug Harvey was godlike—he never made a mistake. Among the managers, what I noticed was how weak Davey Johnson was on fundamentals, compared to Whitey Herzog. No one on the Mets could bunt. Remember Ron Gardenhire, utility infielder? He must have known he wouldn't be around long. He collected signatures from all the players, not unusual, but he got his in his Baseball Encyclopedia.

Part of our duties was to go to Pathmark for snacks and supplies before games—cereal, cakes, muffins, bagels. Part of our privileges was to go on one road trip each year, to ride the bus to Philadelphia, and to travel during playoffs and the World Series. Until '85 we'd be allowed two passes per game—in the auxilliary press box—but when they added the luxury boxes they cut that out, so we had to borrow from the players' allotment of six per game when we needed them.

One time Doc Gooden, when he was coming off rehab but not playing yet, came to our neighborhood, played whiffle ball in front of our house as a crowd gathered, came on in for a barbecue, and then shot hoops with us afterwards. Yeah, I'm the batboy who struck out Dwight Gooden.

Paul Greco works in the Government Operations Department of Sanwa USA on Wall Street.

MIKE RUFINO ....

I started with the Yankees in '82, and then during spring training in '84 Bobby Valentine said to me, "You want to be on the elevator going down with the Yankees or going up with the Mets?" I was a Mets batboy through '87, and Paul Greco and I got to lead the World Series parade carrying the banner in '86. I wouldn't sell my World Series ring for a million dollars.

Baseball players are like kids, always playing and joking around. With the Yankees, Pete Sheehy sent me for a bucket of steam, for left-handed wrenches, for the key to the batter's box. I remember seeing Danny Heep throw Paul into the dryer. And then there was the sour cake routine. You'd smell the cake and yell that it was sour and when someone else would sniff you'd push his face in it. I saw Bill Robinson pull it on all the rookies. On the Mets they got Hubie Brooks with it, but when they tried it on Kevin Mitchell his neck was so strong they couldn't push his face down.

There was no joking around with Davey Johnson. He was all business. When Mike Scott pitched against us, he told me he wanted to see any balls thrown out of play by the umpires.

Paul and I were both hockey players, so it was a thrill when Wayne Gretzky came into the clubhouse. I met Rodney Dangerfield, too, and Glenn Close and George Bush. But it's the players who have the biggest impact. Wally Backman and Lenny Dykstra were favorites—I like the get-down-and-dirty type. When they were traded it felt like losing part of the family. HoJo used to take us out to dinner. And Clint Hurdle took us out in Chicago when we got to go on our road trip.

When I graduated from Iona, the Mets offered me a job in the accounting department. But there was no money in it and no future, so I went to work in Wall Street. But the people on the Stock Exchange always wanted to meet me because I worked for the Mets.

Mike Rufino is Supervising Senior Examiner
for the New York Stock Exchange.

STEVE LABATT ....

There's a Minnetonka legacy of Twins batboys passed down originally from Mark McKenzie. I became part of it through a friend of my brother, and I worked from '82-'86, including three years as visiting-team batboy. I was initiated by being sent to find the key to the visiting dugout—it's a tradition of the visiting clubhouse, and it's part of that tradition not to tell about it.

I was surprised at how nice the players were. George Brett was my favorite, and I still visit with him when he comes to town. Scott Fletcher was a nice guy, too, and it was ironic that one day—it was getaway day for the Rangers—I swung the lead bat over my shoulder and caught him in the face. He had to be taken to the hospital for stitches in his lip.

The most exciting three days were in '85 when we had the All-Star Game. I was with Brett when he met Barry Bremen, "the great imposter," at the loading dock. We hid him in a back room and then he showed up for batting practice wearing a Yankee uniform. Later he sent me an autographed copy of his book, *Official Mascot*.

The Twins' clubhouse was looser than any other I've ever been in. When those guys weren't playing baseball they were out fishing or hunting or playing golf. On road trips Kirby Puckett, Gary Gaetti, and Kent Hrbek took me under their wing. But it was Randy Bush who ran the kangaroo court. He kept finding me guilty of fraternizing with opponents and it would cost me a six-pack. But once, when I was talking to my girlfriend in the stands while working down the left field line, Gaetti had to retrieve a foul ball, and that one cost me a whole case.

You learn to grow up fast in the clubhouse.

Steve Labatt, who wanted to be a police officer
since he was 10, is now with the Deputy
Sheriff's Office in Hennepin County, Minne-
sota, in the Patrol Division.

CLAYTON WILSON ....

I have three older brothers and I've always been in love with baseball. I've been a Twins fan since I was five. In '86 I visited my friend Jeff Resnick in the clubhouse, and when he went to Stanford at the end of that season, I filled in for him in the umpires' room. Next season I began batboying.

Among the umps, Dave Phillips was my favorite, and I thought a lot of John Hirschbeck too. As for Ken Kaiser, he's funny and fun to watch, but he's just not a nice guy.

Kent Hrbek is the funniest guy I've ever met. Blyleven is also funny—I got to stay with him on a trip to California. You can't help but like Kirby Puckett—he taught me respect for my elders.

What happened to me in the clubhouse, though, was that I switched the focus of my attention from the superstars to the ordinary players. I got to like Wayne Terwilliger and Gary Gaetti a lot, and my favorites were David West and Tommy Nieto— I'd have long talks with them.

I was impressed with how good a life the players have. They work hard and earn it, but lots of people take care of them. My life has been the best because of them, they've been the best influence, and I learned respect for others. Yes, they are positive role models.

Clayton Wilson majored in Marketing at the University of Minnesota, is now equipment manager for the Minnesota Timberwolves.

Jimmy Triantas ....

My friend Fred Tyler was equipment manager for visiting teams at Memorial Stadium, and he got me a job helping out in the Orioles clubhouse during the '83 World Series. Then I was visiting-teams batboy in '84 and Orioles batboy from the '85 through the '88 seasons.

Terry Crowley was the person that inspired me the most. I met him when I went over to the Orioles side in '85 and was sort of shy. He sorta took me in, got me to talk to the fellows, and after a while it was just like I was one of the guys—pretty cool for a batboy. I played a lot of baseball from the third grade on, but I had trouble hitting for a long time. Terry Crowley, a Major League hitting coach, helped me out. And we'd sit on the bench next to each other in the dugout and he'd tell me things about the game—he sorta had baseball ESP and nine out of ten times he'd be right. Everybody liked him, and unlike the other coaches, the younger players would ask him to go out with them.

Jim Dwyer, one of Terry's closest friends, is another really great guy. J.J. had a personality, a funny man, and he taught me a lot. I never saw anybody who could pinch-hit the way he did. Hit a home run in his first time at bat in the World Series in '83, but the game I remember was against the Tigers, with Jack Morris pitching. It was the eighth inning and Morris still had all his stuff going and had a 3-0 lead. With a guy on first, Larry Sheets hit a foul off his foot and could hardly walk. Earl Weaver looked down the bench for a pinch-hitter and called Mike Young. The other guys laughed—not loud enough for the manager to hear—because he has to go in there with an 0-2 count. I was getting his batting helmet for a left-handed at-bat, when Earl said, "Now, wait a minute, Mike, we'll put Dwyer in there." And Dwyer had been one of the guys laughing, so Mike had his chance to laugh at J.J.

It was a different story when Dwyer got in the box. He had a great at-bat, worked Jack Morris real well. He fouled off four pitches in a row, worked the count to 3 and 2, and hit a slider in the right field stands about ten rows back. That was weird, but not as weird as the game that both Dwyer and Sheets hit grand slam home runs in the same inning but the Orioles lost the game on a grand slam by Toby Harrah for the Rangers.

Lots of games and plays go around in my mind. Fred Lynn hitting home runs in the ninth, making great catches in center field. Brady Anderson made some great plays, too, that I'll never forget. And Cal Ripken, Jr. turning a double play in the middle to change a whole game around. There's something about Cal—you can tell by the way he plays the game how much he really loves it. It's not just the consecutive game streak but the guy never misses infield or batting practice. And I remember a game in Rochester, just a scrimmage against the AAA team, and Cal, Sr. told him he'd pinch hit for him to give him the last few innings off, and Cal said, "Naw, I'll take another hack at it." I always remember that. It tells you how much he really cares about the game of baseball.

And I remember another time, when the team had just come home from a long road trip to play a weekend series and after the Sunday game a lot of the players were going out to dinner with their wives or just going home to spend a night with their families. I was hanging up some clothes, about the last thing I do, and Cal is the only one there, dressed up with a suit on. I said, "Is everything OK, Cal?" And Cal said, "Yeah," in a down voice, and that wasn't like him. What had happened was he kept signing autographs as long as anybody wanted it, and now he was about two hours late for dinner. He had made everybody happy outside, and now he had to make an explanation to his wife.

There's so many outstanding personalities you meet. For instance, Rex Barney, the p.a. announcer for the Birds, who'd sit with me in the dugout during batting practice and could tell me little things about what players were doing, right and wrong. I think he knows the most about the game of anybody in the media or press. And then there were the trainers. Richie Bansells, who really looked after me, works harder than just about anybody I've ever seen in the clubhouse. And Ralph Salvon, who passed away during the '88 season, who'd sometimes slip me a twenty-dollar bill and say, "Hey, Jimmy, buy yourself something nice this weekend."

I didn't really get to know a lot of managers, probably because I had a great fear of them. I never really talked to Earl Weaver a lot. I was so nervous about going in there to get balls signed that Coach Ray Miller would take them in for me. And then, when I went on a road trip, Earl was sitting in the back of the plane with the guys scattered all over the place on a charter flight. I walked by Earl and he called out, "Jimmy?" There were a couple of Jimmies on the Orioles—Traber and Dwyer— and I just walked past, but when I looked back a couple of coaches were looking at me. And Earl got out of his seat and walked over to me, and said, "Hey, Jimmy, have you ever been to Chicago?" and I said, "No, I haven't, sir." He said, "Here's a twenty-dollar bill. Go buy yourself a steak on me." When he did that, you know, it felt great, because I had never really talked to him, and he came out of his seat and talked to me.

Sparky Anderson's a great person. Each time he came in he knew my name. And if I was over in the Orioles clubhouse, Rex Barney would say, "Hey, Jimmy, Sparky was asking about you." And that's a really good feeling. When he found out I was going to visit my grandmother during the winter in Thousand Oaks, California, he insisted I call him. So I did and he took me out to dinner. I don't think there's many batboys that get a chance to have dinner and talk about baseball with Sparky Anderson.

I haven't mentioned Eddie Murray, but he's a terrific person. People, especially the media, said a lot of things about Eddie, about the way he played or acted, but they were all completely wrong. I know he went through a lot of things, people booing him when he was down because his mom died. You know, some ignorant fans would put long scratches on his car and he'd tell me about it and there was just nothing I could say. I think he was dealt a bad deal at the end of his career in Baltimore. He deserved more credit than he got. He was definitely a first-class guy and he still is.

The thing I remember most about him as a player was his home runs, lefthanded or righthanded, which were different from anybody else's, not line drives down the line but home runs anywhere. I remember when he made the last out of Juan Nieves' no-hitter, when Robin Yount made a diving catch on a line drive. But I also remember when he broke out of a slump to beat the A's with a grand slam off a Jose Rijo fastball.

One of my best friends was Norris Jones, a batboy for the visiting teams for about four years. We had a pretty neat relationship, always ready to help each other out. We had a way of giving signs to each other if we needed a rosin bag or an extra weighted bat, especially when players needed things for some superstitious routine. I've known Norris since we were eight years old, played ball with him and against him, but being batboys together was the greatest of all. One time we went on a camping trip together and had a great time, and then back at the ballpark we were talking about it behind the cage during batting practice. Eddie Murray came over and asked us what we were laughing about, and when we told him he joined in. I remember looking over in the stands and seeing some kids just staring at us. At that point I realized how good I had it—me and my best buddy and Eddie Murray kidding around behind the batting cage, while other kids could only stare.

Here are the details of my daily routine, which was tough during the spring because of school. I was an Accounting major in high school and was on the baseball team. School started at 7:50, and if I didn't have a school game I'd go straight to work at 3:30. I'd run errands for players till 4:30 and then get ready for batting practice—bring out the bats, helmets, catchers' equipment, pine tar, rosin bag, and weighted bat. Sometimes during batting practice I'd either shag fly balls or stand behind the cage and watch the guys hit. Starting pitchers were supposed to work the bucket behind second base, but most of them didn't want to so they would ask me. Then at the end of batting practice I'd have to clear all the bats and stuff so the other team could hit. After batting practice I'd get everything straight for the game. Once the game starts, I'd just sorta take it easy. While the Orioles were in the field sometimes I'd go back in the clubhouse and hang up some of the clothes from batting practice. Then after a game I had a lot of stuff to do usually, sweep and mop the clubhouse, hang the clothes in each locker after they were washed and cleaned, polish the shoes every night. Sometimes I wouldn't get done at a night game until about 1:30 or 2:00 o'clock in the morning, and then had to get up at 6:30 for school.

During the summer the traveling secretary would ask me what road trip I wanted to go on, and that was great. It's a little bit different from working at home. You can catch the team bus with the guys and get there like a half hour before batting practice, because they would have kids there to run errands for the players. And it's more relaxed, you know. They gave me my own hotel room and I could go out to lunch or a movie with one of the players. Everybody's real nice to you, and you get to see so many great towns. One of my favorites was Anaheim. Arlington, Texas and Chicago were great towns to go to. Yankee Stadium is a great experience just to walk in. You can feel the atmosphere of all the great players that played there. During batting practice I got a chance to walk out behind the fence and look at all the monuments. It's a great baseball place. And then once in Texas there was a great old-timers game and I got autographs from Willie Mays and Hank Aaron and Joe DiMaggio. You know it's just great when you get to meet guys like that. I realized how lucky I was, how fortunate I am to meet people like that. It's just a great experience.

Jimmy Triantas works as an electrician in construction.

MARK SASSETTI

I've always been involved with sports. In high school, St. Joseph in Westchester, I was the basketball manager, but I missed Isiah Thomas by two years. Then at Illinois State I did the same, under coach Bob Donewald. Meanwhile, I joined my younger brother at Comiskey, though I worked mostly on the visiting side.

We were both close to Harold Baines and his family, and were upset when he was traded to the Rangers. When he put on the Texas uniform in our visiting clubhouse it brought a tear to my eye. I slept over in the clubhouse for the Sunday game and heard they were going to retire his uniform number, so when he came in that day I said, "H.B., congratulations." "For what?" he said. "They're gonna retire your number today." "You're crazy, you're kidding me, they're not gonna do that." "You better start writing your speech," I said.

A sign in the clubhouse says, "What you see here and what you say here stays here." But people in sports don't hold things back. And baseball is filled with personalities, in the clubhouse and the front office. With the managers, you have to discover their likes and dislikes by trial and error. I found Doug Rader to have a loose attitude. With Frank Robinson, you have to be careful every step you take, what you say, how you say it. Dallas Green, ditto. Tom Kelley is a great guy, but you don't get too crazy in his clubhouse. Nothing bothers Sparky Anderson as long as there's respect for all. And with Tony La Russa, I remember the strange faces he'd make in the clubhouse.

Batboys are gofers in the clubhouse. We're like babysitters for millionaires. More of them smoke than you'd think. I remember Lee Mazzilli with the Blue Jays, with his locker between two rookie Dominicans who kept yapping in Spanish across him, smoking five packs during a three-game series. And some go through two or three tins of chew a day.

There's not much alcohol in the clubhouse, but lots of it in lobby bars on the road. I never saw any prescription drugs or steroids or narcotics, but there were blue movies in the back rooms and we'd be running phone numbers back and forth. There'd be some gambling among the players on NFL pools and some gin and poker, but no betting with bookies. The Illinois Lotto got up to 42 million when the A's were in town, and players gave me twenty- or fifty-dollar bills to buy tickets for them. Jose Canseco peeled off two from a roll of about fifty hundred-dollar bills, and I ended up buying $480 worth of quik-piks at the Greek liquor store on Halstead Street.

When I asked Canseco to sign a picture for me, I said, "but please, no 'best wishes' bullshit." He said OK and signed, "Kiss my ass, Jose Canseco." Reggie Jackson was always a tough autograph. I once brought some balls to him to sign, and he said, "You can take those balls and stick 'em up your ass." I said, "As long as you sign them first I'll put them wherever you want me to put them." After that, he'd always say, "Get those balls out yet?"

Anyone without jock and cup is prime game for Kirby Puckett's "cup-check." Mark Hill and Neil Allen are pranksters too, but Bert Blyleven is the worst—or best. Every clubby in America tries to stay away from him, but sooner or later he'll sneak up and get you, shaving cream in the ear, set fire to some of your clothes. In September, when rookies come up, he steals their clothing and hides it, pants in the ice cream freezer, shoes in the fruit bowl, and he'll set off firecrackers in the walkways and the dugout.

Some guys were low-key, like Floyd Bannister, Vance Law, Scotty Fletcher, and Ricky Horton. Ron Kittle was outspoken but had equal respect for everyone, kids and teammates alike. Carlton Fisk likes to be left alone—he's a baseball businessman. The Dominicans and Venezuelans are interesting. Ozzie Guillen brings a sixteen-year-old's attitude every day. With Carlos Martinez and George Bell you never know what to expect. And Julio Franco and Ruben Sierra like their gold, and they are like gold.

The Equitable Old-Timers Game is always a high point of the season, passing out the Ben-Gay and hot towels for Billy Williams, Ernie Banks, and Minnie Minoso. There aren't many high points with the White Sox—Ozzie Rookie of the Year in '85, Seaver's 300th win. Low points? Six managers and four g.m.'s and eighteen coaches in just a few years, Greg Walker's seizure, H.B. traded, LaRussa fired.

I always liked to spend a week in Sarasota during spring training, hanging out with Ozzie Guillen, who's just like a kid going to video arcades and movies and Putt Putt. One night, after two rounds of miniature golf and blowing fifty bucks on video games, he got in the batting cage and started putting on a clinic, calling his shots, and attracting a crowd. Some old guy says to me, "This guy's good—he might be able to play semipro ball in the Coast League." I go, "You a coach?" "Yeah," he says, "What's his position?" "Shortstop." "No," he says, "he's too small to be a shortstop."

At Comiskey everything was old, even the vacuum cleaners. We'd take turns vacuuming the clubhouse with this ancient lawn-mower type machine. One night I found Roger Clemens' wedding ring just before he called from the airport to ask about it. But for the new Comiskey, my brother Jim and I were asked to contribute suggestions for the clubhouse. So if they have a swimming pool for rehabilitation there, they can thank two old batboys.

Mark Sassetti's first job out of college was as a special events rep for Pepsi, in charge of the Wrigley Field operation, but it still let him off in time to get across town to work in the Comiskey clubhouse.

JIM SASSETTI......................................

I began five years as a White Sox batboy in 1984 when I was thirteen. I've been interviewed on radio and TV and in the papers, and I've met Jimmy Carter, Jim Belushi, George Wendt, Mr. T, the San Diego Chicken, and the *Sports Illustrated* cover girl. It's been great working for Chicken Willie Thompson, the funniest and best clubhouse man in baseball. He's big, bald, and afraid of snakes. When Richard Dotson brought a live snake in, Willie ran so fast he almost turned white. And then Floyd Bannister brought him a live chicken.

In my experience on the road, Yankee Stadium stands out for the outrageous fans there. Also I was on hand for Tom Seaver's 300th win in New York. That tops my list of thrills, including his big welcome home in Chicago—I felt ecstatic.

Spring training is always great. I got to hang out with Ozzie Guillen. One night at the Sarasota County Fair, a crowd of fifty to a hundred gathered around the booth when Ozzie and I posed with another batboy as a couple of wranglers and a tied-up lady for photographs.

I never saw alcohol or drug abuse. Our g.m. in '89 had chewing tobacco taken off the shelves—the club no longer supplied it, so the players had to buy it on their way to the ballpark. You know, three-fourths of the White Sox attend "baseball chapel" on Sundays.

On the field I was no different from any fan—everyone thinks strategy. I liked watching the fans be characters, like the rowdy drunks during rain delays. And there were some bad moments, like when Julio Cruz got hit in the head by a line drive in the dugout and was out for a couple of minutes. Or when Greg Walker had a seizure when he was taking ground balls during b.p.—the whole team was scared, and Greg missed most of the season.

I was ballboying for an NBC Saturday Game of the Week when I became the focus of attention. There were two on in the eighth inning when a wild pitch headed right for me. I did what I was supposed to do, moved out of the way and took my chair with me. But the ball bounced into the ball bag, and play was stopped while they figured out what to do.

I don't know what I'd be about if I wasn't around baseball.

Jim Sassetti is a Cicero policeman, but continues to work in the White Sox clubhouse.

TED ZEIGLER ....

When I was twelve years old I got to be a ballboy for one game in 1979, but I had three full seasons as batboy from '82-'84.

It was the humor that appealed to me most in the clubhouse. Funny guys like Doug Rader. Tricks on batboys like the kid at Comiskey who was told to cover the foul lines with toilet paper during a rain delay—and did. And I'll never forget Steve Comer, a righthanded pitcher, doing imitations of the whole "Saturday Night Live" crew, especially Dan Aykroyd doing Tom Snyder interviewing Sammy Davis, Jr.: "What the heck are the blues and who gets 'em?"

Buddy Bell became a good friend. And Wayne Terwilliger would pitch batting practice to us, had an arm like a machine, never got tired, kept throwing strikes. As a player, a lanky lefthanded first baseman, I found that the hardest lesson to learn was to discriminate between the bad advice I'd get from my high school coach and the good advice I'd get from someone like Terwilliger.

I can't imagine being out of baseball. I'll play in amateur ball as long as I can, and when I graduate from U-T at Austin I hope to be a math teacher and baseball coach.

My graduation from my dad was a trip to Boston for Ted Williams Day. He arranged for us to get together, and it was quite a thrill for me—I hadn't seen him since I was four.

Kim Zeigler ....

I guess I was about two when I first heard from Dad the code of the clubhouse: what you see here stays here. Still I wasn't prepared for some of the things that happened when I started work, four years as batboy through the '86 season, my junior year at Arlington High School. Like my first game as ballboy, when I was so happy to be out there in uniform down the line that I gave away the first eight or nine balls, till Dad said, "Cut it out." Or like the game when I was fourteen and a woman in the stands kept yelling "I want your hat" at me through all the innings I was on the field. The security guards were all laughing and cheering, especially after the game when she came down to the dugout and said, "I'll give you a kiss for it."

One vivid memory is of a bench-clearing brawl with Kansas City. Afterward, umpire Steve Palermo came over to the dugout and was yelling at me.

Toby Harrah and Buddy Bell were my favorite players. They'd always play through slight injuries. I'd take infield and Buddy would work with me. I played third base—threw right, batted left—for Western Oklahoma Junior College one year, Vernon Junior College one year, and then Tarleton State in Stevenville, Texas. Being in the clubhouse made me realize how hard you have to work as a player. Out of a million guys playing baseball, only six hundred each year are in the Bigs. What I'd like to do is coach baseball at the college level.

DAVID ZEIGLER . . . .

I worked part-time in the home clubhouse in '84 and '85, then was visiting team batboy in '86 and '87. I ended up, though, graduating from high school in Vici, Oklahoma, so that I could play for the Woodward Travellers American Legion team. Then I went to Vernon Junior College.

I'm a young student of the old school. Buddy Bell was my all-around favorite—a family friend and my idol. He and Larry Parrish would stay around the clubhouse after games. The young guys like to go out.

Dick Howser used to keep the humor going in the clubhouse. And I saw Tim Foli pull the sour pie trick. Oh, and I was there when they got Pete Incaviglia as a rookie with the three-man-lift routine. It was fun to be around players like Eddie Murray and Kirby Puckett. Steve Buechele knew I played third base and kept advising me to stay relaxed. One great memory was going to Boston on a road trip—to see Fenway Park, to be in that ballpark, and to think of Ted Williams.

Bill Zeigler was a graduate and trainer at Florida State before becoming trainer for the Senators, then the Rangers. His son Ted is named for Ted Williams, who would critique batting tapes of him and his brothers, all promising schoolboy players. Kim Donald is named for Kim Hammond, Seminoles quarterback, and Don Fauls, head trainer at FSU. David is named for FSU's own Dave Cowens. At present, Ted teaches and coaches at Nichols Jr. High in Arlington; Kim is earning his Master's in History at Tarleton State in Stephenville, planning to teach and coach; and David, who will graduate from U-T, Arlington, having completed his baseball eligibility at TCU, hopes to teach and coach. David made it to spring training once, but as one of only four players without a contract among 150 in camp, he knew he was there as a courtesy and enjoyed every minute. Bill Zeigler is now a year-round trainer on the rodeo circuit.

FRED COSTELLO ....

Through a friend of a friend I got to work in the visiting clubhouse at Candlestick Park. I suited up as batboy for the Giants a couple of times, but I preferred the visiting side because I enjoyed the different atmosphere of different teams. I was surprised at how loose it was, like a party. They were always playing games on each other, and they were always happy. I couldn't wait for the players to get there every day.

I was so in awe of them. I was a big card collector, and I had memorized all their stats. They were like gods to me, and then sometimes I get to know one and I'd think, "Oh, what a jerk." A lot of them had fun with me, would send me to get the key to the batter's box or ask me where the fork balls were, and they'd have me running from the visiting dugout out to Murph in the Giant clubhouse, which is about a twenty-minute run in Candlestick.

Joe Sambito was one player who was always super to me. Now he's my agent. The one who stands out most is Terry Forster, the nicest, funniest guy. He still owes me about $500,000 from playing cards—I was on a roll one day. Once when I was pitching in a DiMaggio Tournament game and the Braves were in town, Forster and Bruce Sutter actually came out and saw me throw for about six innings before they had to leave. That's how nice they were to me.

I was embarrassed more than once. Like the time I tripped over the bullpen mound and fell when I was carrying a water cooler. Another time I was ballboying down the left field line and went for a foul ball. The Phillies third baseman missed the ball because I was late getting out of his way—but neither of us got an error. Once on a Saturday afternoon I delivered a message to Terry Kennedy from a fine-looking lady. "I need to talk to Mr. Kennedy," she said, real sweet. The other guys looked up and saw that she was really good-looking and egged him on until he went up to meet her. And then she starts cussin' and screamin' at him, while the players were all biting their lips to keep from laughing. "Who paid you to do this?" was all he could say to her, and he never found out if it was a set-up. If it was, I wasn't in on it.

The players were not allowed to smoke in the clubhouse or on the field, but they'd sneak into the bathroom to smoke. Batboys would get a fifty-dollar reward for turning them in, but I never would, although other players would tell me who was doing it and try to get me to turn them in.

I actually worked in the clubhouse one season after I signed, so that I was a clubby and a professional player at the same time. I got to face Ozzie Smith and Jose Oquendo one spring, but I don't know if they remembered me as a kid who had shined their shoes. After two seasons in Asheville with the Astros organization, though, I made the 40-man roster for spring and got to play with Danny Darwin, Larry Andersen, Jim Deshaies, and Rick Rhoden, who was always big on my list. They knew me, all right. They'd be throwing their bags and dirty uniforms at me, putting their jocks in my locker to be washed. It was pretty neat to be able to tell them, "I'm not a clubby no more."

My dream in life is to roll into Candlestick Park to pitch against the Giants. I know they've got lots of stuff planned for me, like putting my locker in the shower, but it'll be great. I was on a fast track for a while, my star was shining bright. But I was just a thrower, and I think that's why I got hurt. Now with a reconstructed shoulder I'm hoping to move up to Tucson this season, and then we'll see.

As a batboy I learned so much about how to fill up spare time. As a pitcher that's very important, because you could drive yourself crazy sitting around with nothing to do between appearances.

Fred Costello is still considered a bright pitching prospect, but has gone from the Houston Astros organization to the Giants, so his dream will be modified to wearing the home uniform in Candlestick.

MIKE MULLANE . . . .

I was a batboy for the San Francisco Giants from 1983 to 1986. I always saw baseball as magical, larger than life. I was so in awe my first day, I couldn't speak. The grass of Candlestick seemed like a magic carpet, and those feelings were just enhanced as a batboy. It gets in your blood, becomes part of your life, and you never want to give it up.

It's also a job, a tedious one with long hours, but whenever it would start to get to me I'd tell myself I'm where a million others would love to be. And I'd volunteer to stay late to help unpack on the visitors' side, because it was a thrill to unpack and hang Dale Murphy's uniform. In preparation for the '84 All-Star Game at Candlestick, after the Sunday day game, I packed up for the Giants, cleaned out every locker, washed down the clubhouse including the bathrooms, finished at 3 a.m., slept in the clubhouse, was up at 6 for the work-out day, unpacked all the all-stars, finished the day about 10 p.m.. The game was at 5 the next day, I arrived at 8:30 a.m., and the day ended at 1:30 next morning.

My first game was a pre-season exhibition against Oakland, and at first there was no uniform for me. Then they gave me the smallest they had—size 30 waist, 40 shirt—to ballboy down the line. I soon learned to wear two or three thermals and my Little League pants underneath, to make the uniform fit, and one day I almost passed out from overheating.

I was just in the seventh grade, and in June I asked for a Friday night off so that I could go to a school dance. The players heard me and started kidding me, kind of chanting, "Aren't you queer for the yard?" I misunderstood at first, then realized the true meaning and that being taunted meant they liked me.

I learned so much so fast, a thirteen-year-old hanging around grown men. My dad had warned me about the language I'd hear, things like "fuck" and "shit" and I was really surprised because I had never heard my father use those words. But more important than a new vocabulary I learned values like punctuality, commitment, job before fun, respect not intimidation, responsibility, and sacrifice. I learned that it wasn't all easy, that life's not like "Leave It to Beaver," how to act and talk, to keep eyes and ears open but mouth shut. And I also learned about dippin' and cussin'.

I'll never forget the Saturday afternoon that pitcher Bill Laskey sat next to me in the dugout, the first time I talked with a big-league ballplayer during a game. Bob Brenly was my all-time favorite. He took care of me, giving me gloves and shoes, teaching me fundamentals of catching and hitting, and generally encouraging me. Milt May was another good guy, who'd come out early to throw batting practice to his son and the batboys. Then there was Chili Davis, who finally spoke to me after half a season, saying "What's your name?"

Danny Ozark was the only coach who stayed in the cramped locker room with the batboys, and when he took over as manager in '84 he maintained friendly relations with the kids. It was a change from Frank Robinson, who actually did us a big favor when he removed post-game spreads from the clubhouse after a losing streak. But the real unsung hero of the clubhouse is Murph, our equipment manager Mike Murphy. He puts in untold hours at the ballpark, and we all love him.

The initiation-type pranks are all part of growing up fast at the ballpark. They sent me for the key to the batter's box, for a bag of left-handed curve balls, for a bucket of steam from the trainer—and I fell for them all. But the time I was most embarrassed was late in the '84 season when I ran out to pick up the rosin bag from the mound after the top of the ninth and to shake reliever Mark Davis's hand, thinking he'd saved the game. I didn't realize the game had been tied, it wasn't over. So I pretended I was just checking out the rosin bag. I may have fooled some people in the stands, but I didn't fool any players and they let me know about it.

I've always known that baseball is more than a game. I learned that the clubhouse is a shrine, and I was living out a fantasy being there. There's a passage in Roger Kahn's "Good Enough to Dream" that hits home—he calls baseball "the door to the world of men." It's a comfortable, safe feeling, sitting around any clubhouse with baseball people, just talking.

Mullane stayed on as bullpen catcher with the Giants, while pursuing a degree in Business at St. Mary's with the hope of a front office job in baseball.

MIKE MACKO ....

My dad, Joe Macko, was the business manager of the Dallas-Fort Worth Spurs in Arlington. In '72 he was offered a choice of jobs with the Rangers and took the equipment manager job to get closer to the field. My brother Steve was one of the first Texas batboys. I practically grew up in Arlington Stadium, got to put on a uniform, go on the field, and shag flies as a boy.

Shagging is an important assignment for Texas batboys because of the heat, so that the players don't have to chase a lot of balls during b.p. And Dad says we also have to have lots of substitute batboys available because most of the kids are playing ball themselves. I worked the seasons from '83-'87, then part-time as a clubby in '89 after playing summer ball in '88.

I batboyed for Mike Witt's perfect game against Texas in '84, and for Nolan Ryan's 5,000th strikeout (Rickey Henderson)—I had to keep track of the balls he used, and the one he gave me was the second strike. He's an outstanding guy. I feel fortunate to know him. The day after he pitches he's in the clubhouse at 9 a.m. to lift.

Jim Sundberg's an outstanding citizen, and so is Buddy Bell. I remember when Buddy sold his Jaguar because it needed some work—he ran it without oil. Mickey Rivers was one who always talked to us kids. In fact, the batboys and the players' children were his best friends. He'd go to the race track a lot, but he'd always be giving money to poor people.

Some guys got a bad rap. People didn't like Pete Incaviglia much, but he's a good guy who never dogged it. I remember when they got him with the three-man-lift trick in the clubhouse. Doug Rader got a bad rap in the media, but he'd joke around with the batboys. He's definitely a character, though, he'd pull the phone out of the wall, and we learned to stay out of the dugout when things weren't going well.

Funny things happened on the field and off. I learned not to be too gullible, seeing the sour-cake trick, the bucket of sliders, the key to the batter's box pulled on other kids. I saw Cecil Espy come out of the dugout with a tail on his uniform, made of tape and string and stuck on without him knowing. Guys like Toby Harrah, Mike Hargrove, and Jeff Burroughs might launch water balloons into a marching band in Anaheim. And there was Don Zimmer one day, out to argue with the ump, reaching to throw his tobacco chew on the ground and throwing his false teeth instead.

My best trip was to Milwaukee and Baltimore, with Cooperstown in between for the Hall of Fame Game. From Baltimore Bobby Valentine, who went to school with Larry Speakes, arranged for us to visit the White House. A dozen of us went in two big limos and through a series of security checks. What impressed me most was how we were in this long room and the photographers came through one door at the end, and on cue, like clockwork, the door opens at the other end for President Reagan. He shook hands with each of us and we have the pictures to prove it.

I played at McClennon Jr. College and TCU, but I was never drafted. In 1993 I got my one shot at spring training with the Cardinals in St. Petersburg. But being only one of three in camp without a contract out of a hundred and eighty, I knew it was just a courtesy. I had a great time, but the dream of professional ball was over.

Graduating from TCU, Mike Macko is pursuing a graduate degree in physical therapy.

Ron Nedset ....

Everything I've done for the first time in my life had to do with this job of being a batboy, from '83 to '85 on the home side—my first beer, my first cigarette, my first chew, my first time with a woman. And they all had players in on it.

It all started during the strike of 1981. Jerry Augustine, Cecil Cooper, and some other players worked out at a school near my home, and I got to know them. I asked for a job, and Bob Sullivan said I could help out in the clubhouse until I was sixteen, and then I could get on the payroll and into uniform.

Coop took me under his wing, and though he was never big with the press, he was a classy guy, just like Robin Yount. They never badmouthed anybody, though everyone in baseball talks about others. Jim Gantner, Charlie Moore, Rick Manning, Ted Simmons, Jamie Easterly, Jerry Augustine—these were all good guys. And Danny Darwin, another classy guy but a joker. That team won when everybody pulled for each other. Rod Carew was nice to me, gave me several bats. And Mike Caldwell was a good guy who helped me out, although he may have been a slob with a drug problem. On the other hand, Paul Molitor, who always comes across as a good, straight guy, I found to be selfish and didn't care for him.

Rene Lachemann was really good to me—you know, he had been a batboy. When he bought a station wagon from Robin, I got to drive it to Arizona for him. I still look up to Lach. He'd take me to dinner after a Sunday day game when he came back to Milwaukee with an American League team.

My first road trip was to Seattle, and it was my first long plane flight. Rick Manning was sitting next to me, and when they brought hot towels I asked him what they were. He said, "Oh, after you've had a couple of beers, you roll it up, put it in your mouth, suck on it like breath mints, and no one will know you've been drinking." So I did it, and it squirted all over my clothes.

After I graduated high school in '86 I went to Phoenix College in Arizona for a while, but baseball was my life. I got to appear in the movie *Major League*, as a catcher for the A's, as an A's baserunner in the scene where Corbin Bernsen deliberately boots the ball, and then with mustache and long hair in the Yankees dugout. I had also worked winters at Mike

Hegan's "Grand Slam" facility in Milwaukee, and in '88 I got to catch in the bullpen for the first time. Ted Higuera, Juan Nieves, and Bill Wegman were all on the d.l., and I caught for them at the Stadium when the team was on the road. Dan Plesac told them I could do the job, too, and I was hired as bullpen catcher.

I gave up on being a player when I was offered that job. I had a Major League uniform with my name on the back, and I was making more than I would playing A ball. Gantner, for one, pushed me to try making it as a player, but I see too many guys with more talent who don't get the breaks and never make it up to the big leagues. So here I am, and I know I'll stay in baseball somehow, maybe go into college coaching.

Ron Nedset is promoting athletic shoes and was an assistant baseball coach at the University of Wisconsin-Milwaukee in the 1994 season.

CRAIG BEATTY......................................

When we lived in San Diego I wrote a letter to the Padres, and I was interviewed by their equipment manager Brian Prilaman. When we moved to Washington, he recommended me to Henry Genzale, and that's how I got to be Mariners batboy. My little brother Kevin came aboard in mid-'88.

Two things surprised me at first, the amount of smoking in the clubhouse and the way players snapped after poor performances. Then there were things like scuffed balls. After Rick Rhoden pitches, I'd find balls that were covered with what looked like thumbtack scrapes.

I was lucky the first game I ever worked that John Hirschbeck was the ump, a really nice guy. Of all the players, the one I got closest to was Jim Presley. He'd have me shave his bat handles, sand his bats, and clean off the pine tar. I'd get the bats to be just the way he wanted them.

I was never embarrassed on the field, and I escaped most of the hazing in the clubhouse. I saw new kids tossed into the hot tub, but not me. At the end of my first season though, I did get really embarrassed. Coach Billy Connors had put some clothes for drycleaning in plastic bags in the hallway, and I thought they were garbage and threw them out in the dumpster with the other trash. We discovered next day what had happened, and I remember everybody laughing, especially Mike Schooler and Gene Walter. Well, the story got out and was on the air and in the paper, but Connors was a good sport. He said, "Some bum is happy today, walking around in a $500 suit."

I'd like to be a broadcaster. I've learned as a batboy the lesson of being partial to the home team, as a fan and employee, but being able to report as well.

Craig Beatty is majoring in Communications
at Washington State University.

BEN GRIEVE ....

I got my job with the Texas Rangers through my dad, who is the general manager of the club. I always enjoyed baseball as a Little League player, so being a batboy hasn't really changed my feelings about the game at all. I enjoy going out early for batting practice every day before a game, hitting with some of the players' kids. And every few days I get to throw to the pitching coach, Tom House.

I guess probably the funniest things to me are whenever the players tease the batboys, like when Jeff Russell told a new batboy to go out and find the key to the batter's box. Players do funny things to each other, like putting shaving cream on their hats without them knowing. During the game, in the dugout, they spray alcohol on each other's shoes and then use a lighter to set them on fire. You never know it till you feel the fire coming up your leg. I should know because they've gotten me with it a couple of times.

If I ever have grandchildren, I think I'd tell them that the best thing about being a batboy was just being around the players, getting to go out with them, shag fly balls, take a little b.p. with them, and stuff like that. And I could tell them about Bob Brower, who had this pet boa constrictor that he always used to bring into the clubhouse. Cecilio Guante hated it, and every once in a while Bob would put a fake snake into Cecilio's locker and scare him half to death. The one guy I'd pick who is different from what people think is Pete Incaviglia. People in the media get on him a lot for being mean to the fans, but to everyone around the clubhouse he's just a nice funny guy who is always fun to be around.

I haven't seen any serious vices in the clubhouse, though some players do chew tobacco. Players have a pool down in spring training every year for the NCAA basketball tournament but none of them are heavy bettors.

Center fielder for Arlington Martin High School,
Ben Grieve was the second player chosen in the
1994 amateur draft—by the A's.

LUKE FERA......................................

My dad runs the communications at County Stadium. I was at Arrowhead High School when I started working in the visiting clubhouse in June of '87. Then I was on the home side from mid-'88 through '89.

What surprised me at first was that I could be physically so close to the players. My first experience with an umpire on the field had to be with the whiniest big baby around—I won't say who. Someone was called safe on a close play at second, and I was walking balls out to the ump when I saw the replay on the screen. I muttered, "Wow, he really was out," and the ump heard me and growled, "You better keep your mouth shut." But most of them are good guys—Steve Palermo and Rich Garcia were my favorites.

Another time I got yelled at on the field was when a passed ball came right to me at the screen, and I reacted as if it was a foul ball so I caught a ball that was in play, with B. J. Surhoff screaming, "Don't touch it!" The runner was awarded an extra base, but it didn't really matter—the White Sox were beating the Brewers 10-1.

The visiting clubhouse was a lot of fun. The greatest time was telling jokes for hours with George Brett. Reggie was nice to me. Once, he was walking through the clubhouse with his shower shoes on, and I was carrying a pile of towels and stumbled over his feet. He pushed me, pretty hard, but then apologized and explained that his feet were very tender with ingrown toenails. On the Blue Jays, George Bell, Dave Stieb, and Ernie Whitt were all nice guys—but they had the one player who gave me a problem. He accused me of stealing his bats, but another player had put them in his own locker. Minnesota was a great team to work for. Puckett, Gaetti, Hrbek, Blyleven, and Viola were all a lot of fun. Tom Kelley was a joker, too—he yelled at me once to get the phone and I got an ear full of shaving cream.

The whole experience taught me when to keep my mouth shut, not to question things when you don't fully understand the situation, what hard work is all about—"You're there for them" is the message—and not to take things personally, to keep a sense of humor.

Luke Fera played a batboy in the movie Major League. *He works as a standup comedian, but keeps baseball out of his act to "keep that experience for myself."*

PAYTON MORRIS ....

My dad had worked as an equipment man in Chicago, and he got me an interview with the Braves. I started as batboy in '89.

Lonnie Smith was especially friendly to me. Dale Murphy was a real good guy. I hated to see him go, but not long afterward I was watching him play for Philadelphia against the Mets on TV and it was as if he'd never been here.

Jerry Crawford is one ump who likes to play around with the bats with batboys. I think he was working the Sunday game with the Mets when I was down the foul line during a long afternoon of intermittent showers. A line drive came toward me and I caught the ball in my glove, just barely out of my chair in a half sitting position, and got a big hand from the few fans who were left.

I had a birthday during a Fourth of July road trip, and Dad had a cake delivered for me in the Phillies visiting clubhouse. Everyone had a good laugh because they got me with the old sour cake routine, and I ended up with my face in it.

The main lesson I got from the job is that hard work pays off.

Payton Morris transferred from Georgia Tech to Liberty University for a double major in Sports Management and Athletic Training, and right after graduation he will go to the Red Sox club in Lynchburg as assistant trainer.

DAN O'ROURKE ....

For three years I worked in the Phillies clubhouse and got to suit up maybe five or ten times, but I was a regular batboy in '88 and '89. I was also playing ball at Northeast High School. We went undefeated my senior year, but I couldn't start for that team and gave up on my hopes for a career as a player.

One of the first things I remember in the clubhouse is thinking, "Holy cow, this is Mike Schmidt sitting next to me." But he turned out to be moody and not one of the guys. Larry Bowa and George Vukovich were the guys I admired. They had the fire in their eyes and the will to win, and they cared about the little things and the little people, too. Then there's Lenny Dykstra. He's such a slob we had to put a spittoon in his locker or he'd just spit on the floor.

There were a lot of funny things—John Kruk doing his Knute Rockne routine, Roger McDowell setting fire to Tony Taylor's shoes during the anthem, umpire Jerry Crawford teasing me with the bat at the plate. The funniest of all was pitcher Dave Palmer, a pretty good hitter when he was with the Phillies, stealing third and tripping himself up on a pop-up slide and landing on his head.

If there's any negative to the experience, it's the treatment of and attitude toward women that you see—it's not what I'd want to follow. But everyone who likes baseball should see the inside stuff—the cars, the talk, the clothes, the reality of players as men.

Dan O'Rourke is an assistant in the Houston Astros clubhouse.

TONY PASTORE ....

After three years as a clubby I got to be home batboy, but it was a connection in the front office that got me the job in the first place.

Kenny Howell treated me like a big brother. He was the best tipper, too, along with Roger McDowell. Lenny Dykstra was real quiet when he first came over from the Mets. The next year he got more uppity, calling team meetings and like that. Everything has to be perfect for him. And he does strange things, like putting the donut on the bat before going onto the field. I asked him why he does that, and he said, "No reason." Maybe it's a ritual for him.

I learned a lot about players' lives. That it's not just the game, that baseball is the first thing they do in a working day. They do benefits and they work for the Players' Association, and often the game itself is the least important thing. For me, I can't wait for the game to start, so I can rest a little.

Tony Pastore was in the Sports Management
program at Temple University, and is now
pursuing an acting career in New York.

TIM MURNIN ....

In the fall of '87 I wrote a letter to Buddy Bates, the Cardinals equipment manager, and he called me in for an interview in December. I was hired about a month later.

I was a fan before but not really a knowledgeable one. The players are more normal than I thought they'd be, a bunch of kids really, down to earth and not arrogant. Ozzie Smith is quiet in the clubhouse, but Tony Pena kids around so much, so aggressively, making fun of everyone, that I was almost scared of him in my first year. By the second year we got along and then I was sorry when he was gone. He had written to me, "To Tim, my man, anything for you."

Whitey was a brilliant manager, able to psych up his players. His clubhouse is different from most. There's no cardplaying after two-and-a-half hours before game time, no TV, no radio, no games, no videos, no video games—he wants concentration on baseball. And there's no post-game spread—which makes our job easier. I saw no race problems in our clubhouse, no drinking, no drugs, and the only gambling was NFL pools, Indy 500 pools, and Kentucky Derby pools.

Several of the players impressed me—Bob Horner for his cleverness in financial matters, Tom Brunansky for his incredible memory for every pitch in every game, and Danny Cox, who got a bad rap in the press when the public didn't know the facts behind his pushing of a photographer. Ken Dayley and Todd Worrell were fun. On our road trip to Chicago in '88, they took me and Tony Simokaitis to a congenial, fun-loving place where the waitresses and customers yell at each other. Dayley wouldn't let us sit down until Worrell's name was pronounced correctly.

My best clubhouse story is about Joe Magrane. When Brunansky came over in '88, he took measure of Magrane right away—a big, good-looking guy quite confident about his attraction for girls—and planned an elaborate hoax. Sent him a telegram from GQ asking for a photo spread, to come out to the ballpark at 10 a.m. with all his suits. It's 96 degrees in August, and Magrane is modeling suits and bats for a couple of hours, with the team photographer doing the shoot.

Magrane is all excited and rushes out to buy the magazine the next month. Nothing there. Then he gets another telegram. "Roses are red / Violets are blue / You've been had by your teammates / There is no GQ." Joe threw a plate full of shaving cream in the photographer's face, but it took him awhile to figure out who was behind it. The next spring, when he was featured in GQ, he sent a framed copy of the piece to Bruno.

Those three years as batboy was the greatest experience of my life. When I applied to St. Louis University, it was Buddy Bates who wrote my letter of recommendation, and my scholarship application got a recommendation from Whitey Herzog.

Tim Murnin's transition from Cardinals
clubhouse to college campus was smooth.

BOB MICAL ....

I was seventeen when I started in 1980, and Jim Schmakel told me three basic rules. First, I had to maintain the level of my grades in school. Second, my main job was to cater to the players. Third, I had to clear things with him, and if he said no to what they asked for he'd take the rap with the players.

I learned that no matter how big you are it's important to display professionalism, to enjoy the camaraderie, and to be a team player. Alan Trammell, for example, was very down-to-earth, liked to give me shoes since I was a shortstop in school. Larry Herndon took care of me, Lance Parrish played catch with me, and there were other real nice guys including Darrell Evans, Dan Petry, Johnny Grubb, and Tim Brookens. Some of the umps were good guys, too—Durwood Merrill and Tim Haller.

They fooled around with me, made me feel like I belonged. Gates Brown asked me for the key to the batter's box, sent me to Don Zimmer, who went along with it. The one exception was Ricky Peters. He was a nice guy at first, when he was on the bench, but when he became a starter in the outfield in '80 his whole attitude changed. He didn't last long.

I had an especially good relationship with coach Dick Tracewski. We're both Polacks. Sometimes Jim Schmakel would ask my mom to prepare the clubhouse food for the players, and Dick always would say to me, "When are we gettin' some good perogi?"

I was always embarrassed when I was asked for an autograph, like walking out to the bus with the team after a game on the road. But one time, I just said, "No, I'm the batboy," and pointed out Dave Cowart, the other batboy, who signed as if he was a player.

After '84, I found I just couldn't go to the ballpark and watch the game in the stands with the rest of the fans. It was too much of a comedown. But that last season was the ultimate—being on the field in uniform when we won the World Series championship. Nothing would ever match that high. We batboys divided a full share, about $12,000.

Bob Mical graduated from Lawrence Tech
with a degree in Electrical Engineering.

DAVE COWART ....

In 1980 my mom cut out a clipping and wrote to the stadium operator. Jim Schmakel saw the letter and first called my principal—Sister Anne Marie at St. Andrew's—about my grades. He interviewed me and I got the job and then my friend Bob Mical. Sister was a pretty good baseball fan and would let us out early to work for the Tigers.

I learned a lot about life from Jim Schmakel. He was concerned about our education, our direction, and also our finances. Every year he has a reunion for batboys. When Roger Craig became manager of the Giants, Jim gave me the chance to go to San Francisco to work. He saw to it that we got to go on road trips, but he'd never take us to New York. And we couldn't shag flies at home because a kid had gotten hurt.

It was a thrill to shag flies in Fenway Park and stand at the plate looking out at the wall. I loved Boston, Bunker Hill and all. I also loved a trip to Anaheim, where I'd gotten nine tickets for my relatives out there, and we saw Rod Carew come up in the last of the ninth with the bases loaded, and hit what looked like a game-winning grand slam until Chet Lemon caught it right out of the stands. It was a happy trip home.

Everybody cared on that Tigers team. We helped Milt Wilcox move after his divorce, and he took us out on his boat. Walt Terrell would goof with the kids and stay around while we unpacked after a road trip. Billy Consolo, the utility coach, teased everyone, but especially Gibby about his Maalox. He started blowing a whistle for batting practice, but after a couple of days the whistle didn't sound—Gibby had taken the ball out of it.

Sparky Anderson was one of the best guys, a real motivator. He came to my house after my high school graduation. He always made us feel good, would never leave the clubhouse without looking around and pointing to the kids and saying, "Three of the greatest ever right here." Still, the first real conversation I ever had with him, was after I'd graduated from college and come back from working overseas in China for a year.

One interesting story stands out. On Opening Day in 1982, Richie Hebner, who had just been traded to the Tigers, became ill prior to game time and I was asked to drive him back to his hotel. He told me that when he was trying to find the ballpark he thought the stadium was a factory. Richie was quite a character. After Sparky pulled him for a pinch hitter one time he proceeded to the locker room and took a bat to the scale that was next to the bat rack, bending it in half. Next day he found a bill for it on his locker stool and his uniform jersey draped over the scale. The whole team made good fun of the incident.

Dave Rozema was also good for stories. One time after Dan Petry pitched during the 1984 World Series, Rozema sat on Petry's locker stool and put on Petry's uniform jersey. There were so many out-of-town reporters during the Series that it was common for some of them not to recognize players. Rozema conducted an entire interview and the reporter didn't realize his mistake till Petry came out of the shower.

I think Bob Mical's impression of Ricky Peters is based on just a misunderstanding. When Ricky came to the park a little late for batting practice, his jockstrap was misplaced in his locker. He sorta lost it, started cussing, and threw a chair in my direction. We found the missing jock in his locker, but I was pretty shaken up about the incident. When Sparky got wind of it, he called me into his office and explained the pressures of the big leagues to me.

My biggest thrills as batboy came in the 1984 World Series—the fourth game when Alan Trammell hit two home runs; then the Tigers winning it in the fifth game, with my parents in the stands. That was the last ballgame my mom ever saw, because she died of cancer later that year. During that period baseball sure helped me get through a lot of hard times.

On a visit back to Tiger Stadium in 1990, I brought my son Alex and nephew Brian into the clubhouse. I got to introduce them to Sparky, Walt Terrell, and Alex Grammas, who gave little Alex a ball (probably thinking I had named him after him). Jim Schmakel asked if I would mind working for him again. I thought maybe one of his kids had gotten sick or something. I said, "Sure, I'd love to work for you again." "Just kidding," he said. "I'd never let anyone come back—all the shoe-shining, picking up after everyone, etcetera, would only erase all your fond memories." That's why I now sit in the stands as just another fan, but in years past it seems like I was so much more.

Dave Cowart earned his degree in Electrical Engineering from the University of Detroit in 1985.

TONY ANTONIO ....

I took over for my cousin Dave Cowart in '85 and worked five seasons. My family wanted me to stay, but I learned that I could make more money cleaning rugs.

The first couple of years were fun, but then I lost interest. I was surprised at how much time was spent on cleaning clothes, toilets, and shoes. I liked being there but not doing all that stuff. They'd kid me and ask me to smile.

I liked Kirk Gibson. Jim Schmakel says that Gibby never liked batboys, but he seemed to like me, talked to me like a normal person. Mike Henneman, Jeff Robinson, Mike Heath, and Dave Bergman were all good guys, good tippers too. Walt Terrell and Lou Whitaker were nice, laidback guys, and there was classy Alan Trammell. Then there was Hernandez. If you called him Willie he wouldn't answer, would give you a dirty look—he only knew you if you called him Guillermo.

The most exciting moment was the four-game sweep of Toronto in '87. For winning the division, four batboys split a half-share. The most embarrassing moment was missing the infield ball tossed back to the dugout. And there were other moments of fun—spring training and getting only five hours' sleep a night, seeing Jack Morris in the whirlpool at eight in the morning, having fun with the visiting White Sox—especially Ozzie Guillen, having dinner on the road with Sparky Anderson and trainer Pio DiSalvo, watching practical joker Dave LaPoint giving hotfoots and burning shoelaces, having Mike Heath joke around with me with the bats.

What did I learn? Nothing much, really.

Tony Antonio attends Henry Ford Community
College and stays away from Tiger Stadium.

TRACY (RED) LUPPE ....

I worked as a paperboy at the press entrance to Three Rivers, and with two weeks left in the '85 season John Houlahan, the equipment manager, asked me to fill in as batboy. I did a good job, so I started full-time in '86. I also became assistant trainer for the Penguins.

The players would send me for a couple of feet of white line or the key to the batter's box, and you fall for it because you're a kid, in awe of the players at first, and you're happy they want you to do something for them, and then you realize it's a joke.

I got closer to the hockey players—they're closer in age. But the groupie girls are there for both—they'll do anything to be around players. My first road trip to Montreal was a big thrill, maybe moreso because of hockey. But on a twelve-day trip later on, to Houston, Atlanta, and Cincinnati, I learned what it's like to be on the road. The Astros equipment manager, Dennis Liborio, is a great hockey fan and I was able to give him signed sticks from Mario Lemieux and Paul Coffey. They were real signatures, by the way, though I can sign some baseball and hockey names pretty well. I had heard about the mongoose trick in Cincinnati so they didn't get me with that one, but they got our strength coach, Warren Sipp.

It really is fun, and especially exciting when the team's winning. My biggest worry was always tripping and falling out on the field, but it didn't happen. I learned to be very guarded about mentioning players' names—that's part of the code of the clubhouse—but I can tell you that everyone calls Wally Backman "Dirtball" and I don't mind saying a couple of things about Dave LaPoint. For one thing, he has a full-length Bartles & Jaymes poster on the front of his locker. And for another, he has this laughing box that he brings out to ride anyone who has a bad performance, going 0 for 4, and like that.

Tracy Luppe graduated from Point Park College with a degree in accounting, is working as an accountant at the University of Pittsburgh while working toward an MBA at Robert Morris University—but continues to work the Pirates and Penguins clubhouses during their seasons.

ERIC WINEBRENNER ....

Bill Beck, who was the Royals travelling secretary at the time, belonged to our church, and he told me how to go about applying for the job. I was 12 when I was hired in 1980, and my first job was chasing balls in the stands during batting practice. What surprised me most was that big-league players would talk to a twelve-year-old. It was a neat experience to have Jamie Quirk and then George Brett come over and introduce themselves to me.

They sent me for a bucket of steam, for the key to the batter's box—I got all the old initiation jokes. Then there was one new one. One time I threw the lead bat into the on-deck circle and it split in half. Dick Howser had equipment manager Al Zych write a note to me, saying I had to pay for it, that $50 would be deducted from my pay, and it was signed Herk Robinson, Vice-President. I showed the letter to Brett and he was livid, screamed at the public relations v.p. Dean Vogelaar, "It's my goddam bat, if he pays anyone he'll pay me, and he ain't gonna pay." All this time, Howser was taking it in and giggling. He rarely did anything like that. His death was rough. He was a very special man to me.

The worst part of the job was unpacking late at night after a road trip. I also hated taking balls around for autographs. Fortunately we had one clubhouse guy who could do all the signatures.

The best part was getting to know the players. Sometimes they'd escape the media by hiding in the training room after a bad game, and they'd send us for their beer. George Brett gets a lot of things said about him that he doesn't deserve—that he's stuck-up, that he's gay—but he isn't either. He's one of the nicest people I've ever met—he'd do anything in the world for you. He'd invite us for barbecue, Bret Saberhagen would have pool parties for us, Bo Jackson would have us over to dinner at the end of the season, and Buddy Black was a great guy, too.

I don't remember much about my first World Series in 1980, just Pete Rose and playing catch with Bake McBride in the outfield, and media people running around everywhere. But 1985 I remember very well. Quarterbacking for my high school, on the first play of my senior year I broke my ankle, and I had eight screws and a plate put in. I couldn't batboy because I couldn't run, but I was out of the cast then and drove to St. Louis, suited up, and sat on the bench.

I was shocked by the drug scandal in '84. I never knew what was going on, never saw any evidence of drugs. Willie Aikens was kinda different, didn't talk with us, and U. L. Washington the same. You could tell there was some kind of racial problem, but usually one on one—not like St. Louis where I hear the blacks and whites don't talk. By the way, I thought it was a good idea when they made Brett and Frank White co-captains.

My biggest embarrassment came one game against the Brewers when I was working down the right field line. It was either Cecil Cooper or Ben Ogilvie who hit one down the line and Steve Palermo gave a circle signal that went from foul to fair. With Clint Hurdle playing the other way it should have been a triple, but I tried to play it and it bounced off my glove. They teased me some about that, especially Zych, who was always mumbling and grumbling with a cigar in his mouth.

I can't sit down and watch a baseball game any more. It just bores me. For eight years, when the game was on I had something to do. My last season was '88, and by the next summer I was in the Police Academy. I learned some good lessons: that you gotta set priorities, that you have to work for what you want, that you gotta treat everyone else the way you wanna be treated. Even if you had a rotten day at the plate or on the mound you treat other players and reporters with decency and respect, like Brett, Black, and Saberhagen. I use that now, the lesson of mutual respect.

Eric Winebrenner drives a squad car in the Central Patrol Division of the Kansas City Police.

STEVE FRIEND ....

From 1986 to 1988 I was a batboy with the Montreal Expos. My Uncle Mike came to me one day when I was mowing the lawn with news of the job. My first instinct was to say no—I was only thirteen and very shy, eh? But I talked with my brother and my father, and they told me to go for it, that it was the chance of a lifetime.

Before I got the job, going to Olympic Stadium to see an Expos game was like an adventure for me. My parents would pile me and my brother in the car, and I'd hardly say a word on the way because I was so excited. When you're young, seeing Olympic Stadium is a thrill, and even though you're growing through the years the Stadium seems to grow along with you. They were still constructing the tower which we hoped would hold the roof, but that came much later. People in Montreal often complained about this billion-dollar stadium that still didn't have a roof, but I can still remember the feeling of awe, sitting in the stands, just to be looking at the field. It was pretty spectacular, and I never imagined in those pre-batboy days that one day I'd be running out on the field.

Opening game 1986 came a lot faster than I thought it would. I remember waiting to be taken into the clubhouse for the first time—one of the longest moments of my life. But then, despite the feeling of being so much smaller, I was introduced around and began to feel like I'd be one of the guys to people I'd been watching for years. I soon learned that players were special for athletic abilities, but they were just ordinary guys doing what they enjoy doing and what they do best. They immediately made me feel at home.

The first time I suited up, put the Expo uniform on, it felt pretty weird. I'd played Little League, but it was a lot different putting that uniform on—and not just because everything was too big. Game time approached and for the first time I walked slowly onto the field through the tunnels, hearing everyone in the stands, the players walking out patting me on the back.

The instant I saw the stands I panicked. I felt like everyone was looking at me—which you soon learn is completely false. I walked over into the dugout, not knowing what to expect. The national anthems came on. What to do? I looked around at all the players to see what they were doing—taking off their hats and lining up in an official manner—and I did the same thing.

Uh-oh, 7:35, game time. I worked the first game as ballboy. The first time a foul ball went to the backstop I ran so fast I couldn't believe it. I was only on the field for two seconds, but it felt like an hour. Never ran so fast in my life. Get the ball and get off. Try and be in the eye of people as short a time as possible. I remembered what the old batboy had told me as he left with a smile, that he'd slipped once on the pitcher's mound during a rain delay, fell on his back and dirtied his uniform, with everyone watching because nothing else was going on. I kept thinking about that, but the first game went better than I thought. Next day, cleaning shoes in the clubhouse, several of the boys came over, patted me on the back, and said good job. The feeling of relief was nice, eh?

With a guy like Tim Raines on your team, so many things happen every day, funny little stories, it's ridiculous. His nickname is Rock. Bob Seger's song "Like a Rock" is one of his favorites. That song came on the radio and he was doing lip-sync, wearing only his towel. Had the facial expressions down, too. Had a lot of other hobbies—video games, movies, wrestling. Rock was also a great card player, good at bluffing. When they played cassino he was the guy to beat. You had to hear him laugh, the kind of laugh that's impossible to describe. Irritating, when you hear that laugh echoing through the clubhouse when he'd go on a winning streak.

I guess the practical joke master used to be the guy who wore No. 5, Reid Nichols. Used to call him Jughead, because he looked like the character from Archie Comics. He brought us the famous dead mouse sandwich. He found a dead mouse someplace and all that week that dead mouse kept appearing in people's gloves, shoes, caps—everywhere.

A memorable year for me was 1987, the year of the creation of Zilla. Zilla was the one creature that could induce fear in all the players. Zilla was the symbol of their errors on and off the field. A one-foot statuette of Godzilla, he was passed along to players when they did stupid things like tripping, missing an easy catch, or eating too much. At first he was just naked Zilla there, green and red, but then we got him a cap and Expos uniform, number 0 on his back, little glove made from a strip of leather, little bat.

Once Rock was running home from third base on a knock way deep in left field, and he tripped about four feet from the plate, fell right on his face. After the game he went into the clubhouse and saw Zilla sitting on his locker as the symbol of his trip. It was that kind of thing—errors that people in the stands wouldn't get, like missing signals, running when he wasn't supposed to, trying to steal when it was definitely impossible. But also times in the clubhouse, like dropping a plateful of food, would automatically get the Zilla for the day. It was part of my job as batboy to bring Zilla out every day and put him on the bench so he could watch the game and pick his next victim. Actually the person that got Zilla last got to choose, and some players wondered if it was worth it, because if nothing earned it they were stuck with Zilla for another day.

That was the year I took my first and only road trip with the guys, to Pittsburgh and New York. It was my first plane ride and I was really nervous, hardly said a word on the bus ride to the airport, though I was sitting with Wallace Johnson, Herm Whittingham, and Dave Engle, all players I was pretty close to. It was a chartered flight. The players climbed in, fixed chairs so they could play cards, talk, heckle the stewardess, and all that. A good time. I just sat in the back of the plane with the guys I liked.

I was nervous when the sign came on to tie your seatbelts. I looked around and no one was nervous, no one was tying their seatbelts as we went to the runway. These people travel, they're always on the road, in the air, for them it's nothing. We were picking up speed and Hubie Brooks stood up and leaned forward, sticking out his arms, hovering around. I loosened up, the flight went well, and the bus ride into Pittsburgh was unbelievable, with singing, the guys in a really good mood, adding their own variations about [manager] Buck Rodgers.

Five days in Pittsburgh, then off to New York. Wallace Johnson was telling me that when they play "We Will Rock You" in Shea Stadium you need seatbelts in the dugout because people in the stands would shake it so much you'd fall off the bench. I knew it was a joke, playing on my anxiety about going to the big city. He said people in the stands would throw switchblades and bring in twelve-gauge shotguns, stories like that, just to make me nervous. I was.

It was the night of a big storm, and flying just above the thunderheads we could see lightning all around. There was some turbulence, but the only one to get a little queasy was Jim Fanning, Expos manager a couple of years back in the time of Warren Cromarti and Bill Lee, the Spaceman, now one of our radio announcers. Coming in on New York the thunderheads cleared a little and I got my first glimpse of the city. I couldn't believe it, all the lights at 2 a.m. I'd never seen anything that big man-made—hard to describe how I felt.

Next day I saw the big difference between working at Olympic Stadium and at Shea. At Olympic, 20,000 was a good day. No comparison to Shea—the atmosphere, the people in the parking lot with barbecues making a day out of going to a baseball field. They were all there at 3 p.m., four or five hours before the game. Buses stopped beside the entrance, crowded with people wanting autographs. Guards had to push the way through people so we could get in.

On the first day in New York, guys from the visiting clubhouse decided to play a little joke on me. They came over and said I should go see the visiting clubhouse manager and ask him about his mother who is a famous ballerina. I kind of wanted to fit in, and I guess I was kind of innocent, so I went over to see him and start talking to him. Then out popped the question: "The guys were telling me about your mother, a ballerina...." He got mad, just started yelling at me, "You guys are always getting on me." He really rubbed my nose in it, and I felt like dirt.

I went back to the clubbies, said, "What's the deal? He chewed my ass off for that." They said, "You didn't really ask him that?" They were all acting surprised, then said that his mother was crippled, couldn't walk, had been in a wheelchair twenty years, and he was really sensitive about it. For three days then I felt like dirt, and every time I passed the man he'd give me a dirty look.

On the last day I knew I had to go see him, and I explained the clubbies had told me to say it. He said, "What? They didn't tell you? It's all a joke. There's nothing wrong with my mother. It's just one of our tricks—we had one guy going for over a week." I never felt that bad. Hard to believe. They said they only did it to confirm the rumor that guys from New York had no heart.

That little trip brought me closer to the guys—Wallace Johnson who was always looking out for me, Herm Winningham who took me out for my first taste of buffalo wings in Pittsburgh, Dave Engle who used to go to the movies with me. Then there was Jeff Parrett—used to call him "The Bird"—was always the last to leave the clubhouse, and for four years we'd talk about anything. George Wright was the first guy I really became close to. He was a bit younger than everybody else and now he's got a successful career in Japan.

It's tough to lose friends like that, but in baseball the movement is so rapid that you just start getting close to someone and they move on. Working on the visiting side, I got to see a lot of them when they came to town. And I get a Christmas card from Wallace Johnson every year.

Steve Friend is off to university now, studying
Administration Science.

Wes Patterson ....

I was thirteen when I started working for the Royals in 1983 as a shag boy in the visitors clubhouse, then moved up to batboy and ballboy, and retired from the field at age 21.

A routine day goes like this. I get to the ballpark at 3 p.m. and I'm runnin' around with my hair on fire. Help put out uniforms from the dry cleaner, check on lockers and straighten them up, run errands, pick up mail from upstairs, press releases, stats on other ball clubs, get it all to coaches. Then I walk around, make sure each player has sanitary hose, help Joe Corona (George Brett calls him Meatball) who takes care of umpires, too. 3:30: take baseballs to umpires' room, clean it up, shine their shoes, hang up their underwear and T-shirts from the evening before, put out fruit, sandwiches, ice, Cokes, coffee.

Batting practice usually starts at 5, but at 4 you have guys who hit extra. So I have to hustle back to the clubhouse, make sure that all cracked bats are taken out of the mobile bat rack, get plenty of rosin and pine tar, the doughnut, the weighted bat, and I push all that down to the dugout. I designed the bat rack down there. I put out the gamers for each player in his own personal slot, the veterans and the regular starters. The rest are put in the extra rack. Then I bring down the helmets, leaving them in the bag, and the catcher's gear, and then the towels. Next come the batting practice balls, the water jug, and Gatorade.

At 4:30 I'd go get dressed if I was batboy and return to the field for b.p., play catch with coaches while the guys are stretching, then shag balls while they hit till 5:45. Then I'd clean out the home run balls hit during b.p. That turf is like a heat wave in b.p., especially in August when the humidity in Kansas City is really bad, and there's no breeze on the field. They quit at 6:10 and I'd pick up extra bats, pine tar and stuff, put them in their spot. While the visiting team is hitting, two of us would shine the catchers' gear, shine the helmets, and put them in the rack in order for batters.

If you're working inside, you take care of the manager, get him what he needs, chew, sunflower seeds, gum, scouting reports. In the clubhouse you pick up dirty clothes, get their bags if they're going on the road. Got to take care of the coaches—they're the ones who act like they're your dads—shine their dress shoes if they wore them. When the team goes out for b.p. there's a lot of preparation in the clubhouse. Cut up fruit (Bo Jackson can eat a whole watermelon) and prepare for the meal after the game. Some guys need their cars washed. You have to keep the locker room clean.

When b.p. is over you go from first gear to fifth gear, no in between. When those players hit that door, they're thirsty, they got the munchies, they start peeling clothes off. Thirty-five are declothing, with guys saying, "Hey, Wesley, I need this, that, I lost my T-shirt, I need socks, I need gloves," and you're separating uniforms to be washed and picking up clothes.

6:30 to 7 is free time, but it can be taken up by taking baseballs and bats around to get autographed, p.r. stuff, or running small errands. Sometimes George Brett, if he's in a slump, asks me to come out to the cage and I'll set balls on a tee for him for thirty minutes and watch the most beautiful swing in baseball. Or sometimes, because I pitched for a year in junior college, one of the pitchers will ask me to play longtoss with him. But this can also be a critical time to get an education. A lot of guys go into the video room and relax. We call it "the Village" and the two guys who run it are called "Three Card" and "Village Idiot."

Game time as batboy: go to the umpires' room, pick up baseballs. I'd take Gatorade and towels to the bullpen, wipe off the bullpen coach's special chair, and take a minute to jack around with the "right field gang," a bunch of groupies, people who are in lawn chairs waiting to buy tickets at 2 p.m. even though they don't go on sale until 6:30—night workers, I guess, who are big fans.

7:15: go back to dugout, make sure there are plenty of towels, chew, seeds, gum. 7:25: national anthem. 7:30: umpires come out, I place ball and rosin bag on top of pitching rubber, come back to dugout, manager comes back with lineup and I take it to the pressbox. It's weird to think that a guy who makes six bucks an hour is the man who controls the start of the game. Everyone thinks it's the umpire saying "play ball" or the pitcher throwing the first pitch. Nope—it's me.

I stand outside the dugout, and when the pitcher says he's ready, I twirl the towel, and they start their little theme song and they take the field. It's really a weird feeling to be in control, Opening Day in front of 42,000 screaming fans, and you got the towel, getting ready to make 'em erupt. It makes you feel like you're body-slinging Hulk Hogan in Madison Square Garden heading for the title. Well, I guess it's not that exciting, but it's a neat feeling. I do that, they take the field, the rest is cake.

The batboy takes balls out to the umpire. We do it sprinting, two balls at a time. I'm not bragging but I've had every Major League umpire say that we were the best in the league at staying on top of the game. I always blew that off until we were in the playoffs and World Series and National League umpires were asking me why I don't teach the guys in the NL to do this. It's a tradition and reputation that's been passed down here.

I feel that we are the best because we take pride in what we do. Our motto is, if you're not tired at the end of the ballgame from sprinting to the plate, you didn't work. It's the batboy's discretion if a ball stays in the game or not—that's another neat thing. You get good at this when you can pick up a foul ball and feel it and tell if it's gonna stay in the game or not. If you take it to the umpire and he doesn't throw it back, you know you've learned how to do it.

Before the first inning is over you have to make sure the shower has plenty of soap and shampoo, you start washing the clothes from b.p., and you run some personal errands for players, like giving keys to a wife, cash a check, or George Brett says, "Take my golf clubs and put 'em in Gleaton's car."

If you're working in the clubhouse during the game, it's hard to know who's winning unless you hear it on the radio. You're washing clothes, making salads, setting the table for dinner. Time flies. There's barely enough time to finish errands and put out clothes. Sometimes as clubhouse guy you get to play psychologist or group therapist. Pitcher gets knocked out of a game, sometimes they go on a tirade, start throwing things. Here I am, making five bucks an hour, and I'm sitting next to Mark Gubicza making a million, and I'm telling him to relax, calm down, and if I'm lucky I cheer him up. Meatball's good at this, too, he's a stand-up comedian.

After the game they make a total mess. Looks like the movie "Animal House." I clean up the bench, get the balls, bats, Gatorade, gloves, hats. It's hard to find someone's can of Copenhagen or contact case after the lights go out on the field. In the clubhouse there are errands to run, messages to deliver. Some guys have friends on the visiting team. Brett will say, "Tell Wade Boggs I'll be out in ten minutes." And when an umpire says he wants something, he means he wants it now.

After all the players are gone, eleven or midnight, we can relax, get to eat the food, clean up, wash dishes, do the shoes, straighten the lockers, hang up uniforms—a pitcher can go through six shirts a day. Leaving the clubhouse around 2 a.m., in the summertime it's great, because you can sleep till noon the next day. But it becomes a problem for high school kids in September. It's hard when you have to go to class at 8 a.m. On Saturday you get to sleep in and it's great again.

I keep a journal, you know, with lots of anecdotes and a list of baseball terminology. There are words for everything and names for everybody in the clubhouse. I'm gonna write a book myself one day. There's so much joking around, but the more they get on you the more you know they like you. A batboy is usually like a silent member—you see what goes on but can't really explain it. And I'd like to tell my best baseball story—off the field, a week in Palm Springs at George Brett's house. Other stories are incriminating, not to ballplayers but to me. I've done several things that could have gotten me fired, but then again I've done things that I feel are worth getting fired for, like donating autographed baseballs to charities.

The most memorable thing I can tell was my first day on the field. I was 5'1", 90 pounds, my shoes were two sizes too big—I had toilet paper stuffed in 'em, tape to hold my socks up. My pants were huge, baggy, the crotch came to my knees, and I had to cut an extra hole in the belt. On the jersey, where it says "Royals," the bottom half of the lettering was tucked into my uniform. And then there is nothing more embarrassing than to have the first ball hit to you down the foul line, 30,000 people watching, go between your legs. General admission goes nuts, and they are on you till you make a play.

Two years later, when batboy Eric Winebrenner broke his ankle playing football, I got to batboy the rest of the season and on through the playoffs. For the first playoff game, I was sixteen years old, my hair on fire, ready to go, can't sleep. I don't know how players take that kind of pressure. With a man on second in that game there was a passed ball and I'm so gung ho to get the ball I get about a step away from it before I hear the umpire yelling at me, "Don't touch it, don't touch it, don't touch it!" and I back off. I felt about half an inch tall in front of 42,000 screaming fans, and it was worse next day at school where everybody had seen me on TV.

I got a little pride back in the World Series that same year, twice. In Game 5 in St. Louis, I was the one who caught George Brett's legs when he slid into the dugout—you should see how far a drop that is. Then, in Game 7, Darryl Motley's up at bat. He yanks one down the line—foul. He does it a second time, and banging his bat on the ground he breaks it. Comes over to me and I bring him two bats, and he says, "Which one would you use?" I said, "The black one's got a home run in it." I handed it to him and on the next pitch he hammers it out of the ballpark. He doesn't just shake my hand, he picks me up.

The next year, Mr. Winebrenner, who was called "Consensus All-American" in the clubhouse because he was such a perfect kid, was making his comeback as batboy, and I was back down the line as ballboy. One day, still during the school year, the club came back late from a road trip and I was up all night unpacking, went out to breakfast, went to school, skipped lunch to do a track workout because I was running cross country, came to the game, and I'm so dead tired that when I sat down in my chair in the third inning I fell asleep. The right fielder didn't even ask me to play catch. I slept through the whole inning, and then umpire Ken Kaiser came down and scared the shit out of me. I didn't think that much of it, really, but three days later I got in the mail a photograph of me sleeping on the job, taken by a young photographer I used to play soccer with. He kidded me about blackmail.

Kaiser's not the most fit umpire in the American League, but you gotta like him, because where else but in America can a guy that fat and ugly make a hundred grand? A beautiful country, isn't it? Kaiser used to wrestle and he'd show his moves to other umpires, using me as a guinea pig. He showed them a body slam, and it really doesn't hurt.

My favorite ump is Steve Palermo, probably the best. Durwood Merrill's another good guy. In fact they're all good guys as a whole, with great baseball stories. People say how hard it must be for the players to be on the road, but the umpire is in a different town every three to five days, from the moment spring training starts, and unless his family lives in a big-league city, he doesn't get to see them till the season's over.

One of the players once had me take umpire Jim Joyce a glass of water with a little vodka in it during a hot Sunday game. He takes a drink, spits it out, and starts screaming, "Who did this?" and everyone's laughing. Two or three years later, another hot Sunday, about 130 or 140 degrees on the Astroturf and no breeze, he's working the plate, and I bring him a whole glass of vodka. He takes a little sip, and starts yelling, "You can't be doing this shit!"

People don't realize how nice someone like George Brett or Bret Saberhagen is. People only see what goes on on the field, and sometimes it's hard to swallow what stories and opinions get reported in the media. You never hear about how Bo Jackson had the entire clubhouse staff over to his house after the 1988 season. This man slaved over a stove, made us grilled catfish, homemade hushpuppies, salad. That is something. I felt I had a relationship with him, as a friend not a fellow employee, and his little boy calls me Uncle Wes.

Baseball has been an amazing game to me. I've been to spring training twice, had a lot of adventures on the road, met people like McLean Stevenson, Billy Crystal, guys from REO Speedwagon, and Huey Lewis—Brett took us to a Huey Lewis concert. I can't speak bad about anyone in baseball, they've been very good to me. Oh, sometimes a rookie comes up and he's got an attitude about signing autographs. I remember Scott Bankhead, his one year in Kansas City, thought he was Joe Cool and wouldn't sign balls for one of the younger club-house guys. We thought, fine, we've been in the league longer than you, pal, and we can fix that. It's amazing how one guy can lose so many shoes, socks, shirts, belts, gloves, etcetera. They catch on real quick and conform with the activity. It's all a learning experience.

There are three kinds of education. There's the kind you can get in an Ivy League school, where if you have the money you can get a great education and go on to make all kinds of money. Then there's the good street education that you can get in the kind of blue-collar neighborhood where I grew up, and it's especially good for a future police officer. And finally there's baseball education, which is hard to come by. Not many people have the opportunity to get a baseball education. I've had it and I'll never forget it.

Wes Patterson had a double major in college—Criminal Justice and Public Relations—and he graduated from the Royals Stadium club-house into the Kansas City Police Academy.

About the Author

Neil D. Isaacs is a professor of English at the University of Maryland at College Park. He has also taught at the University of Tennessee, the University of Connecticut, CCNY, and Brown University, where he earned his Ph.D. in 1959. Aside from scholarly publications—which include books on Old English poetry, Tolkien, Grace Paley, and *Fiction into Film: A Walk in the Spring Rain* (with Rachel Maddux and Stirling Silliphant)—his essays, stories, poems and columns have appeared in the Washington *Post*, Boston *Globe*, Washington *Star*, *New York Times* and Baltimore *Sun*.

His books also include *All the Moves: A History of College Basketball* (Lippincott, 1975, revised and updated for Harper and Row, 1984); *Checking Back: A History of NHL Hockey* (Norton, 1977); *Jock Culture USA* (Norton, 1978); *Covering the Spread: How to Bet on Pro Football* (with Gerald Strine, Random House, 1978); *Sports Illustrated Basketball* (with Dick Motta, Harper and Row, 1978); and *The Sporting Spirit: Athletes in Literature and Life* (with Jack Higgs, Harcourt, 1977).

His novel, *The Great Molinas*, was published in November of 1992, by the WID Publishing Group and the Sport Literature Association.

Besides teaching literature, Isaacs practices as a family therapist (MSW 1989, LCSW-C, 1993). He lives in Colesville, Maryland. with his wife Ellen and their two children. His four older children and four grandchildren live in Oakland, California; Bethesda, Maryland; Novi, Michigan; and Washington D.C.

Hit A Home Run With Masters Press!

Béisbol
Latin Americans and the Grand Old Game

Michael M. Oleksak & Mary Adams Oleksak

Major League rosters of the 1990s include many names such as Rijo, Canseco, Sierra, Guillen, Alomar, Fernandez, Higuera, and Tartabull. *Béisbol* explains how these men and other greats from "south of the border" broke down cultural, racial, and linguistic barriers to survive and thrive in Major League Baseball.
$22.95 • cloth • 320 pages • b/w photos
ISBN: 0-940279-35-5

Baseball Trivia
So You Think You Know Baseball?

Bob Alley

Find out how much you know about the National Pastime in *Baseball Trivia, So You Think You Know Baseball?*

This book is filled with hundreds of questions guaranteed to challenge the most dedicated baseball buff. But this is more than just another trivia book. Author Bob Alley also takes you on a unique tour of baseball's history which includes pages of photos and fascinating anecdotes about the game's biggest names of yesterday and today.
$12.95 • paper • 160 pages • puzzles and b/w photos
ISBN: 0-940279-85-1

Hit A Home Run With Masters Press!

Baseball Crosswords

Mark Roszkowski

Test your knowledge of the Major Leagues!
Each chapter of *Baseball Crosswords* includes a two-page history of a Major League team, diagrams charting the team's finishes for the last 10 seasons, and stats for the previous year's leaders. Combine that information with a crossword puzzle for each team and photographs of your favorite Major League players, and you've got a home run for baseball and puzzle fans everywhere!
$12.95 • paper • 192 pages • puzzles, diagrams and b/w photos
ISBN: 0-940279-83-5

All Masters Press titles are available in bookstores nationwide or by calling Masters Press at (800) 722-2677. Catalogs are available upon request.